"I love this book in terms of both content and tone. Neil Shenvi has thought deeply about these issues and provides a reasoned case for Christianity. He also responds to some of the most common objections with clarity and precision. I hope *Why Believe?* gets the wide readership it deserves."

Sean McDowell, Associate Professor of Christian Apologetics, Biola University; author, *Evidence That Demands a Verdict*

"Shenvi's interaction with critics of Christianity is instructive for those of us supporting Christian faith. This is a worthy book for your apologetical library and a great resource for moving forward in a society that constantly challenges us."

George Yancey, Professor of Sociology, Baylor University

"What an outstanding work! Pound for pound this is the best apologetics book I've ever read. Shenvi has done a great service to both the church and the broader culture. Christians will find an excellent resource for both the strengthening and the defense of their faith. Non-Christians will have an accessible pathway to understanding the Christian faith that will challenge their beliefs and presuppositions while engaging their minds."

Pat Sawyer, Faculty, University of North Carolina, Greensboro; coauthor, *Disney as Doorway to Apologetic Dialogue* (forthcoming)

"This book provides a clear and cogent exposition of arguments for the authenticity of Christianity in the light of modern historical and scientific evidence. Shenvi brings a coherent, impassioned, and well-reasoned perspective to a number of challenging topics. His approach is appropriate for anyone—Christian or not—who wishes to know more about why Christians believe what they believe."

Troy Van Voorhis, Professor of Chemistry, Massachusetts Institute of Technology

"Neil is one of our generation's most engaging and forward thinkers. His insights are forged not in sterile halls of academia but through vibrant discussions with students, thinkers, and leaders in today's halls of influence. This is an excellent resource for thorough, sound answers to today's most difficult questions, not yesterday's. I've had the privilege of serving as Neil's pastor now for nearly a decade, and I can attest that he not only teaches the truth of the gospel but lives out its grace."

J. D. Greear, Pastor, The Summit Church, Raleigh-Durham, North Carolina; author, *Just Ask* and *What Are You Going to Do with Your Life?*

T0049506

Why Believe?

Why Believe?

A Reasoned Approach to Christianity

Neil Shenvi

CROSSWAY®

WHEATON, ILLINOIS

Trade paperback ISBN: 978-1-4335-7938-7
ePub ISBN: 978-1-4335-7941-7
PDF ISBN: 978-1-4335-7939-4
Mobipocket ISBN: 978-1-4335-7940-0

Library of Congress Cataloging-in-Publication Data

Names: Shenvi, Neil, 1979– author.
Title: Why believe? : a reasoned approach to Christianity / Neil Shenvi.
Description: Wheaton, Illinois : Crossway, 2022. | Includes bibliographical references and index.
Identifiers: LCCN 2021046658 (print) | LCCN 2021046659 (ebook) | ISBN 9781433579387 (trade paperback) | ISBN 9781433579394 (pdf) | ISBN 9781433579400 (mobipocket) | ISBN 9781433579417 (epub)
Subjects: LCSH: Apologetics. | Faith and reason.
Classification: LCC BT1103 .S5335 2022 (print) | LCC BT1103 (ebook) | DDC 297.2/9—dc23/eng/20211001
LC record available at https://lccn.loc.gov/2021046658
LC ebook record available at https://lccn.loc.gov/2021046659

Crossway is a publishing ministry of Good News Publishers.

BP			31	30	29	28	27	26	25	24	23
15	14	13	12	11	10	9	8	7	6	5	4	3	2

Contents

Illustrations

1

Introduction

What does this babbler wish to say?

ACTS 17:18

"WHY BELIEVE THAT CHRISTIANITY IS TRUE?" It's the kind of question that fuels late-night arguments in college common rooms, awkward silences at holiday dinners, and Internet comment threads that make you vow to never again read Internet comment threads. When discussion wanders into the area of religion, otherwise calm and sensible people seem to lose their ability to think rationally or to use lowercase letters.

Even worse, human history is filled with religious violence, leading many people to believe that assertions of religious truth inevitably produce bloodshed. When Gandhi was asked in an interview why people should avoid urging others to change their religion, he responded, "Proselytization will mean no peace in the world."[1] Those who hold this view often argue that religious truth claims should be discouraged for pragmatic

---

1 Quoted in Arvind Sharma, "Hinduism: Adherent Essay," in *Handbook of Religion: A Christian Engagement with Traditions, Teachings, and Practices*, ed. Terry C. Muck, Harold A. Netland, and Gerald R. McDermott (Grand Rapids, MI: Baker, 2014), 77–78.

reasons. While private religious beliefs are acceptable, we should not publicly insist that they are objectively true. How can we truly love and accept other people while claiming that their deeply held beliefs are wrong?

Other people are apathetic toward religion. Why should they bother with the claims of Christianity if they can live happy, compassionate, spiritual lives without it? And what if we see Christianity as outdated and irrelevant? It may have served some purpose in the past, but it has nothing of interest to say to scientific, modern people. It provides dubious solutions to problems that no one cares about. Worse, it turns people into mindless, dull automatons or angry moralists. Should we really take it seriously?

Setting aside practical concerns, there are also philosophical objections to the claim that one particular religion is true. For example, some people believe that all religions are essentially the same. If that's the case, there's no need to ask whether Christianity is true, because Christianity is true along with every other religion. Others insist that religious beliefs are personal, subjective preferences. Arguing that your religion is objectively true for everyone is as silly as arguing that your favorite brand of mayonnaise ought to be everyone's favorite.

Growing up in a very loving but not particularly religious home, I had many of these same objections. Although I believed in God, I couldn't accept the idea that one particular religion was uniquely true. When I arrived at college as a freshman, I might have called myself a Christian in some vague cultural sense, but only because Jesus's moral example was more familiar to me than that of any other religious figure. I certainly wasn't some crazy fundamentalist who memorized Bible verses, attended church each week, went to prayer meetings, walked around humming worship music, and wrote books about how Christianity is true. Since, apparently, I do all those things today (minus the worship music), what changed? A few things come to mind.

During my second year in college, a Christian group on campus set up a table in front of our dining hall. I had planned to pass by with an air of smug superiority, but my disdain turned into disbelief when I realized that they were passing out free books: the Bible (naturally) and two titles by C. S. Lewis, whom I recognized as the author of The Chronicles of Narnia, a series I had loved as a child. After verifying that I wasn't being asked to sign up for anything, I ignored the Bible, snatched up Lewis's works, and disappeared into the dining hall, not realizing that I'd woefully underestimated God's subtlety.

The two books were *Mere Christianity* and *The Screwtape Letters*. I found *Mere Christianity* moderately interesting, but *The Screwtape Letters* was riveting. The novel took the form of a series of letters written from a senior demon in hell to his inexperienced and incompetent protégé on earth, containing instructions for the successful tempting of a human "patient." Although it was an interesting premise and was suffused with Lewis's characteristic humor and creativity, what floored me was its insight into my own life. When Screwtape described the patient's pride, his sense of superiority, his posturing, his insincerity, and the fears and temptations he struggled to hide, he was describing me. I read the book and reread it and re-reread it and asked, How can Lewis know what's going on in my head?

The next incident that challenged my ideas about Christianity was meeting my future wife, Christina. As chemistry majors, we had crossed paths on occasion, but I knew her primarily as the student who had received the highest grade in our much-dreaded sophomore-level organic chemistry course—as a freshman. She was brilliant. What surprised me, though, was how little she seemed to care whether other people thought she was brilliant. Of course, I *pretended* not to care about whether other people thought I was brilliant. But I did care. Immensely.

Most of my identity, maybe all my identity, was wrapped up in being better than other people: better at academics, better at music, better at sports. At a place like Princeton, it was impossible to pretend that I was the best at nearly anything, even taking into account my prodigious talent for self-deception. So I had a backup plan. When I met someone who was undeniably better than me in every category, I fell back on my spirituality, which was my last resort when all else failed. No matter how smart, athletic, or talented the competition was, I could cling to the idea that I was a good, moral, spiritual person.

In contrast, Christina really didn't seem to think about herself very much. Here was a woman who was beautiful, funny, intelligent, and successful but who didn't seem to regard these things as the essence of her identity. She was also an evangelical Christian. *But I can work around that*, I thought to myself.

The final check to my beliefs occurred during our first few months of graduate school at the University of California, Berkeley. I was convinced that Christina and I could compromise on the whole "Jesus thing." To show her how open-minded I was, I went to church with her. Unfortunately for me, the pastor of her church had a PhD from Cambridge. My quantum physics professor, a renowned cosmologist, sang in the choir. I was surrounded by undergraduates, graduate students, postdocs, and professors who were convinced that Jesus was the Son of God and had risen from the dead. That was a problem.

I had always assumed that Christianity could not possibly be accepted by thoughtful, intelligent people, at least not by people as thoughtful and intelligent as me. Surely, Christianity was for well-meaning and sometimes not-so-well-meaning people with substandard educations and a streak of intellectual fear bordering on dishonesty. This stereotype functioned as an implicit and impenetrable bulwark against Christian claims. But suddenly, my defenses began to crumble. I was forced to consider the message of Christianity without dismissing it out of hand.

I'll say a bit more in the final chapter about how I took the final step from uncomfortable uncertainty to belief. At this point, what's most interesting to me about these events was how little they had to do with what we normally think of as evidence. Why? Probably because I had never rejected Christianity on the basis of evidence in the first place. My beliefs about morality, religion, and God were largely the unreflective product of ideas I had picked up from my peers, my friends, my parents, books, television, and movies. I had never questioned my assumptions about the nature of religious truth or engaged with opposing views. What C. S. Lewis, my future wife, and my church in Berkeley provided was not new evidence but the realization that some of my reasons for ignoring Christianity were highly dubious.

Christianity was not dry, archaic, boring, and irrelevant; it offered a compelling assessment of my own most pressing problems. It did not turn people into lifeless automatons, angry moralists, or raving lunatics; it animated the life of the person whom I loved and admired the most. And it was not an opiate for the uneducated masses; it could thrive in the most rigorous academic environments. Shouldn't I try to figure out whether it was true?

What about the other questions I posed at the beginning of this chapter: Shouldn't we avoid religious truth claims for the sake of peace? Aren't all religions equally true? Can religious claims really be classified as "true" or "false"? And why do we even need religion? Even if we acknowledge that Christianity might, like many religions, include interesting spiritual ideas, and even if we recognize that there are kind and intelligent Christians just as there are kind and intelligent atheists, Muslims, and Hindus, aren't there still good reasons to ignore or deny the claim that Christianity is uniquely true? Let's consider each of those objections in turn.

Should We Avoid Religious Truth Claims for the Sake of Peace?

Most people, minus a few cartoon supervillains and a handful of real-life tyrants, prefer peace to war. But history shows us that competing religious truth claims create tensions that can rapidly turn into armed conflict. In his book *God Is Not Great*, the late journalist Christopher Hitchens devoted an entire chapter to the history of religious violence.[2]

---

2 Christopher Hitchens, *God Is Not Great: How Religion Poisons Everything* (New York: Twelve, 2007), 15–36.

Seeing the potential for sectarian strife, many people conclude that religious truth claims should be eliminated entirely. One appeal of this approach is that it appears to be pragmatic. No judgment is being passed on whether there is one true religion. Perhaps there is; perhaps there isn't. The argument is only that we should refrain from making public claims about religious truth in order to promote human flourishing.

In response, we need to note that religion ranks far below other factors as the primary cause of war. In his *Huffington Post* article "Is Religion the Cause of Most Wars?" Rabbi Alan Lurie notes that of the 1,763 wars listed in the *Encyclopedia of Wars*, "only 123 have been classified to involve a religious cause, accounting for less than 7 percent of all wars and less than 2 percent of all people killed in warfare."[3] The death toll of the bloodiest religious conflicts like the Crusades is dwarfed by deaths from secular conflicts like World War I or from ideological killings like those occurring during the "Great Leap Forward" in China. Even if we recognize that attributing wars to "religious" or "nonreligious" causes can be challenging, we ought to acknowledge that human beings are capable of massacring each other with or without religious motivations.

More importantly, while the assertion that religious claims should be avoided for practical reasons sounds neutral, it actually conceals a deep commitment to a particular ideological claim: namely, that the key to long-term peace and human flourishing is not found in one particular religion. Are we sure that this claim is true? After all, if some particular religion is uniquely true, then its truth could have massive implications for human flourishing. For example, if Buddhism is true, then pursuing our desires for temporal happiness will inevitably lead to a cycle of endless frustration and suffering. To discourage Buddhists from sharing this truth with others would then be seriously detrimental to human flourishing. Other religions, like Islam, Judaism, Christianity, and Hinduism, also make claims that, if true, would radically change how

---

3   Alan Lurie, "Is Religion the Cause of Most Wars?," *Huffington Post*, April 10, 2012, https://www.huffpost.com/entry/is-religion-the-cause-of-_b_1400766.

we understand human flourishing and the best way to achieve it. To insist that we can or should ignore religious truth for the sake of human flourishing is to implicitly insist that none of these religions is true.

In the end, we are led back to our original question: Are any religious claims objectively true? We should discourage public discussion of religion only if we are certain that the answer to this question is no. If it's possible that some religious claims are objectively true, then we must be open to religious debate, just as we're open to scientific, economic, philosophical, or political debate.

Since an appeal to religious violence can't sidestep questions of religious truth, we next turn to philosophical objections to religious truth.

Are All Religions True?

When asked whether Christianity is true, many people respond with eager affirmation: "Sure, Christianity is true because all religions are true!" This belief is often illustrated by the parable of the blind men and the elephant: Five blind men are walking through the jungle and stumble upon an elephant. Each of them takes hold of a different part of the animal. The first blind man grabs his tusk and says, "An elephant is hard and pointed, like a spear." The second blind man grasps the elephant's ear and says: "No! An elephant is soft and flat, like a fan." The third blind man, who is holding the elephant's tail, says: "No, you're both wrong. The elephant is long, thin, and flexible, like a rope." All five continue arguing until a wise man comes and tells them that they are all holding an elephant. Their statements are all true, but each of them has only a portion of the truth. The moral of this parable is that religious truth is too nuanced and complex to be contained within any one religious tradition. All religions are true, but none of them is exclusively true.

The most serious problem with this form of religious inclusivism is that it doesn't take seriously the claims made by actual adherents of different religions. For example, I occasionally have friendly conversations with conservative Muslims about the comparative reliability of the Qur'an and the Bible. We are willing to listen to one another, to correct each other's misunderstandings, and to engage in civil, courteous discussion. Throughout this process, we are both trying to better understand what the other person believes. While our dialogue leads us to conclude that we fundamentally disagree on many issues, we can still do so with mutual respect.

In contrast, religious inclusivism must deny the reality of religious disagreement because it accepts as axiomatic the idea that different religions agree on all essential issues. No matter how much a Christian insists that the deity of Jesus is foundational to Christianity, and no matter how much a Muslim insists that the deity of Jesus is incompatible with Islam, an inclusivist has no choice but to insist that both the Christian and Muslim are mistaken in thinking they hold mutually exclusive views. Although I sympathize with the desire to avoid discord, I can't help but think that honest, loving disagreement is preferable to the insistence that we understand others' religious beliefs better than they do.

A similar point is made by a story that I call the parable of the blind men and the five inanimate objects.[4] Five blind men are walking through a museum and stumble across five inanimate objects: a spear, a fan, a rope, a wall, and a tree. While they argue, a wise man enters the museum and tells them that they are all holding an elephant. A problem arises when we try to determine which parable is the correct illustration of spiritual reality, the first version or the second? The inclusivist can know that the original version of the parable is the correct one only if he is speaking from a position of special religious knowledge that all exclusivists lack. In other words, he would have to say to all religious exclusivists, whether Christian, Muslim, Jewish,

---

4   See Harold A. Netland and Keith E. Johnson, "Why Is Religious Pluralism Fun—and Dangerous?," in *Telling the Truth: Evangelizing Postmoderns*, ed. D. A. Carson (Grand Rapids, MI: Zondervan, 2000), 63–64.

Buddhist, or Hindu: "You are all wrong about the exclusive nature of spiritual reality. My inclusive view of spiritual reality is the correct one." When push comes to shove, inclusivism turns out to be just as exclusive as other religious positions.[5]

Is All Religious Truth Subjective?

If religious inclusivism can't avoid the problem of exclusive claims, is there another way to avoid religious conflict? Yes, there is. Rather than arguing that all religions are objectively true, we can instead argue that all religions are subjectively true. In other words, there is no one religion that is *objectively* true for all people, but each person's religion is *subjectively* true for them. Like religious inclusivism, a belief in religious subjectivism precludes the possibility of conflict between religious claims. No one thinks that my subjective belief that In-N-Out Burger is the best fast-food restaurant in America conflicts with someone else's subjective belief that Five Guys is better.[6] These are subjective opinions, not objective truth claims.

The difficulty with the view that all religions are subjectively true is that some religions really do make objective truth claims. For example, Christians believe that Jesus Christ was physically raised from the dead. To put it as plainly as possible, the Christian claim is that Jesus's dead body was restored to life on the third day after he was crucified, leaving his tomb empty. There seems to be no way to understand this statement except as an objective claim about historical reality. It may hypothetically be false or it may be true. But it would be nonsensical to say that the statement "the tomb was empty" is true for me, but the statement "the tomb contained Jesus's decomposing corpse" is true for you.[7]

---

5 See also, Timothy Keller, *The Reason for God: Belief in an Age of Skepticism* (New York: Penguin, 2008), 8–14.

6 Bad example. In-N-Out Burger is objectively ten thousand times better than Five Guys.

7 Quantum mechanics does not provide some bizarre loophole to this assertion through the infamous Schrödinger's cat paradox. The contents of Jesus's tomb would have been "measured" long ago due to exchange of information with the environment.

The same objectivity is a necessary element of all the biggest religious questions. Does God exist? Did he create the universe out of nothing? Did Moses receive the Ten Commandments on Mount Sinai? Did the Buddha attain enlightenment under the bodhi tree? Did the angel Gabriel visit Muhammad? Did Jesus rise from the dead? Are we reincarnated in different bodies after we die? Will there be a final judgment? While the conflict-averse among us (myself included) might prefer all of these questions to be mere matters of opinion, they are inescapably propositions about objective reality that are either true or false.

In the end, I don't think that either religious inclusivism or religious relativism can deliver on the promise of circumventing all religious conflicts. No matter how much we want to avoid the anger that often comes with exclusive religious claims, we shouldn't pretend that religious differences don't exist. A better approach is to acknowledge that while we may hold different and incompatible religious ideas, we are united in our common humanity. Certainly for Christians, Jesus's command to love our neighbors as ourselves demands that we treat them with love and kindness, whether or not we agree with them.[8]

Can We Just Ignore Religion?

Even if religious claims are objectively true or false, do we really need to bother with them? What if we're not interested in whether one particular religion is true? What if we find that we can live lives of happiness and spirituality without organized religion of any kind? Let me suggest two reasons that we can't avoid looking into the truth claims of religion in general and of Christianity in particular: the tragedy of human existence and the magnitude of the claims involved.

---

8 See Professor Timothy C. Tennant's excellent discussion of interfaith dialogue and the problems of relativism and subjectivism in chap. 1 of Tennent, *Christianity at the Religious Roundtable: Evangelicalism in Conversation with Hinduism, Buddhism, and Islam* (Grand Rapids, MI: Baker Academic, 2002), 9–33.

First, for hundreds of millions of people all over the world, life is an unmitigated horror. From some of our own inner cities to the slums of South America to war-ravaged villages in Africa, life for many people is a tragic succession of misery, hunger, loss, and pain. Even in the wealthiest, most isolated communities in America, tragedy forces its way into almost everyone's experience. Most of us will live to see our parents and our friends die. If we personally manage to escape heartbreak, we will almost certainly see others struggle their way through miscarriages, affairs, divorces, cancer, and Alzheimer's. I know these reflections are not pleasant. I know we would rather think positive, encouraging thoughts. But this is the world we live in.

Am I claiming that the tragedy of human existence is evidence that God exists? No. Instead, I am claiming that the tragedy of human existence absolutely and finally strips us of any claimed right to apathy. Anyone who has honestly and seriously thought about death; who has seen premature infants in the neonatal ward struggling to breathe; who has seen malnourished, barefooted children playing next to open sewers; or who has watched his or her elderly mother slowly drift into dementia can no longer shrug off religion as a matter of indifference.

Second, the claims of Christianity merit our attention, given their magnitude. Some truth claims are not very important. If someone asserts that there are exactly 135 rocks in my garden or that Nicholas Cage owns a first-edition copy of *A Tale of Two Cities*, it makes little difference to me whether he is right or not. However, the truth of Christianity is a matter of great importance. If Christianity is true, then God exists, we owe him our obedience, we will face his judgment at death, and we have no hope for salvation apart from Jesus Christ. Yet it is not at all uncommon to hear people say, "Christianity might be true or it might not be, but it doesn't really matter to me."[9] This stance is irrational.

9   See, for example, Jonathan Rauch, "Let It Be," *The Atlantic*, May 2003, http://www.theatlantic.com.

If your doctor told you that you had stage-4 stomach cancer, imagine her surprise if you declared: "Maybe I do and maybe I don't. I don't really care either way." Given what's at stake, apathy is not an option. The doctor would rightly respond: "Either you don't truly understand what cancer is, or you do understand and are extremely confident that you don't have it. You can't possibly understand the gravity of this claim and not care about it." In the same way, we can reject Christianity as false and then ignore it. Or we can embrace it as true and drastically change our lives in response to it. What we cannot do is shrug our shoulders, yawn, and feign indifference. As C. S. Lewis said: "Christianity . . . , if false, is of *no* importance, and, if true, of infinite importance. The one thing it cannot be is moderately important."[10]

I offer this book to both Christians and non-Christians who are interested in Christianity. It is by no means exhaustive. Each chapter could be expanded into an entire book or an entire series of books. For those who would like to explore particular issues in greater depth, the works cited throughout should prove helpful.

The truth of Christianity touches on issues as diverse as ancient history, textual criticism, metaethics, epistemology, and cosmology. No one can claim expertise in all those areas, and I am certainly no exception.[11] However, I have done my best to read broadly, paying special attention to non-Christian scholars and writers, not because I think that Christians can't do good scholarship but because I want to listen closely to voices that my own theological biases tempt me to discount. I have also tried to present counterarguments to my own claims as evenhandedly and charitably as possible, but where I have failed to do so, I hope that readers will extend grace.

---

10 C. S. Lewis, "Christian Apologetics," in *God in the Dock: Essays on Theology and Ethics*, ed. Walter Hooper (Grand Rapids, MI: Eerdmans, 1970), 101.

11 For those interested, I have a PhD and quite a bit of research experience in the field of theoretical chemistry. Certainly an interesting subject, but not one with immediate relevance to the truth of Christianity!

This book is organized around four distinct arguments for the truth of Christianity. Although the chapters follow an overarching logical structure, each can be read more or less independently of the others. Chapter 2 deals with the question of Jesus's identity, chapter 3 with his resurrection, chapters 4–6 with the existence of God, and chapters 7–9 with the central message of Christianity. Readers who are interested in a particular question or who view a particular issue as an insurmountable obstacle to the Christian faith are encouraged to skip to the relevant section. For example, someone who believes that questions of Jesus's identity are wholly irrelevant since God does not exist might want to begin with chapter 4, while someone who wrestles with the problem of evil might want to start with chapter 6. Similarly, if a particular subsection is confusing (or boring), it can often be set aside without affecting the overall point being made.

One final word about content: while each of the arguments in the book is distinct, all of them point back in one way or another to Jesus himself, because Jesus is the center of Christianity. To see Christianity merely as a collection of rules or a political platform or even a set of religious values and practices is to miss it entirely. Christianity is ultimately about a person: Jesus Christ. I understand that this kind of statement might be easily dismissed as a product of my own twenty-first-century American theology, but doing so would be a mistake. If you were to line up Christian traditions and great theologians across all cultures and all of church history, they would affirm that the beating heart of Christianity is the declaration that "Jesus is Lord"; that is, he is our King, our God, and our Savior. Amid our discussion of reason and evidence and arguments, let's remember that this is not a bare intellectual exercise. Jesus is a real Savior for people desperately in need of rescue. Jesus is a real Savior for people like us.

2

The Trilemma

But who do you say that I am?

MARK 8:29

JESUS OF NAZARETH WAS BORN two thousand years ago in a tiny village in a remote province of the Roman Empire among an oppressed and despised ethnic group. His family was poor, he was not formally educated, and he probably worked as a manual laborer. In his early thirties, he began preaching in the local synagogues. He was known for associating with social and religious outcasts and for befriending those on the margins of society. His public ministry lasted for only a few years before he was arrested by the government, tried for treason, and executed.

Two thousand years later, approximately one-third of the world professes to believe that he is God incarnate. The Western calendar divides all of history by the year he was born.[1] His teaching is so deeply embedded in our culture that we barely notice it. Phrases like "being a Good Samaritan" and "going the extra mile" have entered our popular

---

1   Almost, but not exactly. An error by a monk in the sixth century means that Jesus was probably born around 4 BC.

lexicon from Jesus's teaching as paradigms of goodness and compassion. Even prominent atheists like evolutionary biologist Richard Dawkins or philosopher Daniel Dennett have a difficult time finding fault with Jesus. Dawkins writes that "[Jesus's] Sermon on the Mount is way ahead of its time. His 'turn the other cheek' anticipated Gandhi and Martin Luther King by two thousand years."[2] Daniel Dennett, in an interview with *The Beast*, said: "I think that, actually, Jesus makes a fine hero. . . . In fact, we had some discussion of forming a group called Atheists for Jesus."[3]

Upon reflection, the contrast between the obscurity of Jesus's life and his civilization-shaping impact on history is astonishing. When the passage of time has swept kings, emperors, cities, and even entire nations into oblivion, why is a homeless Galilean rabbi still remembered? That's the question we'll consider in this chapter.

Liar, Lunatic, or Lord

During World War II, Oxford professor C. S. Lewis gave a series of radio lectures that were later collected into the book *Mere Christianity*. Commenting on the identity of Jesus, he writes:

> I am trying here to prevent anyone saying the really foolish thing that people often say about Him: "I'm ready to accept Jesus as a great moral teacher, but I don't accept his claim to be God." That is the one thing we must not say. A man who was merely a man and said the sort of things Jesus said would not be a great moral teacher. He would either be a lunatic—on a level with the man who says he is a poached egg—or else he would be the Devil of Hell. You must make your choice. Either this man was, and is, the Son of God: or else a madman or something worse. You can shut Him up for a fool, you

---

2   Richard Dawkins, *The God Delusion* (Boston: Mariner, 2008), 283.
3   Daniel Dennett, "Domo Arigato, Mr. Ten Trillion Robotos!," interview by Ian Murphy, The Beast, March 2009, https://web.archive.org/web/20090421065952/http://buffalobeast.com/135/Daniel%20Dennett-ian%20murphy.htm.

can spit at Him and kill Him as a demon: or you can fall at His feet and call Him Lord and God. But let us not come with any patronising nonsense about His being a great human teacher. He has not left that open to us. He did not intend to.[4]

Lewis is arguing that we cannot pat Jesus on the head and dismiss him as a "good moral teacher." Jesus claimed to be the Son of God and the Savior of the world. No mere man who made such claims could be considered either good or moral. If Jesus's claims were false and he knew they were false, then he was a tremendous liar. If his claims were false and he sincerely believed they were true, then he was a lunatic. But if his claims were true, then he is the Lord of all humanity. This is the trilemma: liar, lunatic, or Lord. Lewis insisted that we must honestly consider the person of Jesus we find in the Bible and make a decision about his identity.

However, one major obstacle to any engagement with Jesus is skepticism about the Bible. Lewis assumed that most of his hearers believed the Bible to be generally reliable. While that belief may have been common in mid-twentieth-century England when Lewis was writing, it is certainly not widespread today. Most people view the Bible as an incoherent mixture of fairy tales, moral parables, and legends—a cross between Aesop's Fables and *The Lord of the Rings*. Such skepticism is found not only in the culture at large but, to some extent, among academics as well.

Bart Ehrman, a professor at the University of North Carolina at Chapel Hill, who is probably the nation's most well-known New Testament scholar, writes the following about the origin of the Gospels, the four biographies of Jesus found in the Bible:

You are probably familiar with the old birthday party game, "telephone." . . . Invariably, the story has changed so much in the

---

4   C. S. Lewis, *Mere Christianity* (New York: Macmillan, 1952), 55–56.

process of retelling that everyone gets a good laugh. . . . Imagine playing "telephone" not in a solitary living room with ten kids on a sunny afternoon in July, but over the expanse of the Roman Empire (some 2,500 miles across!), with thousands of participants, from different backgrounds, with different concerns, and in different contexts, some of whom have to translate the stories into different languages all over the course of decades. What would happen to the stories?[5]

Paula Fredriksen, a religious studies professor at Boston University, writes of the Gospels:

These are composite documents, the final products of long and creative traditions in which old material was reworked and new material interpolated. As they now stand, they are witness first of all to the faith of their individual writers and their late first-century, largely Gentile communities. Only at a distance do they relate to the people and the period they purport to describe.[6]

The Jesus Seminar, a high-profile group of scholars committed to research into the historical Jesus, concludes that "eighty-two percent of the words ascribed to Jesus in the gospels were not actually spoken by him,"[7] and says,

The gospels are now assumed to be narratives in which the memory of Jesus is embellished by mythic elements that express the church's faith in him, and by plausible fictions that enhance the telling of the

5   Bart D. Ehrman, *Jesus: Apocalyptic Prophet of the New Millennium* (Oxford: Oxford University Press, 1999), 51–52.
6   Paula Fredriksen, *From Jesus to Christ: The Origins of the New Testament Images of Jesus* (New Haven, CT: Yale University Press, 1988), 4.
7   Robert W. Funk, Roy W. Hoover, and the Jesus Seminar, *The Five Gospels: What Did Jesus Really Say? The Search for the Authentic Words of Jesus* (New York: HarperSanFrancisco, 1993), 5.

gospel story for first-century listeners who knew about divine men and miracle workers firsthand.[8]

These claims, if accurate, would lead us to mistrust the Gospels' basic historical reliability. If the Gospels are not even generally historically reliable, then we can discount most of the biblical stories about Jesus as mere fabrications of later Christian communities. We don't need to worry about the claims of Jesus any more than we worry about the claims of Batman or Aragorn. No one lies awake at night wondering whether to surrender his or her life to Darth Vader. Fictional figures might inspire us, but they do not demand our allegiance.

Consequently, in order to restore the relevance of Lewis's trilemma, we must make a case that the Gospels provide a generally reliable portrait of the historical figure of Jesus of Nazareth. To do so, let's focus on six major areas: manuscript transmission, non-Christian documentary evidence, geography, archaeology, Jewish context, and onomastics.[9]

The Historical Reliability of the Gospels

The Reliability of Manuscript Transmission

First, it is sometimes claimed that we can't trust the Gospels because we only have copies of copies of copies of copies. Here, Ehrman's analogy of a game of telephone is applied not just to the stories in the Bible but to the physical copies of the biblical manuscripts themselves. For example, the December 23, 2014, cover article of *Newsweek* was "The Bible: So Misunderstood It's a Sin." The article began with a section entitled "Playing Telephone with the Word of God." In it, the author announced that "no television preacher has ever read the Bible. . . . At

---

8 Funk, Hoover, and the Jesus Seminar, *The Five Gospels*, 4–5.

9 Another interesting category of evidence has to do with "undesigned coincidences" in the Gospels, instances of minor details in one Gospel dovetailing with minor details in a different Gospel. For an extensive treatment, see Lydia McGrew, *Hidden in Plain View: Undesigned Coincidences in the Gospel and Acts* (Chillicothe, OH: DeWard, 2017).

best, we've all read a bad translation—a translation of translations of translations of hand-copied copies of copies of copies of copies, and on and on, hundreds of times."[10] The claim made here is that as the biblical manuscripts were copied by scribes, various accidental and deliberate errors crept in that have fundamentally changed the text we have today. We can't know much about the historical figure of Jesus, not only because the Gospels are works of fiction but also because the texts themselves have been corrupted by the process of transmission.

While it is true that we only have "copies of copies of copies of copies" of the original New Testament documents, we are in precisely the same situation with respect to almost every other book written centuries before the invention of the printing press in the fifteenth century. Among these documents, the New Testament[11] is by far the best attested (see fig. 1). For comparison, the second-best-attested ancient document is Homer's *Iliad*, for which we have only eighteen hundred manuscripts and fragments compared with over five thousand manuscripts and fragments of the New Testament in the original language.[12] The New Testament fares just as well if we consider the time between the original writing of the document and the oldest extant fragment (four hundred years for the *Iliad* versus fifty years for the New Testament)[13] or the time between the original writing of the document and the oldest complete

---

10 Kurt Eichenwald, "The Bible: So Misunderstood It's a Sin," *Newsweek*, December 23, 2014, https://www.newsweek.com/. Eichenwald's claim that our modern English Bible is "a translation of translations of translations" is baseless. All modern Bibles are translated from the original languages (Greek, Hebrew, and Aramaic). See, for example, Michael Brown's response piece published one month after the original article: Michael Brown, "A Response to Newsweek on the Bible," *Newsweek*, January 15, 2015, https://www.newsweek.com/.

11 This issue is complicated slightly by the fact that the New Testament consists of twenty-seven different documents that circulated independently before being compiled into a single volume. Nonetheless, the qualitative conclusions drawn here don't change.

12 Clay Jones, "The Bibliographical Test Updated," *Christian Research Journal* 35, no. 3 (2012); published online at CRI, October 1, 2013, https://www.equip.org/.

13 Casey Dué, "*Epea Pteroenta*: How We Came to Have Our *Iliad*," in *Recapturing a Homeric Legacy: Images and Insights from the Venetus A Manuscript of the Iliad*, ed. Casey Dué (Cambridge, MA: Harvard University Press, 2009), 23.

manuscript (sixteen hundred years for the *Iliad* versus three hundred years for the New Testament).[14]

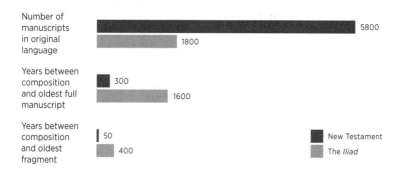

Figure 1. New Testament manuscripts versus *Iliad* manuscripts

It is also true that our New Testament manuscripts are not identical; they contain differences known as "variants," where the text has been altered through the process of transmission. However, the vast majority of these variants are trivial. In his book *Misquoting Jesus*, Ehrman, a former evangelical Christian who is now a self-described "agnostic with atheist leanings," affirms, "Far and away the most changes are the result of mistakes, pure and simple—slips of the pen, accidental omissions, inadvertent additions, misspelled words, blunders of one sort or another."[15] In the relatively small number of cases where there is genuine uncertainty about the contents of the original text, the abundance of manuscripts in our possession comes to our aid. By comparing the quality, age, and "lineage" of various manuscripts, we can usually determine the original wording with a great deal of confidence.

14 Christopher W. Blackwell and Casey Dué, "Homer and History in the Venetus A," in Dué, *Recapturing a Homeric Legacy*, 1.

15 Bart D. Ehrman, *Misquoting Jesus: The Story behind Who Changed the Bible and Why* (New York: HarperCollins, 2005), 55. Ehrman's book provides a good overview of textual criticism and is written in his usual engaging and entertaining style. However, I think he tends to exaggerate the importance of the few remaining textual variants about which there is substantial disagreement.

Despite his skepticism about the historicity of the Gospels, Ehrman himself concedes that the textual data we possess allows us to reconstruct the original documents of the New Testament with a very high degree of accuracy. The famous textual critic Bruce Metzger, who was Ehrman's mentor, said that the variation in the manuscripts of the New Testament does not challenge any essential doctrine of the Christian faith. Reflecting on this statement, Ehrman writes:

> Even though [Metzger and I] may disagree on important religious questions—he is a firmly committed Christian and I am not—we are in complete agreement on a number of very important historical and textual questions. If he and I were put in a room and asked to hammer out a consensus statement on what we think the original text of the New Testament probably looked like, there would be very few points of disagreement—maybe one or two dozen places out of many thousands.[16]

I urge anyone who still has misgivings about the quality of our New Testament texts to consult the footnotes of a modern Bible translation, like the New International Version or the New American Standard Bible. For instance, my one-dollar English Standard Version New Testament contains textual notes whenever translators felt there was significant uncertainty about the original wording.[17] A quick glance shows that textual issues are so infrequent and so minor that they have no bearing on the overall historicity of the Gospels.

While the evidence for the textual reliability of the New Testament does rebut the claim that these documents have been irreparably corrupted by transmission, it does not show that the original documents

---

16 Ehrman, *Misquoting Jesus*, 252.
17 More adventurous readers can consult the NET Study Bible, which includes 60,932 notes, many of which pertain to variant selection and translation. *New English Translation*, full notes ed. (Biblical Studies Press, 2006).

were historically reliable in the first place. A cynic could rightly observe that the existence of accurate copies of *The Amazing Spiderman* is not confirmation that Peter Parker was actually bitten by a radioactive spider. To answer the question of whether the texts of the New Testament reflect historical realities, we'll have to look elsewhere. So, next, let's ask what we can know about the life of Jesus from the works of non-Christian writers.

Corroboration from Non-Christian Authors

Second, what would happen if we burned every Bible in the world and every book ever authored by a Christian? And what if we considered only ancient sources that were composed within a century of Jesus's death? Under these admittedly austere conditions, would we know anything at all about Jesus? Actually, yes. Although we would have few details, we could still learn the basic facts about Jesus's life and about the movement that he founded.

Exclusively from non-Christian sources like Josephus, Tacitus, and Pliny the Younger, we would learn the following: There was a Jewish man named Jesus who lived in first-century Judea. He had a brother named James. He was called the Christ or Messiah by his followers. He did some kind of seemingly miraculous deeds. He was brought to the Roman authorities by the Jewish religious leaders and was crucified under Pontius Pilate. The movement he founded was first checked by his execution but later reemerged and spread as far as Rome. The early Christians chanted to Jesus "as if to a God" and refused to worship other gods, even on pain of death. They met regularly, shared a communal meal, and pledged to live moral lives.[18]

In other words, we would have a very rough outline of Jesus's life and the early Christian movement entirely from non-Christian authors.

18 See, for example, a summary and discussion of the early non-Christian sources on Jesus's life in Mark D. Roberts, *Can We Trust the Gospels? Investigating the Reliability of Matthew, Mark, Luke, John* (Wheaton, IL: Crossway, 2007), 139–50.

The same confirmation is available for many other public figures who play a role in the New Testament narratives. A recent article from the *Biblical Archaeology Review* documented a list of twenty-three political figures mentioned in the New Testament whose existence has been confirmed by archaeological finds, such as inscriptions or coins, or by non-Christian writers like Josephus or Tacitus. These figures include Augustus, Tiberias, Herod the Great, Salome, Philip the Tetrarch, and Pontius Pilate, all of whom are mentioned in the Gospels in the appropriate geographical and political contexts.[19] To them, we could add a handful of nonpolitical religious figures such as Annas, Caiaphas, and John the Baptist, whose existence is similarly confirmed by non-Christian writers.

This corroboration of the historicity of Jesus's life and the Gospels' historical setting by non-Christian authors shows that comparisons to fairy tales or myths are inappropriate. The tale of Hansel and Gretel takes place "once upon a time," not "in Bavaria during the reign of Rudolph I." It seems impossible to argue that Jesus was a fictional creation like Grendel or Sisyphus and yet still found his way into the works of numerous non-Christian historians.

But could the Gospels be similar to legends, which often have some remote basis in history? For example, scholars argue about the degree to which the *Iliad* may be loosely connected to a real war between Greece and Troy. Even if the Gospels are based on the life of a real, historical figure mentioned by secular historians, and even if the Gospels are populated by other undeniably historical characters, could we still insist that they are mostly fictional elaborations of some tiny historical core?

Corroboration from Geography

To answer this charge, we turn next to geography. The biblical Gospels include dozens of geographical landmarks such as the Jordan River; the

---

19 Lawrence Mykytiuk, "New Testament Political Figures Confirmed," *Biblical Archaeology Review* 43, no. 5 (2017): 50–59, 65.

Sea of Galilee; the Mount of Olives; the hill country of Judea; villages such as Bethany, Bethphage, Bethlehem, Emmaus, and Capernaum; and regions such as Judea, Syria, and the Decapolis. From these references, we would at least have to conclude that the authors of the Gospels either were familiar with the geography and general historical setting of Jesus's life or were relying heavily on those who were. Compared with information about major public figures like emperors or kings, knowledge of relatively minor geographical features would be much more difficult to obtain without some kind of firsthand familiarity with Palestine. Most people in the first-century Greco-Roman world had probably heard of Caesar Augustus; it's a good bet that fewer had heard of the Mount of Olives.

It's also interesting to contrast the geographical information we find in the biblical Gospels (Matthew, Mark, Luke, and John) to what we find in later, extrabiblical writings such as the Gospel of Peter or the Gospel of Thomas (see fig. 2).[20] These latter documents contain far fewer and more-general geographical references. Some, like the Gospel of Mary, contain no geographical references at all. The Gospel of Thomas, which many scholars regard as the most historically reliable of the extrabiblical gospels, references only three locations: Israel, Judea, and Samaria (through its mention of a "Samaritan"). The Gospel of Peter makes reference to three major locations (Israel, Judea, and Jerusalem) and one minor one (the garden of Joseph). In contrast, the Q source—a hypothetical document that most scholars believe was used by Matthew and Luke—makes reference to eleven unique geographical locations, not only major regions and cities like Judea or Jerusalem but also small villages like Chorazin and Bethsaida.[21] Likewise, Mark's Gospel uses twenty-four distinct place-names.

20 The results presented here are consistent with unpublished research done by Lorne Zelyck and Julie Woodson under the direction of Dr. Peter J. Williams (personal email to author, September 29, 2021).

21 Reconstructions of Q vary, but the place names included are fairly consistent. See Mark M. Mattison, "The Gospel of Q: A Public Domain Translation," Academia, https://www.academia.edu

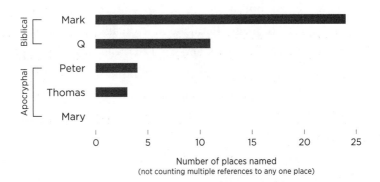

Figure 2. The incidence of geographical place-names in Mark and other texts

While some consideration of the length of the extant texts is pertinent (Q and Thomas are roughly the same size; Mark is three times the length of Q; Peter and Mary are a third of the length of Q), I am not primarily concerned here with whether the biblical Gospels are more reliable than the extrabiblical gospels.[22] Instead, my question is whether it is plausible to suggest, as Ehrman does, that twenty-four geographical references would have emerged from a game of telephone that was played "over the expanse of the Roman Empire (some 2,500 miles across!), with thousands of participants . . . over the course of decades."[23] My suspicion is that a game of telephone involving even fifty people passing along a single sentence in a single auditorium entirely in English over the course of an hour would fail

---

/28395607/The_Gospel_of_Q_A_Public_Domain_Translation. See also Funk, Hoover, and the Jesus Seminar, *The Five Gospels*, 549–53.

22 Most scholars believe that the canonical Gospels, the four biographies of Jesus found in the Bible, are far better historical sources than the apocryphal gospels, biographies of Jesus not found in the Bible. For example, the theologically liberal Jesus Seminar, which includes the Gospel of Thomas as the "fifth gospel" alongside the four canonical Gospels, nonetheless lists only four statements in the Gospel of Thomas that they deem historical but that do not have parallels in the canonical Gospels. In other words, the Gospel of Thomas adds very little, if anything, to our historical knowledge of Jesus. See Robert W. Funk, Arthur J. Dewey, and the Jesus Seminar, *The Gospel of Jesus: According to the Jesus Seminar*, 2nd ed. (Salem: Polebridge, 2015).

23 Ehrman, *Jesus: Apocalyptic Prophet*, 52.

to preserve a single unfamiliar geographical place-name. If the telephone analogy were accurate, would we really expect these kinds of geographical details to have been left intact? Is it really plausible to argue that upon a tiny kernel of historical truth, the early Christian community erected an extensive legendary account of Jesus's activities that included dozens of real historical figures along with dozens of incidental geographical details?

Corroboration from Archaeology

Fourth, archaeology can provide dramatic corroboration of the Gospels, albeit on a more limited scale. It is unsurprising that the existence of a major structure like Herod's Temple in Jerusalem, which is mentioned repeatedly in all four Gospels, can be confirmed by archaeology. What is less expected is the confirmation of very minor details that excavations have unearthed. For instance, we've found the pool at Bethesda (John 5:1–15); the pool of Siloam (John 9:1–7); the synagogue at Capernaum (Luke 4:31–36); inscriptions naming Pontius Pilate, the prefect of Judea, and Lysanias, the tetrarch of Abilene (Luke 3:1); and a first-century house from the village of Nazareth, where Jesus grew up (Matt. 2:23).[24] Other discoveries such as the ossuary of the high priest Caiaphas (Matt. 26:57) and the house of Peter in Capernaum (Matt. 8:14–16) are potentially valid, although their authenticity is still being debated. These finds show that the authors of the Gospels were either generally reliable narrators whose accuracy is reflected in the minor details of their narratives or else extremely clever frauds who filled otherwise fictional works with accurate historical details in order to deceive twenty-first-century archaeologists.

---

24 An extensive discussion of the archaeological finds corroborating the Gospels and the New Testament in general can be found in John McRay, *Archaeology and the New Testament* (Grand Rapids, MI: Baker, 1991). See also Ken Dark, "Has Jesus' Nazareth House Been Found?," *Biblical Archaeology Review* 41, no. 2 (2015): 54–63.

If we expand our discussion to include the book of Acts, which was written by Luke, the author of the third Gospel,[25] we have far more opportunity for confirmation or disconfirmation by archaeology, since Acts follows the growth of the early Christian movement out of Judea into the surrounding Mediterranean world. The narrative in Acts is saturated with historically verifiable features, like cities, ports, bodies of water, and buildings. As in the Gospels, we again find accounts mentioning structures or locations that can be externally verified, like the temple of Artemis (Acts 19:27), the theater in Ephesus (Acts 19:29), Mars Hill in Athens (Acts 17:22), and the Forum Appii (Acts 28:15). Inscriptions have been discovered bearing the names of Gallio proconsul of Achaia (Acts 18:12–17) and proconsul Sergius Paulus of Cyprus (Acts 13:6–13).[26]

One of the more interesting examples of historical confirmation comes from Luke's correct use of regional titles for government officials in various locations. The rulers of Cyprus and Achaia were "proconsuls"; on the other hand, Ephesus was administrated by a "temple-warden," a "proconsul," and "Asiarchs"; the magistrates of Philippi were "praetors," and in Thessalonica they were "politarchs," while Malta was ruled by the "first man of the island."[27] Imagine trying to write a fictional account of a diplomat's journey through Southeast Asia. How accurate would you be in correctly naming the various regional officials, prime ministers, presidents, kings, and governors that you might encounter? Unless you either had accompanied the diplomat yourself or were relying heavily on the account of people intimately familiar with the region, it's very unlikely that

---

25 Most critical scholars reject the idea that the Gospels were written by their traditional authors, Matthew, Mark, Luke, and John. While I see no reason to deny the traditional attribution, the question is irrelevant to the points I make in this chapter. In particular, almost all scholars agree that the author of the Gospel of Luke also wrote the book of Acts.

26 F. F. Bruce, *The New Testament Documents: Are They Reliable?*, 6th ed. (Grand Rapids, MI: Eerdmans, 1981), 83–86.

27 Bruce, *The New Testament Documents*, 83–86.

you'd be able to reproduce the correct titles. The same is true of Luke's account in Acts. While it's possible that Luke was meticulously accurate in his writing of Acts and still largely unreliable in the writing of his Gospel, I think a better option is to recognize that he was a competent historian whose biography of Jesus is generally historically reliable as well.

Corroboration from the Jewish Context

Fifth, the specifically Jewish context and concerns of the Gospels are unlikely to have been invented by later authors. Many examples could be cited under this heading, but I'll confine myself to three: Aramaic words and phrases in the Gospels, Jewish religious details in the Gospels, and the absence of any discussion of Gentile circumcision.

Most scholars today believe that as a first-century Palestinian Jew, Jesus would have primarily spoken Aramaic, the common language of first-century Palestine. Although the Gospels were written in Greek, there are a few places, especially in the Gospel of Mark, where Jesus's words are recorded in Aramaic. Moreover, Mark supplements these "Aramaisms" (*Boanerges*, 3:17; *Talitha cumi*, 5:41; *Corban*, 7:11; *Ephphatha*, 7:34; *Abba*, 14:36; *Eloi Eloi lema sabachthani*, 15:34) with Greek translations for the benefit of his readers, to whom these phrases would apparently have been difficult to understand. One has to wonder what incentive or ability Mark would have had to insert such words into his narrative if these stories were fabricated outside of Palestine several decades after the events of Jesus's life. Isn't it more plausible that he was simply recording what eyewitnesses remembered?

We find ourselves in a similar situation when we examine the Jewish religious details mentioned in the Gospels. Focusing again on Mark's Gospel, we find several instances in which Jesus's conflict with various Jewish groups must be explained to Mark's non-Jewish audience: first in Mark 7:3–4 with reference to the ceremonial washing practiced by the Pharisees; then in Mark 7:11, where the practice of "Corban" must be explained; and then again in Mark 12:18 regarding the Sadducees' view of the resurrection. All four Gospels are replete with tangential mentions of Jewish religious customs, festivals, and quotations from Old Testament Scriptures. It is, of course, possible that Jews living in the Mediterranean Diaspora fabricated these stories, but it would be very odd for them to include details holding so little interest for non-Jewish readers. The best explanation is that the Gospels so clearly reflect a first-century Palestinian context because they have accurately transmitted stories from the life of a first-century Palestinian rabbi: Jesus.

In my mind, the most powerful argument against the large-scale fabrication of Gospel stories by later Christian communities has to do with the subject of Gentile circumcision. The question of whether Gentile (non-Jewish) converts to Christianity had to be circumcised was the most contentious topic in the early church. It occasioned Paul's scathing letter to the Galatians; it is discussed in Romans, 1 Corinthians, Ephesians, Philippians, Colossians, and Titus; and it takes up several chapters in the book of Acts, where it prompted a church-wide council. This controversy almost tore the early church apart. Yet in the biblical Gospels, Jesus says nothing whatsoever about Gentile circumcision. If we really think that early Christian communities were inventing sayings and placing them into the mouth of Jesus to lend authoritative support to their beliefs, why would they neglect to do so in this case?

Most interestingly of all, although Jesus is silent on the issue of Gentile circumcision in Matthew, Mark, Luke, and John, we see Jesus explicitly questioned about circumcision by his disciples in the extrabiblical Gospel of Thomas, where he declares that it is not beneficial (Gospel of Thomas, 53). This kind of dialogue is exactly what we'd expect to see in theologically motivated fictions written by later Christians; yet it is absent from the biblical Gospels. It would then seem that the biblical authors felt constrained to report the actual events of Jesus's life even when they had great incentive to fabricate authoritative teachings.

For all these reasons, the unmistakably Jewish character of the Gospel accounts gives us an additional reason to believe that they accurately reflect the words and teaching of the historical Jesus.

Corroboration from Onomastics

Finally, recent evidence from the field of onomastics—the study of the history and origin of names—strongly supports the reliability of the Gospels. A few decades ago, historian Tal Ilan compiled a database of hundreds of proper names drawn from ossuaries, or burial boxes, of Jews born between 300 BC and AD 200 in Palestine. The data show, for instance, that the most popular name for a Jewish male born in Palestine around the time of Jesus was Simon, while the most popular female name was Mary (see table 1). Using this catalog, biblical scholar Richard Bauckham compared the actual historical frequency of proper names with those of individuals named in the Gospels and Acts.[28] Not only do we find that the most popular New Testament names match the most popular names found on the ossuaries; we even find that the percentages of total names in those two sources roughly agree for both male and female names.[29] For example, about 10 percent of the men named in the Gospels and Acts had the name Simon, and 8 percent had the name Joseph, while only 4 percent had the name Ananias. For comparison, 13 percent of the named male individuals in first-century Palestinian ossuaries had the name Simon, 10 percent had the name Joseph, and 4 percent had the name Ananias.

---

28 Richard Bauckham, *Jesus and the Eyewitnesses: The Gospels as Eyewitness Testimony* (Grand Rapids, MI: Eerdmans, 2006), 85–88.

29 For simplicity, I have included only names taken from ossuaries, omitting the more minor sources employed by Bauckham. His conclusions are unchanged.

Table 1. Frequency of names in the Gospels and Acts versus Jewish ossuaries

	Gospels and Acts		Ossuaries	
Rank	Male Names	Percent	Male Names	Percent
1	Simon	10.5	Simon	13.3
2	Joseph	7.7	Joseph	10.2
3	Judas	6.4	Judas	10.0
4	John	6.4	Lazarus	6.6
5	James	6.4	John	5.7
6	Jesus	3.8	Jesus	5.0
7	Ananias	3.8	Ananias	4.1
8	Herod	3.8	Matthew	3.8
Rank	Female Names	Percent	Female Names	Percent
1	Mary	35.0	Mary	23.5
2	Salome	6.0	Salome	23.0

Why is this data such compelling evidence for the historicity of the Gospels? Most scholars, whether Christian or non-Christian, believe that the Gospels and Acts were written outside of Palestine a few decades after the events they narrate.[30] Suppose we asked four different American authors to write short novels set in Honduras during the Vietnam War, each involving around twenty different named characters. What are the chances that the names of the fictional characters created by the authors would show a good statistical match to the actual names of Hondurans during the 1970s? Extremely low. Would even one of the authors, let alone all four, realize the importance of using realistic names? And even with the benefit of the

---

30 For example, see Bart D. Ehrman, *The New Testament: A Historical Introduction to the Early Christian Writings* (New York: Oxford University Press, 1997), 41, 56, 79, 98, 153. Ehrman places the composition of the Gospels outside of Palestine between AD 65 and 95.

Internet, which ancient authors obviously didn't have, how accessible are foreign census records from a half century ago? In the same way, it seems extremely unlikely that the four authors of the Gospels would have had the foresight, let alone the ability, to write fictional narratives that so accurately yet subtly reflect their historical settings. The best explanation for this data is that the writers preserved the names of actual historical individuals involved in the actual historical events described by the Gospels.[31]

With so much evidence of the authors' meticulous attention to detail, we have good reason to think that the Gospels can be trusted to provide us with at least a generally reliable portrait of the historical words and actions of Jesus of Nazareth. But therein lies the problem.

Jesus's Claims

Imagine you're leaving your favorite coffee shop one morning when you are accosted by a serious-looking man in his early thirties. With little introduction, he begins telling you how you ought to live. He pronounces his authoritative decisions on various theological matters. He announces God's imminent judgment. He tells you that you need to repent so that you do not face God's wrath. The man continues his discourse by demanding that you love him more than you love your father and mother, spouse and children, brothers and sisters, or even your own life. He declares that he is God's chosen King, who will one day judge all of humanity. How would you respond to this encounter?

Chances are you would not extol his good moral teaching. You would back away nervously, climb into your car, and lock the door. If the man began to attract a large following in your city, you would be alarmed. You would warn your family and friends about him. If his disciples grew numerous enough, you might even begin to wonder whether the police ought to be involved.

---

31 See also an excellent extended discussion of additional onomastic evidence in chap. 3 of Peter J. Williams, *Can We Trust the Gospels?* (Wheaton, IL: Crossway, 2018), 51–86.

Yet, once we establish the basic historical reliability of the Gospels, we are forced to conclude that the historical Jesus made exactly the same claims as our hypothetical coffee-shop messiah. Indeed, he made even more outlandish claims on numerous occasions, across all four Gospels and at every point in his ministry:

- Jesus claimed to be the Jewish Messiah, God's chosen ruler of the nation of Israel (Matt. 26:63–64; Mark 8:29–30; John 4:25–26).
- He claimed to be able to forgive sin (Matt. 9:2–8; Mark 2:1–12; Luke 5:18–26; 7:36–50).
- He claimed that he was the only way to know God (Matt. 11:27; Luke 10:22; John 14:6).
- He claimed to have preexisted (Luke 10:18; John 8:57–58; 17:5).
- He claimed that we must love him more than our mothers or fathers or children or even our own lives (Matt. 10:37–39; Luke 9:23–24; 14:26–27; John 12:25).
- He claimed that our eternal destinies depend on our response to him (Matt. 16:24–27; Luke 12:8–9; John 5:24).
- He claimed that he would suffer for our sins (Matt. 26:28; Luke 22:20; John 3:14–15).
- He claimed that he would rise from the dead (Matt. 16:21; Mark 10:34; John 2:19).
- He claimed that he would return at the end of time to judge all of humanity (Matt. 25:31–46; Mark 13:26–27; John 5:28–30).

If a religious teacher were making such statements today, we would not smile benignly. Even if we were convinced that he was sincerely deluded, we would recognize that his demands for unconditional surrender and allegiance were objectively evil. Who could rightly make these kinds of claims and demand this kind of loyalty but God?

In fact, there have been cases in which people like Juanita Peraza, Jim Jones, and Ariffin Mohammed made similar claims to divinity. But in no other case are we inclined to label these individuals as anything other than dangerous charlatans or lunatics. Their names were quickly forgotten or live on only in infamy. Jesus alone changed the course of history. His teaching on caring for the poor and oppressed, living the life of a servant, and forgiving one's enemies has inspired millions to acts of self-sacrifice, courage, and love. How could a lunatic or a liar have made such an impact?

To further illustrate my point, let me simply quote some of Jesus's words from the Gospel of Matthew:

Blessed are the poor in spirit, for theirs is the kingdom of heaven.
    Blessed are those who mourn, for they shall be comforted.
    Blessed are the meek, for they shall inherit the earth.
    Blessed are those who hunger and thirst for righteousness, for they shall be satisfied.
    Blessed are the merciful, for they shall receive mercy.
    Blessed are the pure in heart, for they shall see God.
    Blessed are the peacemakers, for they shall be called sons of God.
    Blessed are those who are persecuted for righteousness' sake, for theirs is the kingdom of heaven. (5:3–10)

You have heard that it was said, "You shall love your neighbor and hate your enemy." But I say to you, Love your enemies and pray for those who persecute you, so that you may be sons of your Father who is in heaven. For he makes his sun rise on the evil and on the good, and sends rain on the just and on the unjust. (5:43–45)

Not everyone who says to me, "Lord, Lord," will enter the kingdom of heaven, but the one who does the will of my Father who is in heaven. On that day many will say to me, "Lord, Lord, did we not prophesy in your name, and cast out demons in your name, and do many mighty works in your name?" And then will I declare to them, "I never knew you; depart from me, you workers of lawless-ness." (7:21–23)

Whoever loves father or mother more than me is not worthy of me, and whoever loves son or daughter more than me is not worthy of me. And whoever does not take his cross and follow me is not worthy of me. Whoever finds his life will lose it, and whoever loses his life for my sake will find it. (10:37–39)

All things have been handed over to me by my Father, and no one knows the Son except the Father, and no one knows the Father except the Son and anyone to whom the Son chooses to reveal him. Come to me, all who labor and are heavy laden, and I will give you rest. Take my yoke upon you, and learn from me, for I am gentle and lowly in heart, and you will find rest for your souls. For my yoke is easy, and my burden is light. (11:27–30)

Truly, I say to you, unless you turn and become like children, you will never enter the kingdom of heaven. Whoever humbles himself like this child is the greatest in the kingdom of heaven.

Whoever receives one such child in my name receives me, but whoever causes one of these little ones who believe in me to sin, it would be better for him to have a great millstone fastened around his neck and to be drowned in the depth of the sea. (18:3–6)

In these statements and dozens of others, we see the shocking juxtaposi-tion of intense moral beauty and hair-raising divine authority. What do you do with a man like this?

Given the evidence for the general historical reliability of the Gospels, the trilemma is just as pressing today as when C. S. Lewis first formulated it. We must come to a decision about who Jesus is and then live out that decision consistently, whether that means surrendering to him as our Lord and rescuer or rejecting him as an evil deceiver.

As Lewis said in another essay:

> Here is a door, behind which, according to some people, the secret of the universe is waiting for you. Either that's true, or it isn't. And if it isn't, then what the door really conceals is simply the greatest fraud, the most colossal "sell" on record. Isn't it obviously the job of every man (that is a man and not a rabbit) to try to find out which, and then to devote his full energies either to serving this tremendous secret or to exposing and destroying this gigantic humbug?[32]

Now, as always, Jesus demands our unqualified allegiance or our unqualified rejection. Try as we might, we cannot escape by expressing our polite approval.

At this point, a skeptic might be tempted to shrug and say: "All you've shown is that Jesus is either God or an evil megalomaniac. Why not just take option B? Perhaps Jesus was an evil megalomaniac after all, a dangerous cult leader whose execution was understandable." While the trilemma by itself doesn't favor one choice over the other, let me offer two considerations that ought to make us hesitant to dispose of Jesus so quickly.

First, the moral teaching and character of Jesus militate against the "evil megalomaniac" response. As I noted in the introduction of this chapter, even many atheists recognize the beauty of Jesus's life and teaching. Of course, it is conceivable that an evil megalomaniac's teaching could be filled with outward moral beauty and that he could dedicate his life to healing the sick and befriending social outcasts before dying with a prayer of forgiveness on his lips. But, *prima facie*, that seems unlikely; evil megalomaniacs rarely live morally exemplary lives. They are usually, well, evil.

---

32 C. S. Lewis, "Man or Rabbit," in *God in the Dock: Essays on Theology and Ethics*, ed. Walter Hooper (Grand Rapids, MI: Eerdmans, 1970), 111–12.

Second, Jesus's tremendous impact on history is quite surprising if he were an evil megalomaniac. Certainly, there are plenty of dictators and tyrants who have transformed history: Hitler, Pol Pot, Genghis Khan. Jesus's world-shaping influence alone does not exclude this option. Rather, it's the *way* in which Jesus transformed history that makes him stand out. Jesus managed to transform the course of human history as a wandering rabbi who led no armies, conquered no kingdoms, didn't have the least inclination to political power, and was executed in his thirties.

What we're left with is a man who (1) traveled around a fiercely monotheistic culture claiming to be God, (2) taught and lived a life of moral beauty, and (3) transformed the entire course of human history for two millennia without recourse to political or military power. If Jesus were merely a run-of-the mill evil megalomaniac, then the last two facts would be absolutely extraordinary. But if Jesus was indeed God, then all three facts are unsurprising. They're exactly what we'd expect if God actually came to earth.

Objections to the Trilemma

In closing this chapter, let me respond to four objections raised to this argument and then offer one suggestion.

"The Bible Is Not Inerrant"

First, one common way to try to avoid the trilemma is by challenging biblical inerrancy, the doctrine that the Bible is without error in all that it teaches. The Internet allows us instantaneous access to "1001 Bible difficulties" and innumerable websites aimed at showing that the Gospels are full of mistakes, often in the form of alleged contradictions between parallel descriptions of the same incident. Similarly, we could claim that there are external contradictions between the biblical accounts and what we know from secular history when it comes to items such as the census of Quirinius, the darkness during the crucifixion, and the date of Theudas's rebellion.

In response to this line of argumentation, it should be stressed that the trilemma does not rely on the inerrancy of the Bible or even its divine inspiration. The trilemma depends only on its general reliability as a normal historical document. The majority of claimed internal contradictions involve minor details, like whether Jesus did or did not forbid the disciples from taking a staff with them on one of their missionary trips (Matt. 10:10 // Mark 6:8 // Luke 9:3) or whether Jesus healed one or two blind men on the road to Jericho (Matt. 20:30 // Mark 10:46 // Luke 18:35); alleged internal contradictions regarding larger issues like the birth narratives are much rarer.[33] The same observation is even more applicable when it comes to alleged external contradictions, given the scarcity of extrabiblical historical sources dealing with first-century Palestine. So, even if we granted that there are factual errors or outright fabrications in the Gospels, we would still have to set those errors against the items I've discussed, which demonstrate the reliability of the Gospels using multiple, converging lines of evidence. The trilemma is valid as long as we can show that the Gospels provide a generally historically reliable portrait of Jesus. Because we have good reason to think that this is the case, doubts about biblical inerrancy would have no relevance to this argument.

More to the point, I believe that objections to the doctrine of inerrancy are approaching the problem from the wrong end. When I first became a Christian, I had very little knowledge of the Bible and attended a mainline church that did not accept inerrancy, although it still had a relatively high view of Scripture. But as I learned more about the Bible, about theology, and about Jesus's teaching, my confidence in the Bible grew. Passages that were once extremely confusing made far more sense once I studied their Jewish background or the cultural context in which they were written. I also discovered that what once

---

33 For a fairly exhaustive discussion of alleged contradictions and an evangelical response, see Craig L. Blomberg, *The Historical Reliability of the Gospels*, 2nd ed. (Downers Grove, IL: InterVarsity Press, 2007).

appeared to be intractable difficulties often had very satisfying solutions. All these experiences gradually led me to accept the doctrine of inerrancy. Of course, that's not to say that even now I can answer all the apparent contradictions in the Bible. I know excellent answers to some alleged contradictions, plausible answers to others, and no really good answers to a handful. But my view of the Bible isn't based on my ability to solve all biblical puzzles, the vast majority of which don't affect essential Christian doctrine anyway; my view of the Bible is based on who I think Jesus is.[34] It might be worthwhile for all non-Christians to take the same approach.

"The Gospels Are Theology, Not History"

A more powerful challenge to the historicity of the Gospels comes from critical scholars like Bart Ehrman, John Dominic Crossan, and the Jesus Seminar. While these scholars would certainly not view the Bible as inerrant, they would go much further and claim that the Bible cannot be trusted to give us even a roughly reliable portrait of Jesus's life and teaching. On what basis do they reach this conclusion?

In general, critical scholars argue that the Gospels show significant theological and narrative development in the accounts of Jesus's life. Critics claim that the earliest sources, which are the Gospel of Mark and Q, portray Jesus very differently than later sources like the Gospels of Matthew, Luke, and John. The internal and external contradictions mentioned above could then be pressed into service not merely to undermine inerrancy but as evidence that the Gospel writers themselves were untrustworthy. They were writing theology rather than history.[35]

---

34 From his teaching, it is clear that Jesus viewed the Bible as fully trustworthy, authoritative, and divinely inspired. If Jesus was indeed God incarnate, then his beliefs about the inspiration of the Bible were accurate. I first heard this argument articulated by Tim Keller, although many others have made it.

35 The dichotomy suggested by the phrase "theology, not history" is a false choice. It's quite possible for an account to be both theology and history. For example, two biographies of a modern historical figure could be perfectly factually correct but still paint vastly different portraits of that

The task of the critical scholar is to clear away later accretions and fabrications to expose the historical kernel, which represents the real, historical Jesus.

Although a full treatment of critical scholarship is beyond the scope of this book, I will offer a few observations in response to this objection to the trilemma.[36] To begin with, critical scholarship often leads to wildly diverging opinions regarding the historical Jesus. At the beginning of his work *The Historical Jesus*, Crossan—himself a critical scholar—says that "*Historical Jesus research* is becoming something of a scholarly bad joke [because of] the number of competent and even eminent scholars producing pictures of Jesus at wide variance with one another."[37] Some scholars identify Jesus as a political revolutionary, others as a magician, others as a Galilean charismatic, others as an Essene, and still others as an eschatological prophet. This "stunning diversity," Crossan writes, is "an academic embarrassment."[38]

To this list, Ehrman adds other scholarly assessments: Jesus was "an ancient Cynic philosopher who had no real interest in Israel as the people of God," "a kind of proto-Marxist," "a proto-feminist," and someone who "taught a completely bourgeois ethic [and who] was married with children." Ehrman remarks dryly that these "are only some of the more serious proposals."[39] The inability of critical scholars

figure based on what material they chose to include and how they chose to present it. Imagine, for instance, biographies of President Abraham Lincoln written by two different biographers, one a close personal friend and the other a historian. Even if the authors made no factual errors in their accounts, their portrayals would differ substantially. In this sense, biblical inerrantists are open to seeing different theological emphases in the Gospels. Inerrantists demur only when critical scholars use the different emphases of the Evangelists to deny the truth or the compatibility of the Gospels. See the Chicago Statement on Biblical Inerrancy, especially the denial in article 18. "The Chicago Statement on Biblical Inerrancy," Moody Bible Institute, https://www.moodybible.org.

36 For an excellent, detailed response, see Michael J. Wilkins and J. P. Moreland, eds., *Jesus under Fire: Modern Scholarship Reinvents the Historical Jesus* (Grand Rapids, MI: Zondervan, 1995).

37 John Dominic Crossan, *The Historical Jesus: The Life of a Mediterranean Jewish Peasant* (New York: HarperSanFrancisco, 1991), xxvii–xxviii.

38 Crossan, *The Historical Jesus*, xxviii.

39 Bart D. Ehrman, *Did Jesus Exist? The Historical Argument for Jesus of Nazareth* (New York: HarperOne, 2012), 11–12.

to reach a consensus on very basic questions about Jesus should cause us to question the reliability of their methodology and the supposedly "assured results of critical scholarship."[40]

Next, even if we were to accept the findings of critical scholarship, there is no guarantee that those conclusions would undermine the trilemma. For example, in *Jesus: Apocalyptic Prophet for the New Millennium*, Ehrman affirms multiple crucial claims about Jesus's radical ethical teaching and his self-understanding. Although Ehrman denies that Jesus claimed to be God, he writes that "Jesus maintained that people who heard his message and followed it would enter into the future Kingdom of God," that "Jesus portrayed himself as the herald of this Kingdom. . . . [And, again,] whoever accepted his message would enter God's Kingdom," that Jesus taught that he "would be the king of God's coming Kingdom," and that Jesus understood himself as "the Messiah, the King of Israel."[41] Ehrman reaches these conclusions despite his belief that the Gospel writers fabricated large portions of the Gospels, retrojecting their own theology onto the life of Jesus. Consequently, we should not assume that critical scholarship is a magic wand that will disappear all of Jesus's radical teachings about himself.

Finally, the conclusions of any critical scholar, no matter how confidently asserted, must be weighed against the evidence. If the Gospels have been so severely redacted, modified, and altered that we cannot trust them enough to give us a historically reliable account of the life

40 This phrase is used unironically in Funk, Hoover, and the Jesus Seminar, *The Five Gospels*, 34. Despite the confident and repeated assertions of Funk et al., their conclusions are far from uncontroversial, even among secular, critical scholars. For example, they insist that Jesus was not an apocalyptic prophet and even say that their non-apocalyptic view is one of the "seven pillars of scholarly wisdom": "Jesus himself rejected that mentality [of impending, eschatological cataclysm] in its crass form. . . . The liberation of the non-eschatological Jesus of the aphorisms and parables from [Albert] Schweitzer's eschatological Jesus is the fifth pillar of contemporary scholarship" (4). Apparently, the community of "contemporary scholarship" does not include Bart Ehrman or Paula Fredriksen or dozens of other non-Christian scholars who see apocalypticism and eschatology as central to Jesus's message.

41 Ehrman, *Jesus: Apocalyptic Prophet*, 217–18.

of Jesus, why do they so clearly reflect a first-century Jewish context? Why have even minor details been confirmed by archaeology? Why do they manage to achieve such accuracy with respect to historical figures, places, names, locations, and customs? In my opinion, the portrayals of Jesus presented by many critical scholars are based on numerous assumptions and speculative reconstructions that are difficult to test. Furthermore, the critics show little ability to account for the actual data we have supporting the historicity of the Gospels.

If we're still doubtful about the historical content of the Gospels, I believe that we can take a pragmatic approach. Let's say that someone views John's Gospel as entirely non-historical. I would suggest that he or she ignore John's Gospel and start reading the other three. Perhaps someone believes that Mark's Gospel alone is the only reliable source and that all the other Gospels include embellishments. In that case, stick with Mark. What people will soon discover is that all four Gospels produce precisely the same trilemma. In all of them, Jesus claims to be humanity's unique Lord and Savior. Even if you picked 25 percent of the verses in the Gospels entirely at random and discarded the rest, you would not be able to avoid the trilemma. The only way to avoid it is to sift through the text and throw away all the verses that make you uncomfortable. That does not strike me as a legitimate way to approach history.

"We Don't Have Enough Evidence to Trust the Gospels as History"

Third, people occasionally have an unrealistic view of historiography and the kind of evidence available to students of history. As in any other work of ancient history, the vast majority of statements in the Gospels are neither substantiated nor contradicted by external evidence. That is to be expected. Most objects, buildings, and writings from the first century have vanished. We are not likely to discover a dusty box somewhere in the vicinity of Nazareth that contains the sandals of Jesus or scraps of bread from the Last Supper. If we insist that the Gospels can be trusted only where they are subject to external verification, we are asking for the impossible. Certainly, we are applying a standard of proof to the Gospels that we would never apply to any other works of ancient history, whether those of Tacitus or Josephus or Thucydides. The evidence I've presented makes it more than reasonable to accept the Gospels' statements as generally historically trustworthy, even in areas where their claims are not immediately amenable to independent confirmation.

"We Can't Trust the Gospels Because of Their Miraculous Elements"

Fourth, it is sometimes claimed that the existence of miracles in the Gospel stories gives us good reason to think they are not historical, since we know that miracles cannot occur. I'll discuss this issue at more length in the next chapter, but for now it's sufficient to observe that this argument is a questionable objection to the trilemma. What we are trying to decide is whether or not Jesus is God. To say that we cannot take the Gospels seriously because they involve Jesus doing the kinds of things that only God could do (miracles) is to have settled on an answer in advance. A more fair-minded approach would be to table the issue of miracles in Jesus's ministry and focus instead on his character and teachings. If we conclude that his claims were valid, then it is not surprising that he performed miracles to authenticate those claims.

A Final Suggestion

Finally, my recommendation to both Christians and non-Christians is to simply read the Gospels. Christians should never be afraid they'll "outgrow" the Gospels or any other part of the Bible. No matter how well versed we are in theology, no matter how much of the Bible we have committed to memory, there is always something new, convicting, and moving to be discovered in the life of Jesus.

Likewise, non-Christians may be surprised to read about the actual character of the historical Jesus. He is not the figure many of us imagine.

If our view of Christ is largely shaped by Renaissance art, television preachers, dim recollections of Sunday school, and pop culture references, then it will quickly collide with the Jesus of the Bible. Jesus was not only compassionate and gentle; he spoke with power and authority. He was scathing in his condemnation of religious hypocrisy. He embraced outcasts and the marginalized, and warned people of God's wrath against sin. Jesus does not fit neatly or comfortably into any of our conventional human categories. Engage him seriously and let him change you.

3

The Resurrection

Returning from the tomb they told all these things to the
eleven and to all the rest. . . . But these words seemed
to them an idle tale, and they did not believe them.

LUKE 24:8–11

GIVEN THE TREMENDOUS IMPACT that Jesus made on world history and the beauty of his life and teaching, most of us are understandably hesitant to write him off as an evil megalomaniac. But could Jesus really have been the Son of God? Many people still find this alternative difficult to accept. In this chapter, I want to examine a second, independent reason that we need to take Jesus's claims very seriously: his resurrection.

The Significance of the Resurrection

For two thousand years, Christians have insisted that Jesus rose physically from the dead on the Sunday after his crucifixion. The historicity of the resurrection is central to Christian theology because Jesus's death and resurrection are both tied to our salvation. While most religions teach that we are saved on the basis of the good things we do,

Christianity teaches that we are saved on the basis of what Jesus did for us. The Bible insists that while we were still far from God, ignoring him, rejecting him, and rebelling against him, God drew near to us in Christ to bear our sin, to take our punishment, and to die on the cross in our place. The resurrection was God's confirmation that Jesus was who he claimed to be, and it is God's assurance to Christians that they have been forgiven.

Because of its theological significance, many people assume that the resurrection is merely an article of religious faith, not an event for which there could be any historical evidence. But that is not the case. In fact, I would argue that even from a purely secular standpoint, the evidence for the resurrection of Jesus is quite strong. For instance, skeptic Jeffery Lowder, a cofounder of Internet Infidels, writes that "strong historical arguments" can be made for the resurrection. Although he thinks that such arguments are insufficient, he agrees that "for theists [people who believe in God's existence] . . . the resurrection is a plausible explanation."[1] Similarly, renowned atheist-turned-deist philosopher Antony Flew affirms that "the evidence for the resurrection is better than for claimed miracles in any other religion. It's outstandingly different in quality and quantity."[2] Jewish scholar Pinchas Lapide even states, "I accept the resurrection of Easter Sunday not as an invention of the community of disciples, but as a historical event."[3]

---

1   Jeffery J. Lowder, "The Historicity of Jesus' Resurrection: The Debate between Christians and Skeptics," The Secular Web, https://infidels.org/library/modern/jeff_lowder/jesus_resurrection/.

2   Gary R. Habermas and Antony Flew, *Did the Resurrection Happen? A Conversation with Gary Habermas and Antony Flew*, ed. David J. Baggett (Downers Grove, IL: InterVarsity Press, 2009), 85.

3   Quoted in Carl E. Braaten, introduction to *The Resurrection of Jesus: A Jewish Perspective* (Eugene, OR: Wipf and Stock, 1982), 13. Lapide's position on the resurrection is particularly interesting because he takes a fairly critical approach to the accounts found in the Gospels, dismisses the empty tomb as a later embellishment, and yet concludes that the resurrection was a historical event on the basis of the radical transformation of the disciples' lives (see 123–31).

Evidence for the Resurrection

What historical evidence was sufficient to convince these non-Christians that the resurrection should be taken seriously and not carelessly dismissed? Although there are other lines of evidence, I'll sketch an argument for the historicity of the resurrection that rests on four main points: the death and burial of Jesus, the empty tomb, the belief of the apostles, and the conversion of Paul.[4]

Jesus's Death and Burial

Contemporary historians are virtually unanimous in their acceptance of Jesus's death on the cross.[5] His death by crucifixion is the single fact most mentioned in all the historical records of his life, both Christian and non-Christian. It is recorded in numerous books of the New Testament, including all four Gospels, Acts, Paul's letters, Hebrews, 1 Peter, and Revelation. It is mentioned by non-Christians like Josephus and Tacitus. It is discussed in apocryphal gospels such as the Gospel of Peter and the Gospel of Truth. And it is referenced by numerous early Christian writings, including 1 Clement and the epistles of Barnabas and Polycarp. Moreover, it is extremely unlikely that the early Christians would have invented the story that their Savior was an executed criminal. Agnostic Bart Ehrman writes:

---

4   I follow the general argument presented in William Lane Craig, "Did Jesus Rise from the Dead?," in *Jesus under Fire: Modern Scholarship Reinvents the Historical Jesus*, ed. Michael J. Wilkins and J. P. Moreland (Grand Rapids, MI: Zondervan, 1995), 141–76. See also Craig, *Reasonable Faith: Christian Truth and Apologetics*, 3rd ed. (Wheaton, IL: Crossway, 2008), 333–404; Gary R. Habermas and Michael R. Licona, *The Case for the Resurrection of Jesus* (Grand Rapids, MI: Kregel, 2004); and N. T. Wright, *The Resurrection of the Son of God* (Minneapolis: Fortress, 2003).

5   I say "virtually" because there is a small movement known as Jesus Mythicism, which rejects not only the idea that Jesus died on the cross but also that he ever existed. See, for example, Robert M. Price, *The Incredible Shrinking Son of Man: How Reliable Is the Gospel Tradition?* (Amherst, NY: Prometheus, 2003). It is difficult to overstate how marginal this idea is among biblical scholars. An excellent dialogue between Price and more mainstream scholars can be found in James K. Beilby and Paul Rhodes Eddy, eds., *The Historical Jesus: Five Views* (Downers Grove, IL: IVP Academic, 2009). See also Bart D. Ehrman, *Did Jesus Exist? The Historical Argument for Jesus of Nazareth* (New York: HarperOne, 2012).

It is hard today to understand just how offensive the idea of a crucified messiah would have been to most first-century Jews. . . . Since no one would have made up the idea of a crucified messiah, Jesus must really have existed, must really have raised messianic expectations, and must really have been crucified.[6]

New Testament scholar Gerd Lüdemann captures the scholarly consensus when he writes, "The fact of the death of Jesus as a consequence of crucifixion is indisputable."[7]

Similarly, there is strong evidence for the historicity of Jesus's burial. Most importantly, Jesus's burial is recorded in all four Gospels. The burial of Jesus is also explicitly mentioned in Paul's first letter to the Corinthians, written in the late AD 50s, around thirty years after Jesus's death, and it probably reflects a much earlier creed.[8] Given that multiple attestation is one of the major criteria by which New Testament scholars adjudicate the historicity of an event,[9] the fact that several independent sources reference the same event strongly suggests that it is historical. Second, the Gospels all claim that Jesus was buried by Joseph of Arimathea, a member of the Sanhedrin, the Jewish religious court that condemned Jesus to death. It seems unlikely that early Christians would have invented this detail involving such a prominent figure, one who was a member of a group opposed to the early Christian movement.[10]

---

6   Ehrman, *Did Jesus Exist?*, 163–64.
7   Gerd Lüdemann, with Alf Özen, *What Really Happened to Jesus: A Historical Approach to the Resurrection*, trans. John Bowden (Louisville: Westminster John Knox, 1995), 17.
8   For example, "[The statement in 1 Cor. 15] was probably formulated within the first two or three years after Easter itself, since it was already in formulaic form when Paul 'received' it. We are here in touch with the earliest Christian tradition, with something that was being said two decades or more before Paul wrote this letter." Wright, *The Resurrection of the Son*, 319.
9   Bart D. Ehrman, *The New Testament: A Historical Introduction to the Early Christian Writings* (New York: Oxford University Press, 1997), 192–93.
10   Craig, *Reasonable Faith*, 364.

If we accept the position that Jesus did actually die on the cross and was actually buried, we must then ask, What happened to Jesus after his death and burial?

The Empty Tomb

Second, the New Testament Gospels claim that the tomb of Jesus was found empty on the Sunday following his crucifixion. While this claim is not universally affirmed, a recent survey of three decades' worth of academic literature shows that it was accepted by the majority of scholars who wrote on that subject.[11] The strongest piece of evidence in favor of the historicity of the empty tomb is the report that it was discovered by women. This detail may not strike us as odd, but it is surprising, given the low status of women in the first century. For example, the first-century Jewish historian Josephus claimed that Jewish law expressed the following sentiment regarding the reliability of women: "Let not the testimony of women be admitted, on account of the levity and boldness of their sex."[12] If the early Christians were inventing narratives to support their own version of events, why not ascribe the discovery of the tomb to witnesses who would have been received as more credible?

Reflecting on this piece of evidence, Jewish New Testament scholar Geza Vermes concludes:

> In the end, when every argument has been considered and weighed, the only conclusion acceptable to the historian must be that the opinions of the orthodox, the liberal sympathizer and the critical agnostic alike—and even perhaps of the disciples themselves—are simply interpretations of the one disconcerting fact: namely that the

---

11 Gary Habermas, "Resurrection Research from 1975 to the Present: What Are Critical Scholars Saying?," *Journal for the Study of the Historical Jesus* 3, no. 2 (2005): 135–53.

12 Josephus, *Antiquities of the Jews*, trans. William Whiston, 4.8.15, Project Gutenberg, August 9, 2017, https://www.gutenberg.org/files/2848/2848-h/2848-h.htm.

women who set out to pay their last respects to Jesus found to their consternation, not a body, but an empty tomb.[13]

Notice that Vermes is not defending the resurrection; he suggests that it may have been an "interpretation" of the disciples. Nevertheless, he recognizes the strength of the women's testimony as evidence that the tomb was really found empty.

A second factor supporting the historicity of the empty tomb is the fact that just seven weeks after Jesus's death, the apostles began preaching the resurrection in Jerusalem itself, the very city in which Jesus had been crucified. Had he been lying in a tomb even for this length of time, his features such as hair, teeth, stature, and the wounds of crucifixion would have still been identifiable.[14] It is difficult to see how the fledgling Christian movement could have survived despite the opposition of the ruling authorities if the corpse of Jesus had been interred within walking distance of the temple. Any skeptic who wanted to refute the claims of the apostles could have silenced them by taking a short stroll to the burial place of Jesus. Yet we have no record of anyone claiming that the disciples lied about the empty tomb. How did Christianity grow so rapidly in the very place where Jesus was buried if it could have been falsified so easily?[15]

Finally, at the end of his Gospel, Matthew provides what amounts to a dialogue between Christians and Jews regarding the body of Jesus.[16] He states that the Jewish leaders of his day insisted that Jesus's body had been stolen by the disciples, a claim that apparently was still circulating in the second century, since it is referenced in Justin Martyr's *Dialogue with Trypho*.[17] But this accusation implies that the Jewish leaders be-

13   Geza Vermes, *Jesus the Jew: A Historian's Reading of the Gospels* (Philadelphia: Fortress, 1981), 41.

14   Habermas and Licona, *The Case for the Resurrection of Jesus*, 70.

15   Habermas and Licona, *The Case for the Resurrection of Jesus*, 70.

16   Craig, *Reasonable Faith*, 369–70.

17   Justin Martyr, *Dialogue with Trypho*, trans. Marcus Dods and George Reith, chap. 108, New Advent, https://www.newadvent.org/.

lieved that the tomb was actually empty; obviously, they would not have accused the disciples of grave robbery if they believed that Jesus's body was still in the tomb. For these reasons, most skeptical responses to the resurrection do not simply dismiss the empty tomb as a legend, but try to provide some alternative explanation for it.

The Belief of the Apostles

Third, the followers of Jesus claimed to have seen him alive after he had been executed. They did not claim to have seen him only once or for a short time; they claimed to have seen him repeatedly over an extended period of several weeks. They also did not merely claim to have had a vision of him but said that they touched him, talked to him, and ate with him.[18] These experiences were not limited to one or two individuals but included large groups of people, including five hundred at one time.[19] What are we to make of these claims?

It is nearly universally accepted by historians that the disciples genuinely believed they had encountered the resurrected Jesus, even if they were mistaken in their belief. For instance, Gerd Lüdemann, who denies the historicity of the resurrection, nonetheless states, "It may be taken as historically certain that Peter and the disciples had experiences after Jesus' death in which Jesus appeared to them as the risen Christ."[20] The reason for this consensus is the persecution endured by the apostles for their belief in the resurrection. The apostles were repeatedly beaten and imprisoned. We have good historical evidence that James, Peter, and Paul were all executed for their faith, and church tradition maintains that as many as eleven of the twelve apostles were eventually martyred.[21] Given the suffering that the apostles faced, it

---

18 Craig, *Reasonable Faith*, 385.

19 "Then he appeared to more than five hundred brothers at one time, most of whom are still alive, though some have fallen asleep" (1 Cor. 15:6).

20 Lüdemann, *What Really Happened to Jesus?*, 80.

21 See a book-length discussion of the apostles' fate in Sean McDowell, *The Fate of the Apostles: Examining the Martyrdom Accounts of the Closest Followers of Jesus* (London: Routledge, 2018).

is difficult to maintain that they knew the resurrection to be a hoax. What would their motivation have been if they knew for certain that they had invented the resurrection stories?

As a parallel, it's reasonable to infer that the terrorists who destroyed the Twin Towers on 9/11 were sincere. If they were certain that Islam was false, why were they willing to kill themselves and thousands of others? What would they have had to gain? Likewise, we can infer that the apostles were sincere. Like the terrorists on 9/11, they would have had little to gain and a great deal to lose by acting upon a known falsehood. But unlike the terrorists, the apostles were in a position to know with complete certainty whether their claims were true. They were claiming to have seen, touched, and conversed with a man who had been executed just days earlier. If they had intentionally invented that claim, they would have known for certain that it was not worth dying for.

Muslim author Reza Aslan, who argues that it's "impossible to know" exactly what happened after Jesus's death, nonetheless recognizes the significance of these considerations. He writes:

> One could simply . . . dismiss the resurrection as a lie, and declare belief in the risen Jesus to be the product of a deludable mind. However, there is this nagging fact to consider: one after another of those who claimed to have witnessed the risen Jesus went to their own gruesome deaths refusing to recant their testimony. That is not, in itself, unusual. Many zealous Jews died horribly for refusing to deny their beliefs. But these first followers of Jesus were not being asked to reject matters of faith based on events that took place centuries, if not millennia, before. They were being asked to deny something they themselves personally, directly encountered.[22]

---

22 Reza Aslan, *Zealot: The Life and Times of Jesus of Nazareth* (New York: Random House, 2013), 174.

When they began to face persecution and even death, why would they continue to affirm what they knew to be a lie? The best explanation is that they truly believed they had seen Jesus risen from the dead, whether or not their belief was correct.

The Conversion of Paul

Fourth, the conversion of Paul is an important datum reported in the book of Acts and by Paul himself in several of his New Testament letters. He had originally been a vehement opponent of the church and had even consented to the stoning of the first Christian martyr, Stephen. While traveling to Damascus to continue his persecution of the early church, Paul suddenly became a Christian, claiming he had encountered Jesus on the road. Unlike the other apostles, Paul had not been a follower of Jesus during his ministry and was clearly no friend to the early church. Thus, his testimony can be regarded as that of a "hostile witness," someone who had no incentive to accept Christian testimony about the resurrection unless he himself had an experience that he could unambiguously interpret as confirmation that Jesus was alive.[23]

The weight of this piece of evidence is significant. First, Paul's conversion put him at immediate odds with the Jewish religious leaders in every city to which he traveled. In his second letter to the Corinthians, Paul recounts how he was whipped, beaten, stoned, and shipwrecked as a result of his faith (11:24–25). Moreover, the physical consequences of his conversion are perhaps even less significant than its spiritual implications. Like many Pharisees, Paul regarded the claims of Jesus's followers—that their Master was the divine Messiah—to be not only false but utterly blasphemous (see Acts 22:2–5; 1 Tim. 1:13). However, Paul underwent a complete religious transformation in a matter of days. He went from regarding Jesus as a false prophet to believing that Jesus was the unique Son of God, who alone offered salvation to all humanity.

---

23 Habermas and Licona, *The Case for the Resurrection of Jesus*, 124.

This event is psychologically surprising. It would have been as un-expected as Richard Dawkins, the vocal Oxford atheist, suddenly announcing that Jesus appeared to him in his study and that he was now a Christian. While we might think he was crazy, it would be hard to deny that something extraordinary had taken place to bring about such a complete reversal. In fact, the conversion of Paul is even more surprising than the hypothetical conversion of Dawkins, given that Paul embraced not a world religion with billions of followers but a despised, persecuted religious sect with no power and few adherents. Therefore, anyone who doubts the resurrection must provide a plausible account of why Paul underwent such a dramatic conversion in such a short period of time.

Naturalistic Explanations

Given the evidence, it is interesting to consider the various explana-tions advanced as alternatives to the Christian claim of Jesus's resur-rection. While many New Testament scholars, regardless of their religious views, accept the four facts listed above, the vast majority of non-Christians obviously do not accept the Christian explanation of those facts: that Jesus rose physically from the dead. If critics reject the historicity of the resurrection, how do they explain these pieces of evidence?

The swoon hypothesis, which originated in the late eighteenth cen-tury, asserts that Jesus did not actually die on the cross but fainted. He recovered consciousness in the tomb a few days later and appeared to his disciples before presumably dying again somewhere else. There are numerous problems with this explanation. First, crucifixion was a form of execution, not just punishment. The burden of proof therefore falls heavily on anyone suggesting that a crucified man managed to survive. Second, it is hard to see how the disciples could have imagined that a badly beaten man had been resurrected to life and immortality. Would a mangled, bloody victim of torture who had spent hours suffocating and who was so close to death that he was buried be able to convince his followers that he was the divine Son of God? Third, the swoon theory is feasible only if we reject a tremendous amount of material in the Gospels, including repeated affirmations that Jesus died, descriptions of Jesus's violent scourging at the hands of the Romans, the testimony of John that the Roman centurion present at the crucifixion stabbed Jesus with a spear to confirm that he was dead, and the fact that Jesus's tomb had been sealed with a large stone. Finally, as with many alternative scenarios, the conversion of Paul must still be independently explained. For all these reasons, contemporary scholars almost universally reject the swoon hypothesis and agree with Jewish scholar Pinchas Lapide that "the death of Jesus of Nazareth on the cross . . . may be considered historically certain."[24]

Alternatively, some scholars subscribe to a variant of the "stolen body" hypothesis, which suggests that Jesus's dead body was stolen from the tomb. The disciples were then subject to repeated mass hallucinations over the next few days, which they interpreted to mean that Jesus had risen from the dead. Many years later, Paul also had some kind of hallucination, which he too interpreted as being an encounter with the risen Christ. The central question for proponents of this theory is "Who took the body?" The sincerity of the disciples' belief and the suffering they endured rules out their participation. If Joseph of Arimathea, the owner of the tomb, removed Jesus's body, why didn't he tell any of the other disciples, especially since he was a follower of Jesus? If Jesus's family stole the body, why did they conceal it from both his brother James and his mother Mary, who were part of the early church?

Even if some plausible account of the stolen body can be provided, other questions remain. Why would Jesus's disciples, including the five hundred mentioned in 1 Corinthians 15, be subject to the same mass hallucination over a period of forty days? What would cause Paul to

---

24 Pinchas Lapide, *The Resurrection of Jesus: A Jewish Perspective* (Eugene, OR: Wipf and Stock, 1982), 32.

so radically alter his views about Jesus that he was willing to be stoned, beaten, and eventually executed for his beliefs?

A similar alternative is the "wrong tomb" hypothesis, in which Jesus's disciples mistook an empty tomb for the tomb where Jesus was actually buried. In addition to the problems of positing multiple hallucinations over the following weeks and years, this hypothesis faces the obstacle of trying to explain why Jesus's opponents did not go to the correct tomb, disinter the body, and use it to refute the apostles' claims about the resurrection. We must also ignore the repeated statements in the Gospels, even in the earliest account in Mark, that Jesus's female followers saw where he was buried, and the claim in Matthew's Gospel that the tomb was sealed and guarded by Roman soldiers, which would have clearly marked it as Jesus's resting place.

Finally, one of my favorite naturalistic explanations is known as the twin hypothesis. Proponents of this explanation claim that Jesus had an identical twin who was mistaken for Jesus after his death, giving rise to a belief in his resurrection. Former evangelical Robert Greg Cavin defended this hypothesis passionately in a debate with Christian philosopher William Lane Craig, even insisting that Jesus's twin probably used makeup to simulate scars on his hands. During the debate, Cavin affirmed that while the twin hypothesis and all other naturalistic hypotheses are highly improbable, they are more probable than any supernatural explanation.[25]

Though the twin hypothesis sounds extremely marginal, it was also proposed by Bart Ehrman, who appealed to it in a separate debate with Craig.[26] After outlining a twin scenario, Ehrman offered the following remark: "[The twin scenario is] highly unlikely. I don't buy it for

25 William Lane Craig and R. Greg Cavin, "Dead or Alive?" (debate at the University of California, Irvine, 1995), http://www.philvaz.com/CraigCavinDebate.mp3. Unbelievably, at one point, Dr. Cavin even mentions the "ET [extraterrestrial] hypothesis" as a potential explanation for the evidence, although he doesn't elaborate on what he has in mind.

26 William Lane Craig and Bart D. Ehrman, "Is There Historical Evidence for the Resurrection of Jesus?" (debate at College of the Holy Cross, Worcester, Massachusetts, March 2006), http://www.reasonablefaith.org/is-there-historical-evidence-for-the-resurrection-of-jesus-the-craig-ehrman.

a second, but it's more likely than the idea that God raised Jesus from the dead because it doesn't appeal to the supernatural, which historians have no access to."[27] We'll discuss this hesitancy to accept a supernatural explanation in the next section. For now, I merely want to observe that Ehrman recognizes that his explanation is "highly unlikely." It's significant that he would propose such a bizarre explanation when, by his own admission, he doesn't "buy it for a second."

These alternative explanations are interesting for two reasons. First, they show that even critics tend to take seriously the facts mentioned above. They do not uniformly dismiss as legend or myth the empty tomb or the appearances to the disciples or the conversion of Paul; instead, they tend to incorporate these facts into their theories. Second, these explanations demonstrate that whatever happened after Jesus's death was very unusual. There simply aren't any naturalistic hypotheses that explain the historical data without recourse to extraordinary events. All the explanations invoke swoons or hallucinations or grave robbers or even identical twins to account for what happened in the days following the crucifixion.

Seeking the Best Explanation

One of the most fascinating aspects of the historical argument for the resurrection is that the pieces of evidence I've presented thus far are entirely non-miraculous.[28] One needn't be a Christian or even a theist to affirm that (1) Jesus was crucified, died, and was buried; (2) the tomb in which Jesus was buried was found empty; (3) Jesus's disciples had experiences they interpreted as appearances of the resurrected Jesus; and (4) the apostle Paul had an experience that he interpreted as an appearance of the resurrected Jesus and that led him to dramatically convert to Christianity. An atheist could easily accept each of these claims on the basis of the historical arguments I've offered in this chapter. The

27 Craig and Ehrman, "The Resurrection of Jesus."
28 Cf. Craig, *Reasonable Faith*, 350.

claim that Jesus died by crucifixion does not—by itself—require a miracle. The claim that Jesus was buried does not—by itself—require a miracle. The claim that the tomb of Jesus was found empty does not—by itself—require a miracle. Even the claim that Jesus's disciples and Paul had experiences that they interpreted as encounters with the risen Jesus does not—by itself—require a miracle. It is only when we try to provide a coherent explanation of these various facts that we are forced to wrestle with the possibility of a miracle.

Moreover, the general historical reliability of the Gospels, which I discussed in chapter 2, gives these four claims additional credibility (see "The Historical Reliability of the Gospels," p. 31). We're not considering statements made by sources of unknown or questionable quality. We're considering claims made by sources we already have good reason to think are generally reliable. While even unreliable sources can yield historical data, reliable sources give us even more reason to accept their claims as accurate.[29]

Figure 3 summarizes our discussion so far. If we accept the pieces of historical evidence I've provided on the basis of the historical arguments I've outlined, we must next look for a unifying explanation. In other words, what is the best explanation of the empty tomb, the experiences of the disciples, and the experiences of Paul? Which explanation is the most comprehensive, the most parsimonious, and the most consistent? Are competing naturalistic accounts of what happened plausible or implausible? And if they are implausible, would it not be worthwhile to consider the traditional Christian explanation: that God raised Jesus from the dead?

---

29 The general historical reliability of the Gospels is itself a good reason to accept the resurrection, which is reported in all four Gospels (in addition to Paul's letters). There is no question that, to the authors of the Gospels, the crucifixion and resurrection of Jesus were the two most important events they recorded; between one-quarter (Luke) and one-half (John) of the Gospels' contents focuses on the final week of Jesus's life, to say nothing of numerous predictions of Jesus's suffering and death that occur at earlier points. Thus, it seems implausible to suggest that the Gospels are generally historically reliable records of Jesus's life and yet are completely unreliable when they report on what they consider its two central, defining events.

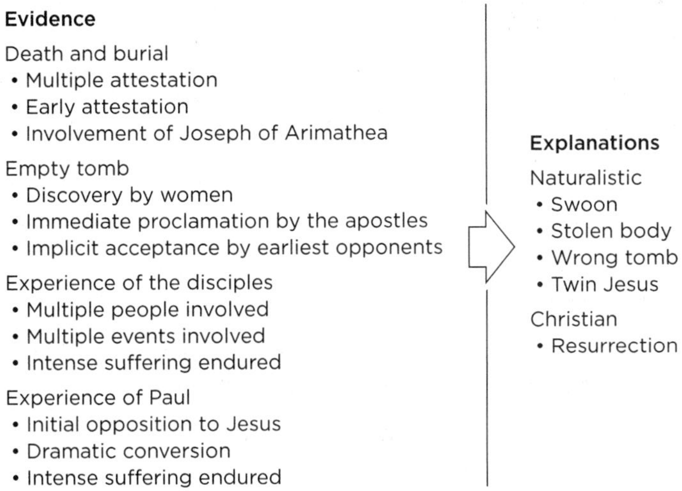

Evidence

Death and burial
- Multiple attestation
- Early attestation
- Involvement of Joseph of Arimathea

Empty tomb
- Discovery by women
- Immediate proclamation by the apostles
- Implicit acceptance by earliest opponents

Experience of the disciples
- Multiple people involved
- Multiple events involved
- Intense suffering endured

Experience of Paul
- Initial opposition to Jesus
- Dramatic conversion
- Intense suffering endured

Explanations

Naturalistic
- Swoon
- Stolen body
- Wrong tomb
- Twin Jesus

Christian
- Resurrection

Figure 3. Historical evidence for Jesus's resurrection and competing explanations

At the conclusion of his essay laying out the cases for and against the resurrection, atheist Jeff Lowder makes the following astute comments:

> Both sides are correct within their worldview. . . . Atheists should not be so quick to ridicule the miraculous and use a Humean attack on miracles to refute the resurrection. Unless atheists can demonstrate that theism is irrational or that the historical evidence for a material resurrection is lacking, they are unlikely to convince many theists to reject the resurrection. Similarly, Christian apologists need to recognize that, *until atheists are shown that theism is plausible*, atheists will continue to regard the resurrection as a highly implausible event.[30]

In other words, Lowder maintains that atheists' rejection of the resurrection is not based on the absence of evidence or on a highly probable naturalistic alternative. Rather, it is a consequence of their belief that God does not exist. I think Lowder is absolutely correct. It is

30 Lowder, *The Historicity of Jesus' Resurrection*, chap. 5; emphasis added.

not evidence per se that leads to skepticism about the resurrection. Instead, it is evidence interpreted in accordance with a prior belief in atheism that leads to skepticism about the resurrection. I would only add that in light of the evidence, the atheist should probably be open to reconsidering his atheism.

Objections to the Resurrection

"Miracles Are Impossible"

From what we've seen in this chapter, the most common reason that people reject the resurrection as the best explanation of the evidence is a commitment to naturalism, the belief that nature is all that exists. If naturalism is true, then miracles are not just unlikely but impossible, since there is no God outside of nature who could perform them.

At first, this position seems eminently reasonable. After all, if we hear a noise in the attic, none of us believes that angels are playing croquet on our roof. We no longer accept explanations for thunder or sunsets based on Thor or Ra. In the words of renowned New Testament scholar Rudolph Bultmann, "It is impossible to use electric light and the wireless and to avail ourselves of modern medical and surgical discoveries, and at the same time to believe in the New Testament world of spirits and miracles."[31] Liberal theologian John Shelby Spong concurs: "There never was an age of miracles [and] the things our ancestors once called miracles were in fact either tales of fantasy that grew over the passing years or misunderstandings of reality based on a lack of knowledge about how the world operated."[32]

Is this view correct? Is naturalism the unavoidable outcome of living in a modern, scientific age? And does modern science render the occurrence of miracles unbelievable? Let me address both of those questions.

---

31 Rudolph Bultmann, *Kerygma and Myth: A Theological Debate*, ed. Hans Werner Bartsch (New York: Harper and Row, 1961), 5, quoted in Alvin Plantinga, *Where the Conflict Really Lies: Science, Religion, and Naturalism* (Oxford: Oxford University Press, 2011), 71.

32 John Shelby Spong, *Jesus for the Non-Religious: Recovering the Divine at the Heart of the Human* (New York: HarperOne, 2008), 12.

First, naturalism is a philosophical position, not a scientific one; there is no scientific experiment which demonstrates that "nature is all that exists." It is true that scientists generally seek natural explanations for the phenomena they observe. This practice is known as *methodological naturalism*. But *methodological naturalism*, the preference for natural explanations over nonnatural explanations, is distinct from *metaphysical naturalism*, the claim that no nonnatural entities exist at all.[33]

Consider a parallel: Scientists also generally seek explanations within the framework of established scientific theories. We assume that existing theories, which have proven successful in elucidating and predicting a wide range of physical phenomena, will be sufficient to explain new data, even when those data at first seem difficult to

---

33 Whether methodological naturalism merely encourages natural explanations or excludes nonnatural explanations entirely is a point of contention. See, for example, the discussion of methodological naturalism in Jerry A. Coyne, *Faith versus Fact: Why Science and Religion Are Incompatible* (New York: Viking, 2015), 91–96. Some scientists see the scientific method as necessarily excluding appeals to the supernatural, while Coyne and fellow atheist Vic Stenger both argue that science can legitimately investigate the supernatural. This position occasionally produces strange allies. For instance, Stenger disagreed with the 2005 *Kitzmiller v. Dover* court decision that classified intelligent design as "not science." Stenger wrote that the decision was "incorrect because science is not forbidden from considering supernatural causes." See Victor J. Stenger, *God: The Failed Hypothesis: How Science Shows That God Does Not Exist* (Amherst, NY: Prometheus, 2008), 60. Contra the ruling on *Kitzmiller v. Dover*, Stenger believes that intelligent design is science, but that it is falsified science.

What is missing from Coyne and Stenger is a discussion of *what kinds* of supernatural entities are accessible to science. For example, one important requirement for any scientific investigation is reproducibility. Science usually assumes that we can observe or control all the relevant variables needed to produce a particular effect. But if supernatural entities are more like persons than forces, this assumption is incorrect. I can predict with great accuracy the path that a ball will take when I roll it down a hill because I can observe almost all the relevant variables (landscape curvature, friction, wind resistance, etc.) and can even control them at will. On the other hand, it would be exceptionally difficult to predict with accuracy the path that my wife and I will take during a stroll in the park because I can't observe most of the relevant variables (our intentions, our emotional states, our preferences, etc.), and I have little control over them. In this way, God's intervention in the natural world is better approached in the same way that we approach historical events. While we can legitimately ask whether a supernatural explanation for a particular event is plausible, we should not expect to be able to reproduce the conditions necessary to probe that explanation experimentally.

reconcile with our theoretical understanding. However, it would be a huge mistake to confuse our *preference* for working within existing theories as *proof*, or even *evidence*, that all other theories are wrong. Indeed, rejecting new theories out of hand would be devastating to the scientific enterprise. Every major advance in scientific thinking, from germ theory to plate tectonics, has depended on challenging established scientific models. In the same way, the fact that scientists generally prefer natural explanations is neither proof nor evidence that all other explanations are wrong.

Second, with the advent of quantum mechanics in the early twentieth century, we can no longer dismiss miracles as impossible because they "violate the laws of nature." According to quantum mechanics, while events may be extremely improbable, very few events can be ruled out as absolutely impossible. For instance, in 2008, *New York Times* science writer Dennis Overbye interviewed physicists to determine whether the LHC, a particle supercollider, had the potential to destroy the world. In the middle of the article, he quipped, "The random nature of quantum physics means that there is always a minuscule, but nonzero, chance of anything occurring, including that the new collider could spit out man-eating dragons."[34] While he was making a joke, he was also technically correct. Almost anything is possible under the laws of quantum mechanics. If God decided to intervene in the universe, he could do so without "violating" any of the natural laws he created.

But given a Christian understanding of God's relationship to nature, it's probably not helpful to think of miracles as "violations" of natural law. The laws of nature are descriptions of how nature operates when it is not acted upon by an external agent, not complete prohibitions on outside agents acting on nature. Imagine that a friend wants to demonstrate the law of gravity to me. He takes me to the roof of his house

---

34 Dennis Overbye, "Gauging a Collider's Odds of Creating a Black Hole," *The New York Times*, April 15, 2008, https://www.nytimes.com/.

and drops a bowling ball ninety-nine times. Each time, the ball takes exactly one second to reach the ground. Before the hundredth drop, I calmly announce that the ball will take thirty seconds to reach the ground. Quite likely, my friend would insist that I'm talking nonsense and that what I propose would be a violation of the law of gravity. But when he drops the ball, I immediately catch it. I wait twenty-nine seconds and then release it, so that it hits the ground thirty seconds after it was dropped. The law of gravity has not been violated; I have merely introduced an external factor into the natural progression of events. This example illustrates God's relationship to miracles. Because God is outside of nature, God no more violates the laws of physics when he performs a miracle than I do when I interrupt the fall of the bowling ball by catching it.

"We Should Reject Miracles Because They Are Highly Improbable"

Because an absolute commitment to naturalism and a complete rejection of the possibility of the miraculous seem extreme, we could seek a more moderate position. Rather than insisting that miracles are impossible, we could insist that they are merely highly improbable. In other words, we could argue that the probability of their occurrence is so low that an immense amount of evidence would be required to convince us that one had taken place. We could then acknowledge that there appears to be some evidence for the resurrection while denying that it is sufficient to overcome the massive improbability we associate with miraculous events. For example, we could argue that someone rising from the dead is necessarily improbable because none of the billions of people who have lived in recent history have risen from the dead. We'd therefore estimate the probability of a resurrection as less than one in a billion and would demand evidence strong enough to overcome this massive improbability.

While this response is certainly more reasonable than an a priori rejection of miracles, it faces a serious problem when we think about how miracles relate to God's intentions. Let's reconsider my bowling ball example. Suppose my friend has dropped the ball a million times over the course of several decades and has always observed that it hits the ground one second after he releases it. It would be tempting to think that there is no more than a one in a million chance that the ball will take longer than one second to reach the ground in any future experiment. But what if, during a particular experiment, my little daughter unexpectedly walks out of the house just as my friend is dropping the ball, so that she is directly in its path? If my friend has this information and knows that I am able to catch the ball, he would not find it at all implausible if I intervened to prevent it from hitting her. In fact, he would expect my intervention and would be amazed if I allowed the bowling ball to hit her. He would not demand extraordinarily strong evidence that I had intervened, given what he knows about my character and my intentions.

Similarly, an appeal to the inherent improbability of any miracle in turn depends on our beliefs about God's intentions, which in turn depend on our beliefs about God's existence. We'll discuss that issue in the next chapter. For the moment, I will only observe that it's more difficult than it appears to dismiss the resurrection as intrinsically improbable without committing to a particular view of God's existence and character. To say that it's unlikely that God raised Jesus from the dead because God did not raise billions of other people from the dead is to assume that Jesus is no more likely a candidate for a powerful, vindicating, authenticating miracle than any other person in history. Even from a purely secular perspective, this assumption is questionable. Jesus is not just some random figure in history, like an extra in the closing credits of a Hollywood B movie. Hence, his resurrection—if it occurred—would have an embedded religious significance that the resurrection of "Confused Bystander in Opening Scene" would not. If Jesus was in fact the Jewish Messiah, then God would have had a compelling reason to validate his ministry through the resurrection.

"If We Accept One Miracle Claim, We Have to Accept All Miracle Claims"

Finally, it's sometimes suggested that accepting the occurrence of one miracle requires us to be equally credulous about every claimed miracle. This concern is unwarranted. Christians do not believe that miracles occur regularly. Indeed, that would undermine the very purpose of a miracle, which is to function as a sign that points to God's extraordinary activity. There can be no interruptions to the regularities of nature if there are no regularities of nature. Thus, from a Christian perspective, we don't expect to see miracles scattered randomly throughout time and space, but look for God's intervention mainly at great turning points, at what C. S. Lewis called "the great ganglions of history."[35] In the Bible, God doesn't intervene aimlessly and unaccountably in human affairs. There are even portions of the biblical narrative in which God's miraculous activity is largely absent.[36] God's interventions accompany God's saving, redemptive acts. If Jesus is the Jewish Messiah and humanity's Savior, then his atoning death is one of those historical turning points at which we expect to see God perform a miracle as a confirmation of Jesus's unique identity.

Therefore, if we're agnostic about God's existence, we must remain agnostic about the possibility of miracles. We can't definitively rule them out and refuse in advance to examine the evidence. But when we examine the evidence for the resurrection, it really does appear that something extraordinary happened, even if we're not sure exactly what. The puzzle is compounded in that this purported miracle is associated with Jesus, who, as we saw in the last chapter, made such colossal claims about himself. Doesn't it strike us as a bit remarkable

---

35 C. S. Lewis, *Miracles: A Preliminary Study* (New York: Macmillan, 1960), 167.

36 Most famously, the book of Esther contains no mentions of God. Apart from the ministries of particular prophets like Elijah or Elisha, the books of Ruth, 1 and 2 Samuel, 1 and 2 Kings, Ezra, and Nehemiah also contain limited mention of God's miraculous intervention, although these books still clearly affirm God's ordering and sovereignty over all events.

that the one miracle which, according to Flew, is the best attested in any religion in all of history happens to be associated with a figure who also had the moral character and impact of Jesus? How do we explain this coincidence?

In Conclusion

Many people ask: "If God does exist, why doesn't he provide us with some miraculous sign? Why doesn't he perform some amazing miracle that would be so inescapable as to leave us in no doubt of his existence?" Well, what if he has? What if there is one clear, central miracle right in the middle of human history? Let me even suggest that the miracles most skeptics imagine are actually far less useful than the one that God has provided. After all, if the message "God exists" were scrawled across the moon in thirty-foot-high letters of fire (apologies to Douglas Adams), that miracle might tell us that God exists, but it would still leave us with no idea who this God is or what he is like. On the other hand, the resurrection of Jesus is God's vindication of his ultimate revelation to humanity, Jesus Christ himself. In Jesus, we do not learn merely of God's existence. We also see his love and compassion, tenderness and holiness, mercy and justice. Like the trilemma, the evidence for the resurrection points us back to Jesus. We are left to grapple with the question of his identity and his claim upon our lives.

4

God and Revelation (Part 1)

Nature

Yet [God] is actually not far from each one of us, for
"In him we live and move and have our being."

ACTS 17:27–28

IN THE LAST CHAPTER, I mentioned that our beliefs about the existence of God will influence our beliefs about the resurrection. We might find the historical evidence interesting, even a bit surprising, but if we think it unlikely that God exists, we will likely reject the resurrection as an explanation. After all, if there is no God, then he could not have raised Jesus (or anyone else) from the dead. We turn now to the question of God's existence. Does he exist? If he does, is there any evidence for his existence? Or do we simply have to take his existence "on faith"?

Let's begin by addressing the nature of faith. It's common to hear vocal atheists like Richard Dawkins and Jerry Coyne pitting religious faith against evidence. For example, in *Faith versus Fact: Why Science and Religion Are Incompatible*, Coyne defines *faith* as "belief without—or in the face of—evidence."[1] In *The Selfish Gene*, Dawkins writes: "Another member of the religious meme complex is called faith. It means blind trust, in the absence of evidence, even in the teeth of evidence."[2] Unfortunately, these authors have misunderstood the word *faith*, at least in a Christian context. The Bible does not use the word *faith* in this way, and this is not how Christians have thought about the concept of faith for thousands of years.

The Greek word *pistis*, which is translated as "faith" in modern English Bibles, can also be translated as "trust" or "confidence." When we examine how this word is used in a biblical context, we routinely see faith being placed in God on the basis of evidence, often in the form of God's miraculous intervention in history. The Bible never assumes or contends that faith and evidence are mutually exclusive.

Moreover, the use of the word *faith* to refer to trust is not some strange religious aberration; we adopt the same usage when speaking about any personal relationship. If I say, "I have faith in my wife," I mean that I trust my wife. My trust is not opposed to evidence but is grounded in ample evidence gathered over nineteen years of marriage that testifies to her goodness, her love for me, and her trustworthiness. The same is true of our trust in God; it is based on evidence that he exists, that he is good, and that he is worthy of our confidence. The common claim that "religion is based on faith while science is based on evidence" is predicated on a misunderstanding of the nature of faith.

We should also remember that what I am offering is not *proof* but *evidence*. Proof is generally confined to the realm of abstract logic or mathematics. When asked to draw conclusions about real-world phenomena, neither the scientist nor the historian nor the economist nor the homicide detective deals in proof. If we demanded a logically

---

1   Jerry A. Coyne, *Faith versus Fact: Why Science and Religion Are Incompatible* (New York: Viking, 2015), 67.

2   Richard Dawkins, *The Selfish Gene*, 30th anniversary ed. (Oxford: Oxford University Press, 2006), 198.

undeniable proof of any proposition before accepting it as true, we'd be paralyzed. In all these disciplines, we gather evidence and then consider various hypotheses before settling on the one that provides the best, most comprehensive, most coherent, and most plausible explanation. In what follows, I ask readers to take the same approach.

Let me offer one more caution: we shouldn't consider each piece of evidence only in isolation. Instead, we need to examine the larger picture painted by the evidence. Theists claim that our universe is best understood as the creation of an infinitely wise, good, just, loving, and powerful personal Being. In contrast, atheists deny that our universe is best understood in this way. The question before us is not Can each of these pieces of evidence be avoided? but Which system of belief best explains the evidence?

The analogy of a puzzle is helpful here. We can work on a puzzle for a long time under the assumption that it is a picture of Degas's *L'Absinthe*. But the more pieces we try to assemble, the harder it becomes to force them into an arbitrary arrangement. If we're basing our reconstruction of the puzzle on a false assumption, we'll be left with handfuls of pieces that don't fit anywhere and a picture that is patchy and confused. Christians are arguing that what we have mistaken for Degas's *L'Absinthe* is actually Rembrandt's *Prodigal Son*. The way to determine whether Christians are right is not to pick out two individual pieces and show that we can force them together if we hammer them hard enough. Instead, we should ask whether the Christian worldview provides a better overall fit of the data. If I began to reassemble the puzzle with an entirely different framework in mind, would the pieces fit more naturally? Would we find fewer unaccountable gaps? Would we see a more coherent and consistent picture? It will be helpful to keep this illustration in mind during our discussion.

In the conclusion to his work *Critique of Practical Reason*, German philosopher Immanuel Kant wrote, "Two things fill the mind with ever new and increasing admiration and reverence, the more often and more steadily one reflects on them: the starry heavens above me and the moral law within me."[3] The apostle Paul points to the same two features of reality as the basis for our knowledge of God: nature outside us (Rom. 1:18–20) and the moral law within us (Rom. 1:28–32). In the next two chapters, I will use the same twofold division. In this chapter, I'll examine the evidence for God's existence from the universe: its mathematical beauty, its origin, its existence, and its fine-tuning. In the next chapter, I'll examine the evidence for God's existence from the moral law: the existence of objective moral values and duties and the goodness of truth-seeking. Let's begin with the universe outside us to see whether it has any features that are better explained by theism than by atheism.

Why Is Mathematics So Successful?

The success of mathematics in describing the universe is a fact that most of us, even scientists like me, take for granted. Yet it is actually extremely surprising. Nobel Prize–winning physicist Eugene Wigner wrote an article over fifty years ago entitled "The Unreasonable Effectiveness of Mathematics in the Natural Sciences," in which he repeatedly used the word "miracle" to describe this phenomenon.[4] Why, he asked, do the same beautiful mathematical equations apply uniformly across all time and space? We could easily conceive of a universe that is wholly haphazard and chaotic, described by no underlying mathematics at all. Or we could conceive of a universe that is sporadically chaotic, where the laws of physics are occasionally suspended or altered every few years. Or we could conceive of a universe in which the laws of physics are not universal; they could vary from planet to planet or from galaxy to galaxy. Instead, we observe a universe with a deep and beautiful underlying

---

3   Immanuel Kant, *Critique of Practical Reason*, trans. and ed. Mary Gregor, rev. ed. (Cambridge: Cambridge University Press, 2015), 129.

4   Eugene Wigner, "The Unreasonable Effectiveness of Mathematics in the Natural Sciences," *Communications on Pure and Applied Mathematics* 13, no. 1 (1960): 1–14.

mathematical structure that appears to be universal in space and time. Wigner asked why this should be the case; what is the explanation for this phenomenon?[5]

In addition to the mathematical structure of the universe, Wigner called attention to another unusual and "miraculous" phenomenon: that human beings are able to perceive and understand this structure. This fact is also quite surprising. After all, while one might argue that evolution would produce organisms with enough intelligence to flee from tigers or to avoid falling off cliffs, why are human beings unique in their ability to comprehend quantum mechanics or molecular biology? Surely, these activities didn't confer any reproductive benefit on hunter-gatherers foraging for fruit and fending off predators. Why should we expect human beings to understand science and mathematics any better than other intelligent animals like chimpanzees or dolphins?

Atheistic Explanations for the Success of Mathematics

"The universe's mathematical structure is necessary." With regard to the first phenomenon, I think the atheist's best response is to say that the mathematical structure of the universe might be *necessary*; that is to say, there is no possibility that the universe could *not* have possessed a deep, mathematical structure. But this idea strikes me as odd. Why think that irregular or unpredictable universes should be impossible? We normally do not make the assumption that there is a necessary connection between mathematical beauty and truth. For example, most physicists insist that even very mathematically beautiful theories like string theory must be certified by evidence. Unlike Keats, we do not

---

5   Physicist Paul Davies echoes this sentiment. He tells the story of a classmate who, when Davies said that he could predict the motion of a projectile using Newton's equations, asked incredulously, "How can you possibly know what a ball will do by writing things on a sheet of paper?" Davies reflects: "Over the years I came to see that her impulsive response precisely captures one of the deepest mysteries of science: *Why* is nature shadowed by a mathematical reality? Why does theoretical physics work?" Davies, *The Goldilocks Enigma: Why Is the Universe Just Right for Life?* (London: Allen Lane, 2006), 11.

simply assert that "beauty is truth, truth beauty" and call it a night. We fairly ruthlessly demand that beautiful theories withstand the scrutiny of empirical testing.

Neither do we reject successful theories purely on the grounds that they are mathematically inelegant. Consequently, we should not insist that the "ugliness" of a nonmathematical universe renders it impossible. Mathematical beauty and structure certainly exist, but they do not appear to be necessary. So why do they exist?

"Language explains our mathematical ability." Explaining the second phenomenon—that humans can perceive and understand the mathematical structure of the universe—is also challenging. It is objectively true that we human beings are unique in our capacity for abstract mathematical and scientific thought. Furthermore, these abilities don't directly contribute to our ability to produce offspring; early humans didn't use particle physics to escape from hyenas. So we can't appeal to the idea that these capacities were evolutionary adaptations. How, then, can we explain their existence?

I believe that the best option for an atheist is to argue that our highly advanced cognitive faculties are an accidental by-product of our ability to use language. The evolution of language, an atheist could argue, allowed human beings to mentally process abstract symbols, which, in turn, led to the development of our mathematical and scientific abilities even though they didn't directly increase our chances of survival. Language was an evolutionary adaptation, and mathematics was an accidental evolutionary by-product.

Unfortunately for the atheist, human beings are just as unique in their ability to use language as they are unique in their ability to understand mathematics.[6] Worse still, the evolution of language is

6   Martin A. Nowak, *Evolutionary Dynamics: Exploring the Equations of Life* (Cambridge, MA: Harvard University Press, 2006), 249–51. Nowak writes: "The emergence of language was the last in a series of major events in evolution, comparable in significance only to the origin of life, the

extremely mysterious. In a 2014 review article cowritten by numerous renowned evolutionary psychologists, biologists, and linguists, including Marc Hauser, Noam Chomsky, and Richard Lewontin, the authors state:

> In the last 40 years, there has been an explosion of research on this problem [of the evolutionary origin of language] as well as a sense that considerable progress has been made. We argue instead that the richness of ideas is accompanied by a poverty of evidence, *with essentially no explanation of how and why our linguistic computations and representations evolved.*[7]

After describing in their paper the various obstacles facing research into the origins of language and outlining possible ways for research to proceed in the future, given certain advances, they conclude: "These are all big IFs about the nature and possibility of future evidence. Until such evidence is brought forward, understanding of language evolution will remain one of the great mysteries of our species."[8]

Appealing to the acquisition of language as a solution to our mathematical abilities only moves the problem back one step: rather than asking why we are uniquely able to understand math and science, we are left asking why we are uniquely able to use language in a way that also allows us to uniquely understand math and science.[9] Because scientists currently have no clear answer to this puzzle, it is difficult to insist that the answer—whatever it is—must be atheistic.

---

first bacteria, the first higher cells, and the evolution of complex multicellularity. Language is the biggest invention of the last six hundred million years" (249); and "Language is the one property that sets us apart from all other animal species" (250).

7 Marc D. Hauser et al., "The Mystery of Language Evolution," *Frontiers in Psychology* 5, no. 401 (2014): 1; emphasis added.

8 Hauser et al., "The Mystery of Language Evolution," 10.

9 See also Fiona Cowie, "Innateness and Language," *The Stanford Encyclopedia of Philosophy*, ed. Edward N. Zalta, January 16, 2008, https://plato.stanford.edu/.

Theism's Explanation for the Success of Mathematics

In contrast, both of these phenomena—the mathematical beauty of the universe and our unique ability to understand it—fit quite naturally into a theistic universe. If God is a rational, infinitely intelligent Being, it is no surprise that the universe he created reflects his reason and intelligence. And if, as the Bible teaches, men and women were uniquely created in the divine image to understand and appreciate the universe that God has created, our capacity for mathematics and science is similarly explained. A rational God gave us our rational cognitive faculties to understand the rational universe he created. At least this one piece of the puzzle seems to fit more readily into a theistic picture of reality than into an atheistic picture.

What Caused the Universe?

The vast majority of modern astronomers now believe that the universe as we know it is not eternal. Instead, it had a beginning about 14 billion years ago in an event known as the Big Bang. Most people aren't aware that this model was resisted for decades because it contradicted the prevalent belief among physicists that the universe was eternal (which went back at least as far as the ancient Greeks).[10] Commenting on the development of the Big Bang theory in the 1920s, string theorist Brian Greene writes that "Einstein refused to take his own theory [of general relativity] at face value and accept that it implies that the universe is neither eternal nor static."[11] As recently as 1989, the editor of *Nature* magazine, one of the most prestigious scientific journals in the world, wrote that the Big Bang is "philosophically unacceptable" and that

---

10 "Aristotle, and most of the other Greek philosophers [in contrast to Jewish/Christian/Muslim traditions] did not like the idea of a creation because it smacked too much of divine intervention. They believed, therefore, that the human race and the world around it had existed, and would exist, forever." Stephen Hawking, *The Illustrated "A Brief History of Time"* (New York: Bantam, 1996), 13.

11 Brian Greene, *The Elegant Universe: Superstrings, Hidden Dimensions, and the Quest for the Ultimate Theory* (New York: Vintage, 2000), 346.

"Creationists and those of similar persuasions seeking support for their opinions have ample justification in the doctrine of the Big Bang."[12]

The reason for this discomfort is apparent: If the universe had existed eternally, it would not have needed a cause. But if the universe came into being in the finite past, then it is meaningful to ask what caused it to come into being. Furthermore, if all time, space, matter, and energy came into being at the Big Bang, then wouldn't the cause of the Big Bang have to be immaterial, outside of time, and outside of nature? Christians, Muslims, and Jews all affirm that this immaterial, eternal, extra-natural cause of the universe was God. Reflecting on the discoveries of modern astronomy, astronomer Robert Jastrow concluded his book *God and the Astronomers* in the following way:

> For the scientist who has lived by his faith in the power of reason, the story ends like a bad dream. He has scaled the mountains of ignorance; he is about to conquer the highest peak; as he pulls himself over the final rock, he is greeted by a band of theologians who have been sitting there for centuries.[13]

In other words, scientists are just now catching up to theologians, who have believed for millennia that the universe is not eternal and was created by God in the finite past.

Objecting to the Argument from the Cause of the Universe

"Who caused God?" By far, the most common atheistic rejoinder to this line of reasoning is the question "If God caused the universe, then who caused God?"[14] One positive aspect of this objection is that

---

12 John Maddox, "Down with the Big Bang," *Nature* 340 (August 10, 1989): 425.

13 Robert Jastrow, *God and the Astronomers* (New York: Warner, 1980), 105–6.

14 See, for instance, atheist philosopher Bertrand Russell: "That very simple sentence ["who made God?"] showed me, as I still think, the fallacy in the argument of the First Cause. If everything must have a cause, then God must have a cause. If there can be anything without a cause, it may just as well be the world as God, so that there cannot be any validity in that argument." Russell,

it implicitly endorses the necessity of causation. Anyone who wants to know what caused God can't simultaneously dismiss the notion of causation as meaningless. However, this objection makes a fundamental mistake about the kind of Being God is. The reason we demand a cause for the universe is that it began to exist in the finite past. In contrast, God never began to exist. God is eternal. Therefore, asking for the cause of God's existence is illegitimate. It would be like asking for the cause of the set of all even numbers. The set of all even numbers never began to exist; therefore, it doesn't require a cause. In the same way, God never began to exist; therefore, God doesn't require a cause.

"Quantum fluctuations caused the universe." There are two other ways that atheists can seek to explain the origin of the universe. Instead of raising the "Who caused God?" objection, an atheist could deny that the universe requires a cause. To support this point, appeals are often made to "quantum fluctuations" to show that particles can pop into existence without a cause. In his book *A Universe from Nothing*, atheist physicist Lawrence Krauss attempts to show that the universe could have indeed arisen spontaneously from "nothing." He writes:

> Modern science . . . can address and *is* addressing the question of why there is something rather than nothing: The answers that have been obtained—from staggeringly beautiful experimental observations, as well as from the theories that underlie much of modern physics—all suggest that getting something from nothing is not a problem.[15]

As a theoretical chemist who specializes in quantum mechanics, I'll simply say that this argument is misguided and that the term "noth-

---

"Why I Am Not a Christian," in *Why I Am Not a Christian and Other Essays on Religion and Related Subjects*, ed. Paul Edwards (New York: Touchstone, 1957), 6–7.

15   Lawrence M. Krauss, *A Universe from Nothing: Why There Is Something rather than Nothing* (New York: Atra, 2012), xxiii.

ing" is being ill-advisedly redefined.[16] In his review of Krauss's book, theoretical physicist and philosopher David Alberts agrees with my assessment. When Krauss complains about being criticized by philosophers for redefining the term "nothing" to mean "the quantum vacuum," Alberts responds:

> Krauss is dead wrong and his religious and philosophical critics are absolutely right. . . . If what we formerly took for nothing turns out, on closer examination, to have the makings of protons and neutrons and tables and chairs and planets and solar systems and galaxies and universes in it, then it *wasn't* nothing, and it *couldn't* have been nothing, in the first place.[17]

To put it bluntly, saying that we can get "something from nothing" by redefining "nothing" to mean "something" is a dubious approach.

"The universe had no beginning." Finally, an atheist could deny that the universe actually began to exist. This objection is usually based on a rejection of the Big Bang. Atheists will sometimes argue that the Big Bang model of cosmology might be incorrect and that the correct model might not predict that the universe had an absolute beginning in time. Because no one currently knows how to reconcile quantum mechanics with general relativity, we do not know how to accurately describe the earliest moments of the universe when it was crushed into a miniscule region of space. It may be that a complete theory of quantum gravity will restore the plausibility of a past-eternal universe.

However, all the current evidence, like the relative abundance of the light elements or the cosmic microwave background radiation,

---

16 Neil Shenvi, "Do Quantum Fluctuations Show That Something Can Come from Nothing?," Neil Shenvi—Apologetics, https://shenviapologetics.com/.

17 David Albert, "On the Origin of Everything," *The New York Times: Sunday Book Review*, March 23, 2012, https://www.nytimes.com/.

certainly makes it *appear* that the universe had a beginning.[18] Until some counterevidence is provided to challenge this claim, asking what caused the universe to begin to exist is a reasonable question. And it's a question that Jews, Christians, and Muslims have answered in the same way for millennia: God created the universe. God is the eternal, uncaused First Cause, who brought the universe into being.

Why Is There Something rather than Nothing?

The question Why is there something rather than nothing at all? can be asked independently of the previous one. For example, let's imagine that the universe did not begin at the Big Bang and has existed for infinite past time. While we could then avoid the need for a First Cause, we could still legitimately ask, Why is there a past-eternal universe rather than nothing at all?

Another way to pose this question is to ask for the universe's explanation. We normally assume that there is an explanation for any entity that exists. If I find a piece of blank paper in my mailbox one afternoon, I am naturally led to ask: Why is this paper here? Why wasn't the mailbox empty? If a forensic pathologist discovers traces of poison in a body, he asks, What explains the presence of this poison? If a paleontologist discovers a fossil on a dig, she rightly asks for an explanation of the fossil. These questions are all entirely reasonable. We would never be satisfied with the response "Perhaps there is no explanation for the paper in your mailbox or the poison or the fossil. They are just there. They are just brute facts with no explanation."

But what if we applied the same reasoning to the existence of the universe? What explains its existence? Why is there a universe instead of no universe? The Christian answer is that God explains the universe.

---

18 When speaking unguardedly, even atheists who would vehemently deny the soundness of this type of cosmological argument still tend to speak as if the universe had a beginning in time. For example, in his afterword to Krauss, *A Universe from Nothing*, Richard Dawkins writes, "The spontaneous genesis of something out of nothing happened in a big way at the beginning of space and time, in the singularity known as the Big Bang" (189).

God is a personal and all-powerful Being, and his choice to create explains why the universe exists; if he had chosen not to create, there would be no universe, no papers, no mailboxes, no fossils, and no *you* puzzling over this argument.

But if everything has an explanation for its existence, then what is the explanation for God's existence? The traditional answer is that God is self-existent. His existence is explained by the nature of who he is, a Being who exists necessarily and is completely independent of any other being. If God were explained by something outside himself, then he would not be God at all. This doctrine of the aseity of God (from the Latin *a se*, "from self") is found in the biblical description of God as a Being who has "life in himself" (John 5:26) and "for whom and by whom all things exist" (Heb. 2:10).

For those skeptical of theology, we could take an alternate route. Let's say we accept the idea that God explains the universe's existence, but reject the idea that God's nature explains his own existence. If God's nature can't explain his existence, then we have to posit the existence of some other entity (call it god 2.0) that explains God's existence. But what explains the existence of god 2.0? We're left positing the existence of a third entity, god 3.0. But what, in turn, explains the existence of god 3.0? We quickly realize that we're left with an infinite regression of explanations, unless that regression is terminated by a self-existent entity. The simplest end point is God himself, which is the same result that Christian theology leads us to expect.

Objecting to the Argument from the Explanation of the Universe

But is the simplest end point really God? If the theist can declare that God exists necessarily and therefore explains his own existence, why can't the atheist insist that the universe exists necessarily and therefore explains its own existence?[19] Alternatively, why can't the atheist

19 One way atheist George Smith avoids the argument from contingency is by denying that physical objects are contingent. He writes: "To say that something exists contingently makes sense

claim that the universe is simply a "brute fact," which requires no explanation?[20]

"The universe explains itself or is a brute fact with no explanation." One response to these suggestions is to observe that the universe is a collection of physical things. All our experience leads us to believe that the existence of physical things or collections of physical things requires an explanation outside itself. To put it another way, physical entities are contingent; that is, they might not have existed at all. Just as it would be extremely odd to declare that a piece of paper in our mailbox is self-existent or is a "brute fact" with no explanation, it seems extremely odd to declare that something in the universe (or everything in the universe) is self-existent. It would be equally strange to declare that either the paper or the universe is a "brute fact," with no explanation.

On the other hand, nonphysical entities do not seem to demand an explanation. We don't normally ask why prime numbers exist or why the law of noncontradiction exists. Given their nature, it's difficult to conceive of a reality in which they did not exist; they seem to exist necessarily. But God is also a nonphysical entity, so even apart from theology, it's plausible to think that if he exists, he exists necessarily.

---

only within the sphere of volitional action. So, for example, we might say that a building exists contingently, meaning that, if certain men had decided to act differently, the building would never have been constructed. With this exception, however, the idea of contingent existence has no application. Everything exists necessarily." George H. Smith, *Atheism: The Case against God* (Amherst, NY: Prometheus, 1989), 251.

20   This is the approach taken by atheist theoretical physicist Sean Carroll in his excellent book *The Big Picture*. He writes:

An obvious place where it's tempting to look for reasons why is the question of why various features of the universe take the form that they do. Why was the entropy low near the Big Bang? Why are there three dimensions of space? Why is the proton almost 2,000 times heavier than the electron? Why does the universe exist at all? . . .

The secret here is to accept that such questions *may or may not have answers*. . . . We have to be open to the possibility that they are brute facts, and that's just how things are.

Carroll, *The Big Picture: On the Origins of Life, Meaning, and the Universe Itself* (New York: Dutton, 2017), 44–45.

In this way, God is a reasonable explanation for a contingent universe, while it's less plausible to insist that the universe explains itself or has no explanation for its existence at all.

If we insist that the universe exists necessarily or that it is a brute fact, we also run into a problem that will recur in the next section: What exactly are the essential attributes of the universe? In other words, what are the properties that make the universe a *universe*? For example, if there were one less atom in the universe, would that entity still be a universe? Presumably, we'd have to answer yes, since there's nothing essential to the nature of the universe requiring that it contains exactly the number of atoms it does actually contain. But what if we subtracted two atoms? Or three? What if we reduced or increased the universe's energy by 1 percent? What if we doubled its number of spatial dimensions? All of the entities that would result from these changes would still seem to qualify as a universe. So exactly which attributes constitute the "essential attributes" of a universe? It's not clear.

The fact that it is difficult to specify these essential attributes casts doubt on whether the universe exists necessarily. A universe might contain more atoms or fewer atoms or no atoms at all. It might contain more energy or less energy. It might contain two spatial dimensions or three or four. If we insist that the universe is necessary, we end up arguing, "We're not really sure what the universe is, but we're sure that it exists necessarily." In the same way, if the universe's existence were a brute fact, we would be left with not just one brute fact but a large number of brute facts, specifying all the nonessential properties of the universe, like how many elementary particles it contains, how much energy it contains, and how many spatial dimensions it spans.

All things considered, the existence of God seems like a better explanation of the universe's existence than any atheistic alternative. Consistent with our intuition, the universe did not have to exist. Its existence is contingent on God, and his decision to create explains why there is something rather than nothing.

Why Is the Universe Finely Tuned for Life?

Finally, the fine-tuning of the universe is difficult to explain in the absence of God. The Standard Model, which is currently our best working description of the interaction of fundamental forces and subatomic particles, includes a number of independent constants and parameters. These values, which include items like the strength of gravity, the electron mass, and the magnitude of the cosmological constant, must be obtained from experiment. Although they are important components of the physical theories that describe the structure of the universe, they cannot be derived from any known equations.

What physicists have recently discovered is that biological life would be impossible anywhere in the universe if some of these constants were altered by even a fraction of a percent. For example, in his book *Just Six Numbers*, atheist Martin Rees, a cosmologist at Cambridge University, identifies six parameters, including the relative strength of gravity, the strength of nuclear binding, and the number of spatial dimensions that "constitute a 'recipe' for a universe." He writes that "if any one of them were to be 'untuned,' there would be no stars and no life."[21] The most dramatic example of fine-tuning is found in the value of the cosmological constant, which is finely tuned to one part in 10^{120} (that is, one part in one trillion trillion trillion trillion trillion trillion trillion trillion trillion trillion).[22] If this value fell outside the life-permitting range, the universe would expand so rapidly that it would consist of nothing more than a "thin soup of hydrogen and helium": no stars, no planets, no complex molecules, no life of any kind.[23]

---

21 Martin Rees, *Just Six Numbers: The Deep Forces That Shape the Universe* (New York: Basic Books, 2000), 4.

22 Luke Barnes, "The Fine-Tuning of the Universe for Intelligent Life," *Publications of the Astronomical Society of Australia* 29, no. 4 (2012): 544–46.

23 Geraint F. Lewis and Luke A. Barnes, *A Fortunate Universe: Life in a Finely Tuned Cosmos* (Cambridge: Cambridge University Press, 2016), 13.

This cosmological fine-tuning is widely recognized by both Christian and non-Christian physicists as a real phenomenon requiring some kind of explanation. As Christian cosmologist Luke Barnes writes,

> There are a great many scientists, of varying religious persuasions, who accept that the universe is fine-tuned for life, e.g. Barrow, Carr, Carter, Davies, Dawkins, Deutsch, Ellis, Greene, Guth, Harrison, Hawking, Linde, Page, Penrose, Polkinghorne, Rees, Sandage, Smolin, Susskind, Tegmark, Tipler, Vilenkin, Weinberg, Wheeler, Wilczek.[24]

These scientists all agree that the universe is fine-tuned, even though they disagree "on what conclusion we should draw from this fact."[25]

To be clear, when physicists say that the universe is "fine-tuned," they are not implying that there must exist a Fine-Tuner. That is one potential explanation for fine-tuning, but not the only one. Instead, physicists are observing that the existence of life anywhere in the universe is incredibly sensitive to the precise values of the fundamental constants of physics. In the same way, if I found a tall stack of delicately balanced rocks on top of a mountain, I could describe the rocks' positions as "fine-tuned" because the stack's existence is incredibly sensitive to the slightest perturbation. However, I would not necessarily be implying that the rocks had been stacked by an intelligent agent; perhaps some kind of physical process could have produced this result.

At the same time, there's no denying that the phenomenon of fine-tuning is provocative. The degree of fine-tuning that we observe in cosmology led British astrophysicist Fred Hoyle to remark, "A common sense interpretation of the facts suggests that a superintellect has

---

24 Barnes, "The Fine-Tuning of the Universe," 531.
25 Barnes, "The Fine-Tuning of the Universe," 531.

monkeyed with physics, as well as with chemistry and biology, and that there are no blind forces worth speaking about in nature."[26] Commenting on Hoyle's remark, agnostic cosmologist Paul Davies writes: "[Hoyle] was right in his impression. On the face of it, the universe *does* look as if it has been designed by an intelligent creator expressly for the purpose of spawning sentient beings."[27]

Objecting to the Argument from Fine-Tuning

"*The universe isn't actually fine-tuned.*" The claim of cosmological fine-tuning sounds so astonishing that it can be tempting to attribute it to the overactive imaginations of a handful of religious apologists trying to find evidence for the divine. Atheist particle physicist Vic Stenger takes this view, writing that "supporters of supernatural fine-tuning [are motivated] more [by] wishful thinking than [by] truthful scientific inference. A proper analysis finds there is no evidence that the universe is fine-tuned for us."[28] However, Stenger's allegation is incorrect.[29] In their book *A Fortunate Universe: Life in a Finely Tuned Cosmos*, cosmologists Geraint Lewis, an atheist, and Luke Barnes, a Christian, emphasize that cosmological fine-tuning is not an obscure field on the outskirts of science but an active topic of research in mainstream physics. Commenting on the findings of over two hundred papers related to the subject of fine-tuning, the authors conclude:

---

26 Fred Hoyle, "The Universe: Past and Present Reflections," *Annual Review of Astronomy and Astrophysics* 20 (September 1982): 16.

27 Davies, *The Goldilocks Enigma*, 3.

28 Victor J. Stenger, *The Fallacy of Fine-Tuning: Why the Universe Is Not Designed for Us* (Amherst, NY: Prometheus, 2011), 294.

29 In more ways than one. Barnes's review article "The Fine-Tuning of the Universe," cited above, provides a scathing rebuttal to Stenger's book. Note that Barnes does not offer a philosophical or theological critique of Stenger's dismissal of fine-tuning, but offers a scientific critique of Stenger's *understanding* of fine-tuning phenomena. For example: "We conclude that Stenger has failed to solve the entropy problem. He has presented the problem itself as its solution. Homogeneous, isotropic expansion cannot solve the entropy problem—it *is* the entropy problem. Stenger's assertion that 'the universe starts out with maximum entropy or complete disorder' is false." Barnes, "The Fine-Tuning of the Universe," 539.

On balance, the fine-tuning of the Universe for life has stood up well under the scrutiny of physicists. . . . Only a handful of peer-reviewed papers have challenged the fine-tuning cases we've discussed in this book, and none defend the contention that most values of the constants and initial conditions of nature will permit the existence of life.[30]

In other words, the scientific literature agrees with the claim that life-permitting values of the fundamental constants and parameters that define the universe are extraordinarily rare. So how else could atheists react to claims of fine-tuning?

"If the universe weren't fine-tuned, we wouldn't exist." Atheists could insist that it's no surprise that the fundamental constants of physics have life-permitting values, because if they didn't have life-permitting values, human beings would not be around to observe that fact. For example, atheist Jerry Coyne writes: "It seems easy to refute [fine-tuning] as evidence for God. If the constants didn't have those values, we wouldn't be here to measure them. *Of course* they must be consonant with human life."[31] In other words, if the fundamental constants of physics didn't permit the existence of life, there would be no one to ask, "Why do the fundamental constants of physics permit the existence of life?" This response, while common, confuses the question Why are we able to observe this phenomenon? with the question Why did this phenomenon occur in the first place?

Philosopher Richard Swinburne invites us to imagine a madman who kidnaps a victim and threatens to kill him unless the victim can randomly draw the ace of hearts from ten different well-shuffled packs of cards.[32] To the man's astonishment, he draws all the required cards,

30 Lewis and Barnes, *A Fortunate Universe*, 241–42.
31 Coyne, *Faith versus Fact*, 161.
32 Richard Swinburne, *Is There a God?*, rev. ed. (Oxford: Oxford University Press, 2010), 57–58. I have modified the thought experiment slightly for ease of explanation.

and the kidnapper lets him go free. When the victim later recounts the story to a police officer, she tells him haughtily, "It is hardly surprising [that you drew] only aces of hearts. . . . For you would not be here . . . if any other cards had been drawn."[33] While the officer's statement is correct, it is answering the wrong question. The relevant question is not Why was the man able to *observe* these ten cards? but Why did such an incredibly unlikely draw *happen in the first place*?

Barnes adds that this kind of selection bias is already well known in astronomy and is not a valid explanation of fine-tuning. He writes:

> Selection bias alone cannot explain anything. Consider quasars: when first discovered, they were thought to be a strange new kind of star in our galaxy. Schmidt (1963) measured their redshift, showing that they were more than a million times further away than previously thought. It follows that they must be incredibly bright. How are quasars so luminous? The (best) answer is: because quasars are powered by gravitational energy released by matter falling into a super-massive black hole. . . . The answer is not: because otherwise we wouldn't see them. Noting that if we observe any object in the very distant universe then it must be very bright does not explain why we observe any distant objects at all. Similarly, [the anthropic principle] cannot explain why life and its necessary conditions exist at all.[34]

"No other fundamental constants were possible." Another possible response is that we can't know whether the fundamental constants could have taken on different values. Perhaps the fundamental constants could not have been different because some as-yet-undiscovered "theory of everything" specifies the precise values of all these constants.[35] Or

---

33 Swinburne, *Is There a God?*, 58.

34 Barnes, "The Fine-Tuning of the Universe," 530.

35 Although we'd then have to explain why the universe's laws are described by that particular theory of everything and not another.

perhaps these precise values are just brute facts about the nature of the universe that have no explanation. Surprisingly, the theist finds an ally in atheist Richard Dawkins, who writes that he finds this answer "unsatisfying." "Why," he asks, "did that one way [for the universe to be] have to be such a set-up for our eventual evolution? Why did it have to be the kind of universe which seems almost as if, in the words of the theoretical physicist Freeman Dyson, it 'must have known we were coming'?"[36] I think Dawkins's dissatisfaction is correct. Saying that it is metaphysically necessary for the universe to have laws that happened to permit life doesn't seem much more satisfying than the police officer telling our kidnapping victim that it was metaphysically necessary for him to turn up ten aces of hearts.

"Fine-tuning is explained by the multiverse." In my opinion, the atheist's best answer to the question of cosmological fine-tuning is to posit the existence of an infinite or near-infinite number of undetectable parallel universes, known as a "multiverse." In each parallel universe, the fundamental constants are slightly different such that every possible value for the constants is sampled somewhere in the multiverse. While the overwhelming majority of universes in the multiverse cannot support life, we live in one of the few universes in which life is possible.

While there are scientific objections to this explanation,[37] I think that its practical implications are particularly hard to accept. If an infinite multiverse exists, then there are actual universes in which pink unicorns exist, or in which Bigfoot is real, or that are composed entirely of Gorgonzola cheese. As appealing as a universe filled with pink unicorns might be to my eight-year-old daughter, it strikes most of us as preposterous. Yet scientists are quite serious about these claims. For example, in a discussion of the implications of an infinite inflationary multiverse, cosmologists Jaume Garriga and Alexander Vilenkin write that in an

36 Richard Dawkins, *The God Delusion* (Boston: Mariner, 2008), 173.
37 Lewis and Barnes, *The Fortunate Universe*, 297–323.

infinite multiverse, "there are infinitely many . . . regions where Al Gore is President and—yes—Elvis is still alive."[38] It seems very odd for an atheist to scoff at the implausibility of God and then to affirm the existence of an infinite, unobserved, and undetectable ensemble of parallel universes.

In an article provocatively entitled "Science's Alternative to an Intelligent Creator: The Multiverse Theory," *Discover* magazine reflects on some of these problems. Near the end of the article, the author asks, "If there is no multiverse, where does that leave physicists?" Cosmologist Bernard Carr responds: "If there is only one universe . . . you might have to have a fine-tuner. If you don't want God, you'd better have a multiverse."[39] I agree and would turn that answer around: if you are hesitant to embrace a multiverse, you ought to consider the possibility that God created the universe and designed it to be inhabited by physical creatures like us.

Objections to a Theistic View of the Universe

"Christianity Relies on a 'God of the Gaps'"

Apart from the specific objections given in each section above, the specter of a "god of the gaps" is the most common general objection to any argument for God based on the observation of nature. The idea of a "god of the gaps" originated with the nineteenth-century Christian evangelist Henry Drummond, who admonished Christians not to use God as a placeholder to fill gaps in our knowledge of the natural world. Even today, this warning is issued to Christians not only by atheists but by fellow believers. For example, in his book *The Language of God*, Christian geneticist Francis Collins, the former head of the National Institutes of Health, writes: "A word of caution is needed when inserting specific divine action by God in this or any other area where scientific understanding is currently lacking.

38 Jaume Garriga and Alexander Vilenkin, "Many Worlds in One," *Physical Review* D 64, no. 4 (July 26, 2001), 10.1103/PhysRevD.64.043511.
39 Tim Folger, "Science's Alternative to an Intelligent Creator: The Multiverse Theory," *Discover*, November 10, 2008, https://www.discovermagazine.com/the-sciences/sciences-alternative-to-an -intelligent-creator-the-multiverse-theory.

... This 'God of the gaps' approach has all too often done a disservice to religion (and by implication, to God, if that's possible)."[40]

The argument against a "god of the gaps" runs roughly as follows: There were once many phenomena that we didn't understand and that we attributed to supernatural agency, including the movement of the sun, the timing of eclipses, and the occurrence of thunder and lightning. Now that we have scientific explanations for these phenomena, we no longer resort to supernatural explanations. If our conception of God is merely "a being who explains whatever science cannot explain," then as science explains more and more phenomena through natural means, our conception of God will grow smaller and smaller. One day, when all the gaps are filled, the very idea of God will vanish.

To decide whether this objection is valid, let's look at several models for how God relates to nature, which are illustrated in figure 4. The bar at the top represents our current understanding of the natural world as provided by modern science. The dark gray lengths indicate phenomena for which we currently have natural explanations. Question marks highlight gaps in our understanding, which occur whenever phenomena do not yet have a natural explanation. So what is happening in these gaps? Different models provide different answers.

Figure 4. Different models of the relationship between God and science

40 Francis S. Collins, *The Language of God: A Scientist Presents Evidence for Belief* (New York: Free Press, 2006), 93.

The first model is naturalism, which holds that nature is all that exists. If naturalism is correct, then there is a natural explanation for all the phenomena we presently do not understand. Consequently, all the current gaps can—at least in principle—be filled in by natural explanations.

The second model, deism, states that although God exists and may have had a hand in creating the universe, he has never interacted with it. Thus, God is placed into a sealed box somewhere outside the universe. Deism retains the idea of God but, like naturalism, affirms that all phenomena have natural explanations.

The third model is a "god of the gaps," which uses God to fill the gaps in our current knowledge of the natural world. The lighter regions represent God's miraculous intervention in the world. The problem with this view is that whenever a gap is filled by a natural explanation, our conception of God grows smaller. Critics of this view, whether atheists or Christians, correctly argue that it diminishes our conception of God.

The Christian model, shown at the bottom, recognizes that God is sovereign over natural processes but also insists that God can and does intervene in the natural order. We find this view throughout the Bible where both natural processes and miracles are credited to God's goodness and power (see Ps. 104 in particular). Given this view, Christians recognize that there are many gaps in our current knowledge that we fully expect to be filled by scientific explanations. For example, no Christian thinks that the mechanism for high-temperature superconductivity, which is currently a mystery, is likely to involve God's supernatural intervention. Understanding a natural mechanism for some event should not threaten our conception of God and should actually enhance our appreciation for his design of the world. Well-known theoretical chemist and Christian Henry "Fritz" Schaefer illustrates this aspect of the Christian worldview well when he says: "The significance and joy in my science comes in those occasional moments of discovering something new and saying to myself, 'So that's how God did it.' My goal is to understand a little corner of God's plan."[41]

On the other hand, Christians also believe there are gaps in our current knowledge that will never be filled by scientific explanations because they have a supernatural explanation. At a bare minimum, every Christian acknowledges that the resurrection of Jesus was a genuine miracle. All events, even those which are the product of natural causes, are ultimately under the authority and providence of a sovereign God. But some events are brought about by God's miraculous intervention into the regular workings of nature. Consequently, the Christian view rejects both deism and a god-of-the-gaps approach.

"Supernatural Explanations Should Never Be Invoked"

Even if Christianity doesn't commit us to a god-of-the-gaps view per se, atheists will sometimes claim that God should still never be invoked as an explanation. On the Internet, the exclamation "GODDIDIT" is used to deride appeals to divine intervention. The implicit claim is that any appeal to God is necessarily an appeal to ignorance and should be rejected.

However, this claim is mistaken. Almost everyone would agree that some conceivable events would cry out for a supernatural explanation. If astronomers discovered tomorrow that the stars in some distant galaxy spelled out the text of John 3:16 in Greek, Mandarin, Hindi, Arabic, and English, it would be preposterous to argue that a supernatural explanation for this event is an argument from ignorance. There are certain phenomena that favor a supernatural explanation, because natural explanations are either difficult or contrived.

Upon reflection, we should note that all the phenomena discussed in this chapter fall into this category. When we ask questions about the deep mathematical structure of nature or the cause of all nature

---

41 Quoted in Jeffrey L. Sheler and Joannie M. Schrof, "The Creation," *U.S. News & World Report*, December 23, 1991, 56.

or the explanation of nature or the fine-tuning of nature, we are asking questions that may require a nonnatural explanation. It would be unwise to rule out any such explanation before inquiry even begins. If we should reject a god-of-the-gaps view which dogmatically insists that every current gap in our scientific knowledge must be filled by a supernatural explanation, then we should likewise reject a nature-of-the-gaps view which dogmatically insists that every current gap in our scientific knowledge must be filled by a natural explanation. Instead, we should lay the supernatural and natural explanations side by side and determine which one is a better fit.

"Theism Is Weird"

A more subtle objection to theism is the perceived "weirdness" of the supernatural. It's not uncommon to hear atheists remark: "An invisible, immaterial Mind who designed the universe and brought it into existence? Surely, that's absurd! How much simpler and more plausible is the idea that there is nothing 'out there' except the normal kinds of objects we can see, hear, and touch."

However, it's naive to think that rejecting the supernatural and embracing science will allow us to remain in the comforting, familiar world of raindrops, and roses, and whiskers on kittens. If modern physics has done nothing else, it has shown us that reality is unavoidably weird. Since the advent of relativity theory and quantum mechanics, which Einstein disparaged as "Black Magic Calculus," physics has revealed to us a cosmos that is increasingly distant from the ordinary world. The largely comprehensible, clockwork universe of Newtonian physics has been replaced by a bewildering assembly of wave functions, matter fields, and dark energy.

Yet, no matter how counterintuitive, shocking, and bizarre the constructs of modern physics become, many in our culture continue to insist that whatever it portrays is "ordinary" while the supernatural is "extraordinary." We balk at the existence of immaterial realities but seem curiously unconcerned with the proliferation of ten-dimensional strings, parallel universes, closed-time loops, and nonlocal entanglement. You can even see this inconsistency in our science fiction, where magical plot devices are barely concealed by a thin patina of scientific jargon. The presence of actual angels or ghosts in *Star Trek* would be exceptionally jarring. But if the captain announces that a "hyperdimensional tachyon-based life-form has materialized on the bridge," we can suspend our disbelief. Why the disconnect?

The answer has very little to do with the intrinsic plausibility of theism or atheism, and far more to do with the ubiquitous influence of naturalism on our culture. We assume that things in nature are "ordinary" and that anything outside of nature is "weird." But why subscribe to this assessment? The two basic propositions under consideration are "Nature is the product of a Mind" and "Nature is not the product of a Mind." When phrased in this way, it's not at all clear which thesis should be viewed as intrinsically more unlikely. Certainly, the choice is not between the "normal" universe of atheism and the "weird" universe of theism. Weirdness is unavoidable, and any claim to the contrary is probably based on an antiquated, nineteenth-century understanding of science.

In the end, we can't dismiss theism solely on the grounds that it strikes us as unusual. We must examine the evidence—some of which has been presented in this chapter—subject it to scrutiny, and decide which worldview provides a better explanation.

Evidence and Worship

While the aim of this chapter is to provide evidence for God's existence, we shouldn't stop there. If God exists, the arguments presented above are more than just arguments; they should also be deep sources of wonder.

For example, what does it mean to say that God is the cause of the universe? It means that he is extraordinarily powerful. Supernovas are like dollar-store sparklers in God's eyes.

Behold, the nations are like a drop from a bucket,
  and are accounted as the dust on the scales;
  behold, he takes up the coastlands like fine dust. (Isa. 40:15)

What does it mean to say that God is eternal? Though men and women
and nations and civilizations die, God has always existed and always
will exist. It means that we can say with Isaiah:

Have you not known? Have you not heard?
The LORD is the everlasting God,
  the Creator of the ends of the earth.
He does not faint or grow weary;
  his understanding is unsearchable. (40:28)

Or sing with the psalmist,

Before the mountains were brought forth,
  or ever you had formed the earth and the world,
  from everlasting to everlasting you are God. (Ps. 90:2)

What does it mean to say that God is self-existent? It means that he is
not a God who depends on us, nor is he "served by human hands, as
though he needed anything," but rather "he himself gives to all mankind
life and breath and everything" (Acts 17:25).

What does it mean that God designed the universe for life and
balanced it on a hair's breadth between emptiness and chaos? It
means that he is wise beyond all reckoning, with "greatness [that is]
unsearchable" (Ps. 145:3). With David, we can stare up at the night
sky and say,

When I look at your heavens, the work of your fingers,
  the moon and the stars, which you have set in place,

what is man that you are mindful of him,
    and the son of man that you care for him? (Ps. 8:3)

Despite our philosophical differences, no one captures the wonder evoked by nature like Richard Dawkins. In his work, it's impossible not to be impressed by his enthusiasm and curiosity. But what if all the glories of this universe were meant to lead us to a greater glory that the universe itself cannot contain but can only reflect? What if nature points beyond itself to the Creator of nature? The Christian claim is that it does. None of us should be content with arguments for God's existence until they lead us to gaze in awe at the God who exists.

5

God and Revelation (Part 2)

The Moral Law

They show that the work of the law is written on their
hearts, while their conscience also bears witness, and
their conflicting thoughts accuse or even excuse them.

ROMANS 2:15

IN THE LAST CHAPTER, we considered evidence for God's existence drawn from the universe: its origin, its existence, and its structure. In this chapter, we'll look inward rather than outward. According to the Bible, God's existence is written not only in the heavens but also on our consciences, in the form of the moral law. Let's ask next how our moral experience can tell us about God's existence.

How Can Objective Moral Values and Duties Exist?

Almost everyone recognizes that there exist objective *physical* facts, which are true whether or not anyone affirms them. For example, statements like "The earth is a spheroid" or "Gravity causes objects to fall" are objective physical facts; they are true independent of whether human beings accept or reject them. I might sincerely believe that gravity is an illusion. I might convince everyone in my community or even everyone in the world that gravity is an illusion. But if I step off a cliff, I will fall to my likely death regardless of my beliefs because gravity is an objective physical fact.

Objective moral facts are analogous to physical facts in that they are true or false independent of our beliefs. A moral statement like "Torturing children for pleasure is evil" is objectively true if its truth does not depend on whether people accept it. The position that moral facts exist is known as moral realism.

Similarly, objective moral obligations are duties, like "You should love your neighbor," that are binding on us regardless of whether we acknowledge them. According to Yale philosopher Greg Ganssle, "to call moral obligations *objective* is to imply that the fact that we are under the obligation is not something that is up to us."[1] An analogy would be the legal obligation we have to pay a speeding ticket. We can tear the ticket to pieces and throw them into our fireplace, but the legal obligation to pay the ticket exists regardless of how we react to it.

But how can objective moral facts and objective moral duties exist? Neither moral facts nor duties seem to be reducible to physical facts. For example, the statement "It is wrong to kill a toddler" is not identical to a knowledge of all the physical facts about the toddler: his height, his weight, or the endorphin levels in his brain before and after we kill him. We could be in full possession of all the physical facts about the toddler and still lack the moral knowledge that killing him would be evil. Moral duties are even more perplexing, because they describe what we ought to do, not what we are actually doing. Consider a physical fact like "The earth orbits the sun" and imagine how odd it would sound to add "but it ought to orbit Saturn." Yet there is nothing at all unusual in saying something like "I stole this

---

1   Gregory E. Ganssle, *A Reasonable God: Engaging the New Face of Atheism* (Waco, TX: Baylor University Press, 2009), 82.

bag of Doritos from the store, but I ought to have paid for it." Physical facts *describe* the universe as it is, but moral duties *prescribe* the way we humans ought to behave. Where do such moral facts and duties come from?

One potential answer is that they come from God. Moral values are grounded in God's nature: qualities like love, compassion, and justice are morally good because they reflect God's character. Moral duties are constituted by God's commands to us: God enjoins us to love our neighbor and therefore forbids actions like murder, theft, and adultery. God is not accidentally good; he is goodness itself. His character is the standard and paradigm of goodness, and his commands, which are necessarily consistent with his moral nature, constitute our moral obligations.[2]

When we reflect on the nature of moral duties, they do seem to strike us as authoritative commands rather than as personal preferences or social expectations. For instance, many of us personally believe that we should exercise regularly. There also exists a social expectation that we will wear matching shoes. But neither of these

---

2   This understanding of God's relationship to morality avoids the Euthyphro dilemma posed by Plato, which asks whether (1) actions are good because they are commanded by God or (2) actions are commanded by God because they are good. The dilemma is whether God arbitrarily chooses certain actions to be good or there is some standard of good independent of God. Divine command theory, which I adopt here, resolves this dilemma by positing that moral goodness is grounded in God's nature and moral obligations are constituted by God's commands. Thus, while God could have chosen to issue different commands, he could not have altered his perfect goodness, with which all of his commands are consistent. Because God's moral goodness is essential to his nature, asking whether God is necessarily good is like asking whether a circle is necessarily round. Any entity that is not good is not God, just as any entity that is not round is not a circle. See a very entertaining and accessible response to the Euthyphro dilemma from a Christian perspective in Glenn Peoples, "A New Euthyphro," *Think* 9, no. 25 (2010): 65–83.

As a side note, atheists are sometimes shocked by the suggestion that there are things an omnipotent God cannot do. This objection seems to arise from a confusion over the meaning of omnipotence. An omnipotent being is one who is all-powerful, but even all-powerful beings cannot do things that are logically impossible, like creating square circles or rocks too heavy for an omnipotent being to lift. Moreover, the Bible is quite clear that God cannot perform actions like lying or tempting to sin, because of his perfect goodness (Titus 1:2; Heb. 6:18; James 1:13). God's omnipotence is always consistent with his other attributes.

standards entails a moral prescription. If someone offered us a million dollars to stop exercising for a week or to wear mismatched shoes, most of us would do it. We certainly would not experience a great deal of personal conflict in making the decision, nor would we be crippled by feelings of guilt afterward. Contrast that response to how we'd feel if we were offered the same amount of money to stab a toddler to death.

While personal standards and social expectations do provide us with incentives to behave in certain ways, those incentives can be outweighed by other considerations, like how much personal benefit we will derive from our choice or whether our community will approve of our actions. In contrast, moral considerations seem to trump all others. No matter how much money we are offered, the knowledge that murder is wrong is prescriptive; it tells us what we *ought* to do wholly independently of whether we *want* to do it. If we violate this prescription, we often feel guilt or remorse no matter how much we gain personally. If there really are moral facts that are not identical to physical facts, and if there really are moral obligations that are prescriptive and binding regardless of our preferences, it seems very plausible to posit the existence of a perfectly good, command-issuing God to account for these realities.

The moral argument could then be formulated as follows:

Premise 1: If God does not exist, then objective moral values and
     duties do not exist.
Premise 2: Objective moral values and duties do exist.

Therefore,

Conclusion: God exists.[3]

---

3   This is a very common formulation of the moral argument. See William Lane Craig, *Reasonable Faith: Christian Truth and Apologetics*, 3rd ed. (Wheaton, IL: Crossway, 2008), 172.

Stated this way, the moral argument is formally valid, meaning that its conclusion is true via modus tollens if both of its premises are true. Conversely, the conclusion can be avoided only if we deny the truth of one or both of its premises.

For comparison, consider an analogous argument with the same valid logical form:

Premise 1: If I had not written this book, then this book would not exist.

Premise 2: This book does exist.

Therefore,

Conclusion: I wrote this book.

If someone denied the claim that I wrote this book and were presented with this argument, he would have to deny either premise 1 or premise 2, or both. For example, he might argue that premise 1 is false; perhaps it isn't true that my existence is required for this book to exist. He could argue that the book exists but was written by another person who used my name or by a complicated computer program. Alternatively, he could argue that premise 2 is false; perhaps this book does not actually exist. The book's apparent existence might be a clever illusion engineered by my publisher, who somehow tricked you into believing that you're reading this book right now. Either way, a person can deny the conclusion of the argument ("I wrote this book") only by denying at least one of the argument's two premises.

Similarly, there are two ways to avoid the conclusion that the existence of objective moral values and duties is evidence for the existence of God. First, an atheist could insist that objective moral values and duties can still exist even in the absence of God. Alternatively, he might deny that objective moral values and duties exist. Let's consider each of those possibilities.

Objecting to Premise 1: "Objective Moral Values
and Duties Can Exist without God"

The most common way to argue that moral facts can exist in the absence of God is to ground morality in temporal human flourishing: behaviors that cause people to suffer are immoral, and those which benefit people are moral. For example, renowned atheist philosopher Bertrand Russell asserts, "The question whether a [moral] code is good or bad is the same as the question whether or not it promotes human happiness."[4] Atheist neuroscientist Sam Harris agrees: "Questions of right and wrong are really questions about the happiness and suffering of sentient creatures. If we are in a position to affect the happiness or suffering of others, we have ethical responsibilities toward them."[5]

This view, though widely held, has serious problems. For one, some immoral actions do not cause suffering. A husband who has a series of affairs and lies about them to his wife to preserve her happiness may not be causing suffering. In fact, one might argue that by bringing pleasure both to his mistresses and to his wife, his actions are morally good and perhaps even morally obligatory. Yet I doubt many spouses would find this reasoning persuasive! Similarly, abusing people in comas or subtly mocking the severely mentally disabled is grossly immoral whether or not anyone is harmed. If we recognize that some actions do not diminish human flourishing but are still immoral, then human flourishing cannot be identical to morality.

A second problem has to do with how we evaluate the suffering and flourishing of groups. For example, most of us recognize that it would be immoral to enslave one person and use his labor to greatly enrich the lives of a hundred other people. But if morality is grounded in human flourishing, why would the suffering of just one individual

4   Bertrand Russell, "Our Sexual Ethics," in *Why I Am Not a Christian and Other Essays on Religion and Related Subjects*, ed. Paul Edwards (New York: Touchstone, 1957), 169.

5   Sam Harris, *The End of Faith: Religion, Terror, and the Future of Reason* (New York: Norton, 2005), 170–71.

outweigh the flourishing of a hundred? Should we really bite the bullet and insist that slavery or organ harvesting or any other morally abominable action is justified provided it brings pleasure to a sufficient number of people?

Perhaps the most difficult problem for this view of morality is explaining why human beings are valuable at all. If we believe that nature is all that exists and that human beings are ultimately reducible to atoms and energy, then our suffering and flourishing are reducible to certain concentrations of chemicals in our brains. But why think that it is morally important to maximize the concentrations of certain chemicals in certain locations? Do we worry about the intrinsic morality of increasing the concentration of sugar in our iced tea or the propriety of salting our mashed potatoes? Without something beyond atoms and energy to ground our value, it becomes very difficult to see why human flourishing and suffering per se carry moral connotations.

For these reasons, many atheists have concluded that if God does not exist, then morality cannot exist either. In the words of the great atheist existentialist Jean-Paul Sartre: "God does not exist [and] all possibility of finding values in a heaven of ideas disappears along with Him. . . . Everything is permissible if God does not exist."[6] Atheist philosopher J. L. Mackie agrees, and puts it this way: "[Moral facts] constitute so odd a cluster of qualities and relations that they are most unlikely to have arisen in the ordinary course of events, without an all-powerful god to create them."[7] More recently, atheist philosopher Joel Marks has written the following about his own decision to reject morality: "A 'soft atheist' would hold that one could be an atheist and still believe in morality [but] the religious fundamentalists are correct: without God, there is no morality."[8]

---

6 Jean-Paul Sartre, *Existentialism and Human Emotions* (Secaucus, NJ: Carol, 1998), 22.

7 J. L. Mackie, *The Miracle of Theism: Arguments for and against the Existence of God* (Oxford: Clarendon, 1982), 115.

8 Joel Marks, "An Amoral Manifesto (Part I)," *Philosophy Now* 80 (2010): 30–33.

Objecting to Premise 2: "Objective Moral
Values and Duties Don't Exist"

The second way for atheists to avoid the force of the moral argument is to deny that objective moral facts exist in the first place. If objective moral values and duties do not exist, then we do not need God to explain them. This view is often expressed as moral relativism, which generally comes in two forms: cultural relativism and ethical subjectivism. Cultural relativism claims that morality is relative to a particular culture, and that no objective standard of morality transcends cultures. Thus, an action that is evil and wrong in one culture could be good and right in another. Ethical subjectivism would go even further and claim that morality is relative to the individual. All individuals have their own equally valid standards of morality, and there is no higher standard that adjudicates between them.

Despite the popularity of cultural relativism, its implications are extremely problematic. First, cultural relativism leads to what is known as the "reformer problem." All great moral reformers were individuals who opposed the dominant moral paradigm of their culture, whether that paradigm included infanticide, the oppression of women, or racial injustice. They insisted that these practices were wrong and needed to be changed. Yet, if we adopt moral relativism, these reformers *themselves* were wrong because they opposed the moral values accepted by their culture, which—according to cultural relativism—is the only arbiter of morality. The very idea of moral progress assumes some objective standard of morality by which society can be judged to have progressed. But the existence of any such standard is precisely what cultural relativism denies.

Second, a cultural relativist cannot consistently oppose practices or ideas in other cultures. Visit any college campus, and you'll find that many people care deeply about justice, both here and abroad. However, many of the practices being protested have deep historical and cultural roots. For example, what we see as the oppression of women other cultures see as a proper understanding of social status. If every culture determines for itself what is right and wrong, then what gives us the authority as industrialized, individualistic, twenty-first-century Westerners to tell agrarian, communitarian, South Asian traditionalists that their values are wrong? Only if there is some objective standard of morality that stands outside both of our cultures and to which both of our cultures are equally accountable is such criticism warranted.

The problems of ethical subjectivism, the idea that each individual creates his own moral standards, are no less serious. First, ethical subjectivism removes any objective ground for moral criticism. No matter how evil you think another person's actions are, these actions are wrong only to you. If the other person approves of his or her actions, then those actions are right to that person. No behavior or attitude, whether racism or sexism or violence, can be labeled as objectively evil, and nothing, whether generosity or compassion or justice, can be extolled as objectively good. Absent objective moral criticism, the only question that remains is whether you have enough power to impose your moral preferences on other people. This fact has devastating consequences for the concept of human rights, which protect people, particularly minorities, from the abuse of power. If human rights are not grounded in objective moral facts, then they can be created or dissolved at the whims of those in power.

Second, the reformer problem also reemerges, albeit in a different form. Although the beliefs of a reformer who opposes the surrounding culture can now be called good, they are good to you only because you happen to share his moral preferences. From the standpoint of the majority of people in the culture who do not share your moral preferences, his beliefs are evil. Furthermore, there is no objective difference between a moral re-former, who is calling a culture to one standard, and a moral de-former, who is calling a culture to the opposite standard. Both are trying to persuade the culture to adopt their own personal moral preferences. The one who amasses the most power will win, and there will be no objective moral standpoint from which to criticize his victory.

Finally, both forms of moral relativism make it difficult to answer two thought experiments, which I call "Cypher's Challenge" and "the amorality pill."

Imagine a decision similar to the one made by Cypher in the movie *The Matrix*. How would you respond if you were asked to perform some moral atrocity, like pressing a button to detonate a bomb that would murder a busload of strangers in some distant country, in exchange for whatever future life you wanted? Your memory would immediately be erased so that you could fully enjoy your newfound money, fame, family, or career without any awareness of your action. What would you choose? Would you accept the offer or reject it? Hopefully, most of us would refuse such an offer. But why? If no action is objectively good or objectively evil, why is an infinitesimally short flicker of revulsion that will be immediately erased from your memory of more importance than the pleasure of money or success or a happy family that you will experience for the rest of your life?

A moral relativist could object that he has a personal, subjective repugnance for actions that harm others. In this way, his decision would be an aesthetic choice, like a preference for Beethoven over Bach, Pissarro over Picasso, or Adam Sandler over Jim Carrey. But is this objection sufficient? If we altered the challenge by replacing the moral atrocity, like killing a busload of strangers, with a nonmoral decision, like watching a curling match from start to finish or attending a middle-school production of *High School Musical*, there is little doubt that even the moral relativist would overrule his personal inclinations and accept the offer. Whence comes the difference? Why would a moral relativist treat moral decisions so differently than he treats nonmoral decisions?

When we reflect on our choices, we realize that moral considerations lie on an entirely different axis than our own goals and preferences or the expectations of our culture. No matter where an action falls on the continuum of our desires, from "I really want to" to "I really don't want to," we find another voice that says, "Thou shalt not." No matter how strongly we desire the bribe being offered and no matter how vehemently our culture disapproves, we feel the constraint of our moral obligations.

Second, imagine that scientists developed an "amorality pill" that would permanently destroy all your capacity to experience negative moral emotions, like sympathetic pain, guilt, and remorse, but would leave intact all your capacities for positive emotions, like gratitude and happiness. You would still be able to love your wife and children, to experience the vicarious joy of giving them gifts, and to feel a rush of tenderness when you kiss them goodnight. However, if you decided one morning that killing them all would give you great happiness, you would be able to do so without the slightest twinge of conscience. The pill would not force you to kill your family; it would just enable you to do so without regret if you decided you wanted to. Would you take the pill? If moral relativism were true, then there would be no obvious reason to not take the pill. It would allow you to pursue your personal goals free from the fetters of an illusory and incriminating conscience. Yet most people, even moral relativists, recoil in horror from the thought of becoming such a person. Why?

While these thought experiments seem extremely fanciful, they are actually quite achievable. For example, we have daily opportunities to commit small moral infractions with almost certain impunity: cheating on our taxes, lying on job applications, shoplifting small items from convenience stores, taking advantage of elderly people with dementia, anonymously vandalizing the cars of people we dislike. A person with minimal prudence could engage in such actions whenever he feels it would bring him the most pleasure with little chance of getting caught. So why does the moral relativist hesitate?

He could argue that acting "immorally" would make him feel guilty and that his conscience, though ultimately an illusion, is an unfortunate fact of life he has no ability to change. But is it? We know from experience that this claim is false. We can dull our conscience by engaging in small but steadily increasing acts of immorality. If we really wanted to reach a point in our lives where we could be largely amoral and free from the bonds of conscience, we could slowly begin practicing quiet, careful acts of rebellion against our moral sense. Today, it might cause you unbearable guilt to tell your spouse a serious lie. But you could begin with small fibs and slowly progress to greater and greater betrayals. Does anyone doubt that we could desensitize ourselves through this process so that one day our moral inhibitions and hang-ups would be greatly reduced, if not entirely eradicated? To put it more pointedly, are there no areas in your life for which your current complacency toward formerly repulsive actions (whether dishonesty or extramarital sex or greed or pornography or drugs) has developed through small but progressive acts of moral compromise? Since that's the case, why not work to deface your moral intuition completely? In practice, most professing moral relativists are just as protective of their conscience as moral realists. Why?

My contention is that no one is experientially a moral relativist. All of us, as human beings, are aware of the existence of moral reality. A recognition of moral duty, good and evil, and right and wrong are inescapable features of our shared humanity.[9] This hypothesis explains why moral relativists are so inconsistent. They support moral reformers; they fight against injustice; they have a conscience they would not obliterate, even when it pains them; they feel shame and guilt. In short, professing moral relativists encounter the same moral reality as everyone else; they merely lack the worldview resources to explain what it is or where it comes from.

In the last two subsections, we've seen that we have good reasons to accept both premises of the moral argument. First, if God does not

---

9   See anthropologist Donald E. Brown's list of human universals, which lists "distinguishing right and wrong," "empathy," "good and bad distinguished," "self is responsible," and "moral sentiments" as items discovered in every human culture; reproduced in Steven Pinker, *The Blank Slate: The Modern Denial of Human Nature* (New York: Penguin, 2002), 435–39.

exist, then objective moral values and duties do not exist. Without a good, loving God to ground the concept of morality, morality cannot be objective; it is merely a human construct. If human beings are reducible to molecules in motion, there is no reason to think that we have any more moral value than any other collection of molecules. And without a God to issue commands, we are left only with our personal preferences and goals, not binding moral duties. Second, objective moral values and duties do exist. Nearly all human beings recognize categories of right and wrong and good and evil. When it comes to issues of fundamental human rights, moral behavior, and the dictates of conscience, even the most ardent moral relativist unavoidably reacts like a moral realist. Given that moral relativism leads to such serious philosophical problems, and given that it flies in the face of our deep, natural intuition, it seems much more plausible to accept the idea that objective moral values and duties do indeed exist.

Consequently, we have good reasons to accept both premises of the moral argument: If God does not exist, then objective moral values and duties do not exist. But objective moral values and duties do exist. Therefore, it follows that God exists.

Common Misunderstandings

"The moral argument slanders atheists." The most common misunderstanding of the moral argument involves confusing moral grounding with moral behavior or moral knowledge.[10] In this section, I've only

---

10 See, for example, Greg M. Epstein, *Good without God? What a Billion Nonreligious People Do Believe* (New York: Morrow, 2009), 1–5. Epstein, a humanist chaplain at Harvard, seems to conflate the question If God doesn't exist, can morality exist? with the questions Can we know what is moral without divine revelation? Do we need to believe in God to act morally? and Do we need to believe in God to have moral motivation? The moral argument for God's existence is concerned only with the first question.

Reflecting on the umbrage taken by many atheists over the issue of moral foundations, Christian philosopher Mitch Stokes writes:

The confusion here is to think that questioning a person's ethical grounds is *ipso facto* questioning that person's moral character. . . .

been asking whether we need God's existence to explain the existence of moral facts. I have not been asking whether we need to believe in God's existence in order to behave morally or in order to know right from wrong. Clearly, many atheists behave morally. Any person can show kindness, love, compassion, mercy, and forgiveness, whether she believes in God or not, because we are all created in the image of a kind, loving, compassionate, merciful, and forgiving God. Nor do people need to believe in God in order to know what is moral. In fact, the Bible says that because we were made in God's image, his law is "written on [our] hearts" (Rom. 2:15), whether we affirm that he exists or not. Therefore we know right from wrong, albeit imperfectly, through our consciences. The moral argument should not be seen as a subtle (or not-so-subtle) disparagement of atheists. I am only asking whether objective morality can exist if atheism is true, not whether atheists can behave morally or whether they can know right from wrong.

"Moral disagreement shows that moral facts don't exist." It is occasionally argued that objective moral facts do not exist because moral commitments vary greatly from person to person. For example, some individuals and some cultures believe that sex outside of marriage is wrong, while other cultures believe that it is morally permissible. This kind of moral disagreement, so the argument goes, is evidence that morality is relative.

Such an inference is unwarranted. Just as disagreement over physical facts does not show that their truth is relative to the observer, neither does disagreement over moral facts show that their truth is relative to the observer. Scientists and nonscientists alike routinely disagree over

---

No one—or no one *I* know—thinks that atheists can't behave. Atheists can love their spouses, care for the poor, desire world peace, and enjoy long walks on the beach. Atheists can behave in accord with traditional moral standards, regardless of whether naturalism can ground these standards. We've all seen it done. The real question is whether naturalism can support or account for the moral standards themselves.

Stokes, *How to Be An Atheist: Why Many Skeptics Aren't Skeptical Enough* (Wheaton, IL: Crossway, 2016), 162–63.

many questions: Do electrons bind to the interior or the exterior of water clusters? Was the first life on earth RNA-based? How many gallons of milk do we have in the fridge? Is it your turn to pick the kids up from soccer practice? The presence of disagreement does not entail that these questions have no objectively correct answer.

A moral relativist could object that physical facts, unlike purported moral facts, can be empirically verified. However, this is not always the case. It may be a physical fact that there are an infinite number of undetectable parallel universes or that King Harold II weighed exactly 170.43 pounds at 9:07 a.m. on June 1, 1066. Even though these claims cannot be empirically verified, they could still be true. Furthermore, many philosophical claims are disputed and cannot be empirically tested but are nonetheless either objectively true or false. Not all philosophers agree on the answers to questions like Is nature all that exists? or Do we have free will? But that's not sufficient reason to conclude that these questions have no objective answer.

Finally, showing that particular moral claims are uncertain is not a sufficient reason to deny premise 2, which only claims that some moral facts exist. Instead, we would need to show that there are no moral facts whatsoever. If there exists even one objective moral fact, like "Murdering innocent people for pleasure is wrong," then premise 2 is true. Since cultures universally affirm that categories of right and wrong exist[11] and even agree on many basic moral issues,[12] it's difficult to argue that moral disagreement constitutes evidence against the existence of objective moral values and duties of any kind.

"Evolution shows how objective moral values and duties exist." A second misunderstanding involves the relationship of morality to evolution.

---

11   Pinker, *The Blank Slate*, 435–39.

12   C. S. Lewis addresses this issue in chap. 2 of *The Abolition of Man*. See also his collection of moral codes from various civilizations throughout history in the appendix. Lewis, *The Abolition of Man* (New York: Macmillan, 1955), 95–121.

Atheists often argue that evolution provides a mechanism for the emergence of moral behavior and our moral sense. For example, Richard Dawkins writes that there are several "good Darwinian reasons for individuals to be altruistic, generous or 'moral' towards each other"[13] and that "our moral sense . . . is indeed rooted deep in our Darwinian past."[14] Atheist particle physicist Vic Stenger likewise maintains:

> Modern thinkers have elaborated on [the evolutionary advantage of cooperation and altruism], showing in detail how our moral sense can have arisen naturally during the development of modern humanity.
>
> . . . When we include cultural evolution as well, we have a plausible mechanism for the development of human morality—by Darwinian selection.[15]

For the sake of argument, let's grant that evolution can entirely account for our tendency toward certain cooperative behaviors and for the existence of our moral sense.[16] Even if we make this concession, it

13 Richard Dawkins, *The God Delusion* (Boston: Mariner, 2008), 251.

14 Dawkins, *The God Delusion*, 254.

15 Victor J. Stenger, *God: The Failed Hypothesis: How Science Shows That God Does Not Exist* (Amherst: Prometheus, 2008), 209.

16 It's not obvious that we can safely make this assumption. For instance, the existence of "true altruism," in which one individual sacrifices his or her own well-being for the sake of a genetically unrelated individual who is unlikely to reciprocate, appears to be something of a puzzle in evolutionary terms. Evolutionary biologists like Jerry Coyne and Richard Dawkins explain its existence as a "misfiring" of our evolved tendency to care for our relatives or those who can reciprocate. It is a "Darwinian mistake," albeit a "blessed [and] precious" one (see Dawkins, *The God Delusion*, 253).

On the other hand, other evolutionary biologists like E. O. Wilson or David Sloane Wilson (no relation) or social psychologists like Jonathan Haidt see this answer as insufficient, given how ubiquitous true altruism is across cultures and how significantly it can harm an individual's fitness, which would produce strong selective pressure against such behavior. They argue that true altruism and other pro-social behaviors demand an explanation in terms of group selection, in which whole communities, rather than individual organisms or their genes, are selected for fitness. For an extended discussion of some of the evidence of group selection, especially as it pertains to morality and religion, see chap. 9 in Jonathan Haidt, *The Righteous Mind: Why Good People Are Divided by Politics and Religion* (New York: Pantheon, 2012).

is not clear how this claim is meant to affect the moral argument we've been discussing.

On the one hand, these claims about the evolution of morality might be intended to demonstrate that objective moral facts can exist without God. In other words, the argument is that our evolutionarily produced moral beliefs are the basis for what is actually, objectively right or wrong. But this reasoning is incorrect. A complete evolutionary description would tell us only that certain pro-social behaviors like cooperation or psychological inclinations like empathy *increased our ancestors' reproductive fitness* (i.e., their ability to pass their genes on to the next generation). These traits were therefore passed on to modern humans. Such an explanation would not tell us whether these behaviors were *objectively moral* (notice that Dawkins himself puts the word "moral" in quotation marks), because evolution might have produced a very different set of behaviors and intuitions. As Charles Darwin said: "If . . . men were reared under precisely the same conditions as hive-bees, there can hardly be a doubt that our unmarried females would . . . think it a sacred duty to kill their brothers, and mothers would strive to kill their fertile daughters."[17] If such hive-bee intuitions had been passed down to humans from our own ancestors, would it then have been objectively good to kill men and fertile women? If not, then we can't insist that whatever behaviors and inclinations evolution has given us are objectively good.

To put it another way, pro-social behaviors and inclinations are just a few of a whole range of human behaviors and inclinations. Human beings also tend to distrust members of the out-group. We display jealousy and envy. We punish rather than forgive those who violate community

---

The dispute between these two factions is extremely heated (see Steven Pinker's essay "The False Allure of Group Selection," *The Edge*, June 18, 2012, https://www.edge.org). With respect to my argument in this chapter, it doesn't matter whether we believe that one of these explanations is true, but it's worth noting that it's not at all certain that we have a good evolutionary explanation for pro-social behavior.

17 Charles Darwin, *The Descent of Man* (Amherst, NY: Prometheus, 1998), 102.

norms. If these behaviors also have an evolutionary origin, then they also once increased our ancestors' reproductive fitness. So, on what basis do we call one set of behaviors moral and the other set immoral? On what basis are we told to suppress our "lower," selfish inclinations and follow our "higher," selfless inclinations? Without some objective standard to decide which inclinations are "lower" and which are "higher," we have no way to know which inclinations we "ought" to pursue, since all of them purportedly came from evolution.[18] To say that one set of behaviors is higher because it promotes flourishing societies raises the question of whether flourishing societies are objectively good and why we ought to pursue anything other than our own self-interest, which are exactly the questions evolution was initially invoked to answer!

Finally, a proposed evolutionary basis for morality suffers from the same liabilities as an appeal to human flourishing. Why think that empathy or cooperation always leads to morality? Cannot nations cooperate to commit horrendous evil? Does empathy toward the many mean that it is moral to torture the few for the benefit of society at large? An evolutionary explanation of moral behavior does nothing to answer these questions.

"Evolution shows that objective moral values and duties don't exist." On the other hand, an evolutionary explanation for pro-social behavior might be used in exactly the opposite way: to deny the existence of objective morality. The atheist could grant that the vast majority of people believe that objective moral facts and duties exist, but he could argue that this belief is a side effect of the pro-social behavior bequeathed to us by evolution. For example, atheist Alex Rosenberg, the former chair of the Department of Philosophy at Duke University, writes: "Our core morality isn't true, right, correct, and neither is any other. Nature just seduced us into thinking it's right . . . because that

---

18 This claim is by no means new. It was addressed by C. S. Lewis in 1943. See his discussion in *Mere Christianity* (New York: Macmillan, 1952), 21–24.

made core morality work better; our believing in its truth increases our individual genetic fitness."[19] According to Rosenberg, morality doesn't exist and is merely an illusion foisted upon us by evolution. There are two responses to this argument.

First, the fact that we can see the evolutionary utility of a belief doesn't mean that the belief is false. For example, we can see the evolutionary utility of the belief that the external world exists (i.e., the belief that our experiences are not part of a Matrix-like illusion or a dream). This belief is evolutionarily advantageous because humans who believed that their experiences of sight, hearing, and pain were all an illusion might have behaved carelessly and died. In contrast, humans who believed that their experiences corresponded to a real, external world would have survived. But does it follow that belief in the existence of the external world is false?

Or consider the belief that other human beings also have conscious first-person experiences of color, pain, noises, and so forth (i.e., the belief that other humans are not unconscious zombies but instead have minds like we do). This belief is evolutionarily beneficial because it helps us predict the behavior of other humans, which helps us survive. Does it follow that the belief that other humans are conscious is false? Of course not.

In the same way, the fact that a belief in the existence of objective moral facts provides an evolutionary benefit does not imply that this belief is false. The atheist has to concede the possibility that moral facts exist even if the belief that they exist has evolutionary utility.

Second, if a belief in the existence of moral facts is an illusion, it is an extremely peculiar illusion. Many illusory beliefs and inclinations have a claimed evolutionary origin, like a tendency to see human faces in random objects, a belief that inanimate objects possess agency, and a fear of the dark. Many atheists claim that belief in God is another

---

19 Alex Rosenberg, *The Atheist's Guide to Reality: Enjoying Life without Illusions* (New York: Norton, 2011), 109.

false belief that once had evolutionary benefits. But in all these other cases, once we realize that our beliefs and inclinations are illusory, we make concerted efforts to modify or eradicate them if they conflict with our other goals.

For instance, it could be argued that our fear of the dark has a natural, evolutionary origin; humans with no fear of the dark were more likely to fall into tar pits and die. In contrast, humans who were afraid of the dark survived and passed their genes on to their offspring. But if a fear of the dark were preventing us from leaving our house after sunset, we would work to eradicate that fear, whether through medication, rational reflection, or counseling. It would make no sense to argue that because there is an evolutionary explanation of our fear, it is therefore reasonable to let it control our lives. We would be extremely puzzled if millions of people admitted that there is no objective reason to be afraid of the dark but still resisted all attempts to eradicate that fear. It would be stranger still if these same people praised those who feared the dark, encouraged others to fear the dark, and criticized anyone who did not fear the dark. Or imagine a tourist at the Grand Canyon who claimed to disbelieve in the existence of gravity yet at the same time clung to the guard rails and refused to leave the marked path for any reason whatsoever.

We see analogous incomprehensible behavior when it comes to belief in the existence of objective moral facts. Moral relativists who claim to have "seen through" the illusion of objective morality continue to behave as if objective morality exists. They frequently follow the dictates of their consciences rather than engaging in behavior they might otherwise enjoy. They make little to no effort to rid themselves of their negative moral emotions, like guilt. They laud moral reformers. They praise beliefs and practices they consider moral and criticize beliefs and practices they consider immoral. Such inconsistency is extremely odd. It would be almost unfathomable if we observed it in relation to any other behavior or inclination we dismiss as an illusory artifact of our evolution.

If our moral experience is, after all, an illusion, then it must be an utterly unique illusion that we cannot throw off and—what's more significant—that we don't seem to want to throw off. Perhaps we ought to consider the possibility that the indelible nature of our moral experience is the consequence of an objective moral standard whose existence we can't escape. But if objective morality exists, then it fits much more naturally into a theistic view of reality than an atheistic view.

Why Should We Seek the Truth?

One surprising area where atheism falters is in the search for truth. Historically, one of the most attractive features of atheism has been its forthright assertion of stark realism. No matter how unappealing a godless universe may turn out to be, atheists insist that they are committed to pursuing the truth at all costs. But why should we seek the truth about the nature of reality? In other words, why should we try to determine what is true by reading books, weighing the evidence, and taking time to reflect on our beliefs? This turns out to be a very interesting question that can be turned into something I call the "transcendental moral argument" for God's existence.

If God exists, then truth is potentially good and there are potentially some truths we are morally obligated to seek. I say "potentially" because it turns out that not any god will do. If some kind of generic Universal Spirit exists, it would not follow that truth-seeking is a moral obligation. Perhaps the Universal Spirit doesn't care whether we seek the truth. On the other hand, the Bible is filled with affirmations of the supreme value of truth: the book of Proverbs insists that knowledge is more desirable than wealth (8:10–11), the apostle Paul condemns us because "by [our] unrighteousness [we] suppress the truth" (Rom. 1:18), and Jesus declares that if we follow him, we "will know the truth, and the truth will set [us] free" (John 8:32). If the God of the Bible exists, then he does care whether we seek the truth, especially as it pertains to his existence and his will for our lives.

Of course, not all truths are equally important, nor are we morally obligated to seek them. I have no moral obligation to seek to know the millionth digit of pi or the number of ice cubes in my freezer. The question is not whether we are morally obligated to seek all truths indiscriminately, but whether there are certain specific truths we are morally obligated to seek. In particular, I am interested in whether we have a moral obligation to seek to know the answers to questions like why we exist, whether life has meaning, whether or not God exists, and whether he has revealed his will for our lives. When I talk about "truth-seeking" in what follows, I'll be referring primarily to these truths about the ultimate nature of reality.

On the one hand, I am arguing that if the God of the Bible exists, then we can explain why truth is intrinsically good and why we are morally obligated to seek true answers to these ultimate questions about reality. On the other hand, if a truth-loving God does not exist, then it is difficult to see why truth is intrinsically good or why we are morally obligated to seek it.

Formally, this transcendental moral argument can be expressed as follows:

Premise 1: If a truth-loving God does not exist, then truth is not intrinsically good and truth-seeking is not morally obligatory.
Premise 2: Truth is intrinsically good and truth-seeking is morally obligatory.

Therefore,

Conclusion: A truth-loving God exists.

As in the last section, because this argument has a valid logical form, we can reject its conclusion only if we reject one or both of the premises. Either we will have to argue that truth can be intrinsically good and truth-seeking can be morally obligatory even in the absence of a truth-loving God, or we will have to argue that truth is not intrinsically good and that truth-seeking is not morally obligatory. What are the problems with each of those alternatives?

Objecting to Premise 1: "Truth Can Be Intrinsically Good and Truth-Seeking Can Be Morally Obligatory without God"

As I mentioned in the last section, most atheists who believe in the existence of objective moral facts argue that morality can be grounded in human flourishing: what is good is whatever benefits human beings, and what is evil is whatever harms them. I argued that if we are reducible to molecules and energy, then it's difficult to see why human beings are morally valuable or why certain configurations of matter and energy carry any moral connotations. But as difficult as it is to make the connection between human flourishing and moral good, it is even more difficult for an atheist to make the connection between truth and moral good.

If our thoughts are *true*, then there is a correspondence between our thoughts and reality. From the perspective of naturalism, this means that there is a correspondence between the configuration of certain particles in my brain and the configuration of certain particles in reality.[20] Let's say that I believe the proposition "There is a penguin in my living room." I have a true belief if (1) there is actually a penguin in

20 Here I'm granting, for the sake of argument, that if naturalism is true, then thoughts can still be true or false. However, many atheists are suspicious of the idea that human thoughts can be true. For example, Rosenberg spends several chapters in *The Atheist's Guide to Reality* rejecting the notion that our thoughts are "about" things and, consequently, that they can be true or false. Some sample passages: "The mistake [made by our introspection] is the notion that when we think, or rather when our brain thinks, it thinks about anything at all" (170). "When consciousness convinces you that you, or your mind, or your brain has thoughts about things, it is wrong" (172). "Consciousness is just another physical process. . . . Introspection certainly produces the illusion of *about*ness. But it's got to be an illusion, since nothing physical can be *about* anything. That goes for your conscious thoughts as well. The markers, the physical stuff, the clumps of matter that constitute your conscious thoughts can't be *about* stuff either" (193).

my living room and (2) the configuration of particles in my brain corresponds to a penguin being in my living room. But why exactly do we think that there is something intrinsically good about some particles (those in my brain) corresponding "truly" to other particles (those in the penguin and in my living room)?

To use an alternate example, why should I think that it is *good* if I arrange a pile of rocks to resemble the solar system, but *not good* if I swap the positions of the rocks representing Neptune and Mars? And why think that I have a moral obligation to arrange particular rocks in particular configurations? These claims seem preposterous when applied to rocks. Surely, I have no obligation to shuffle rocks around in a particular way. But then why do I have an obligation to shuffle the particles in my brain around in a particular way? Why should I waste my precious time pursuing the truth, whether it's the truth about penguins, the solar system, or the existence of God?

The naturalistic answer is that truth is valuable because it so often produces human flourishing. Having true beliefs allows us to discover new medicine, improve farming techniques, predict natural disasters, and perform other activities that greatly improve the lives of billions of people. Thus, the claim could be made that truth is good and that we are obligated to seek it because it promotes human flourishing. There is nothing intrinsically good about making a rock model that accurately represents the solar system. But if my rock model enables me to colonize Mars and thereby promotes human flourishing, then the model is indeed good, and I am morally obligated to construct it with this goal in mind.

Unfortunately, this account makes truth an *instrumental* good rather than an *intrinsic* good; in other words, truth is good not because of what it is, but because of what it can produce (see fig. 5). However, a serious difficulty arises when one of our instrumental goods comes into conflict with our intrinsic good. For example, papayas and smooth jazz can also be instrumental goods because they also can contribute to human flourishing. But what happens if a person is allergic to papayas or loathes smooth jazz? In that case, these things are no longer good, because they no longer produce human flourishing. Indeed, we'd now be morally obligated to avoid papayas and to flee from smooth jazz, since they detract from human flourishing rather than enhancing it. So, what happens when truth and truth-seeking come into conflict with human flourishing?

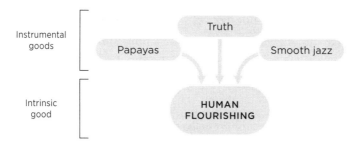

Figure 5. Instrumental good versus intrinsic good

Suppose that you are an atheist, and your Christian grandmother is lying on her deathbed. Her only comfort is that she believes she will soon be in the presence of God. She tells you: "I'm sad that I'm dying and I'm in incredible pain. The only thing that enables me to endure this illness and even to have joy in the face of my suffering is knowing that I'll soon be face to face with Jesus and that I'll be reunited with my husband and my children. But tell me, atheist grandson, I've heard that some people don't even believe in God. Is that claim true? And should I seek to know whether that claim is true?"

As an atheist, how do you respond? Do you tell her the truth? Do you urge her to seek the truth? Not if her happiness is your highest priority. Telling her that atheism is true will diminish her flourishing. Indeed, if she presses you for an answer, it seems that you are morally obligated to affirm her religious beliefs. If human flourishing is the ultimate good, then why shatter her happiness for the sake of truth?

This example shows that setting up human flourishing as the ultimate good cannot account for the intrinsic goodness of truth or for our moral obligation to seek it. Even if we grant—for the sake of argument—that it is good for the particles in my brain to take on states that correspond to happiness, it is not at all clear why it is good for the particles in my brain to take on states that correspond to truth.

This counterexample and many others like it show that, in the absence of God, it is extremely difficult to argue that truth is objectively good or that we have a moral obligation to seek it. In particular, if we believe that the ultimate good is human flourishing, then there are situations in which truth is objectively bad and we are morally obligated to ignore or even to lie about the truth for the sake of people's flourishing.

Given the difficulties inherent in denying premise 1, perhaps we can deny premise 2? Perhaps truth is not intrinsically good and truth-seeking is not morally obligatory after all. Let's consider that possibility next.

Objecting to Premise 2: "Truth Is Not Intrinsically Good, and Truth-Seeking Is Not Morally Obligatory"

To see whether we can avoid the conclusion of this argument by denying the second premise rather than the first, let's return to the example of the dying Christian grandmother.

Most atheists wouldn't think twice about lying in this situation. In reflecting on this "dying grandmother" scenario, atheist Jerry Coyne writes: "If . . . faith eases her last moments, it would be churlish to attack it, for the costs are high and the benefits nil. . . . I know of no nonbeliever who would sanction that, or say there's anything wrong with allowing the dying to retain their faith."[21] Here, Coyne argues quite explicitly that we ought to weigh the costs and benefits to human

21   Jerry A. Coyne, *Faith versus Fact: Why Science and Religion Are Incompatible* (New York: Viking, 2015), 253.

flourishing when we consider questions of truth or falsehood. However, atheists sometimes fail to see the far-reaching implications of this idea.

What if atheists like Bertrand Russell and Jean-Paul Sartre were right in thinking that atheism is a terrible, miserable, agonizing truth? What if the purposelessness of life, the meaninglessness of suffering, and the certainty of death are psychologically unbearable for most people? And what if it happened to be empirically true that most people would be happier believing religious delusions than conceding the truth of atheism? In that case, a commitment to human flourishing as the ultimate good would require us to conceal atheism from as many people as possible and to promote harmless religious beliefs we know to be false, as long as they make people happier.

Of course, the atheist could argue—as Coyne does—that existing religions are far from harmless and therefore should not be exempt from considerations of their truth or falsehood. But this objection faces several major hurdles. First, it is not clear that religion makes people unhappy. Data is mixed, but many studies show a positive correlation between religious belief and happiness.[22] Second, even if there were evidence that existing religions are harmful, the atheist would have to make the case that there exist no false religious beliefs at all that promote human flourishing. This seems highly unlikely. We can all think of seemingly harmless religious beliefs that could greatly increase people's happiness, like the idea that when we die, we will all go to Pastry-heaven to feast on croissants and éclairs for all eternity. An atheist who rejects the intrinsic goodness of truth (and who consequently only views truth as an instrumental good) would have to support and champion such beliefs. Is that a bullet he's willing to bite? Rather than committing his life to the search for truth, will he commit himself to the search for and promulgation of whatever false beliefs tend to maximize people's happiness?

---

22 Christopher Alan Lewis and Sharon Mary Cruise, "Religion and Happiness: Consensus, Contradictions, Comments and Concerns," *Mental Health, Religion, and Culture* 9, no. 3 (2006): 213–25.

Most significantly, I question whether the atheist really wants to shift the ground of the debate from whether religion is true to whether it is helpful. If an atheist insists on denying that truth-seeking is intrinsically good or morally obligatory, then he will have to approach the question of religion not primarily in terms of truth but in terms of its practical impact on humanity's overall flourishing. If the atheist rejects notions of objective morality altogether, the implications are even more extreme. Claims will then have to be evaluated not in terms of human flourishing but in terms of the atheist's own personal goals. For instance, when he hears someone say, "Christianity is true," he should immediately respond: "Well, I don't really care about its truth, per se. My real questions are Will it meet my own personal needs? Will it help me achieve my own personal goals? Will it help me lose weight, make more money, and become a better salsa dancer?" If truth is not an intrinsic good, then these are the questions he ought to ask not just about religious claims but about all claims.

Furthermore, the position that truth is not intrinsically good explicitly contradicts the foundational tenets of free thought and the modern atheist movement. As I've pointed out, one of the most legitimately attractive features of atheism is that most atheists today claim to be on a quest for truth. Atheists are quite right when they say that we ought to seek true answers to the ultimate questions about life, the universe, and everything. They are correct in saying that it is wrong to bury our heads in the sand and comfort ourselves with false beliefs. But if we can't explain why truth-seeking is good or obligatory in a universe without God, then our moral obligation to seek the truth actually undermines atheism. On what basis do freethinkers urge others to seek the truth or to abandon religious dogma if atheism can offer us no reason to think that truth-seeking is obligatory?

To put it another way, as a Christian, I can affirm that truth is intrinsically good and that truth-seeking is morally obligatory because God loves the truth and commands us to seek it. But if an atheist were to urge me to throw off my religious delusions and to embrace the truth of atheism, I would be well within my rights to respond: "Why? I am happy as a Christian, and Christianity has made me into a more loving, compassionate, and generous person. If Christianity is true, then I understand why I am obligated to seek true answers to ultimate questions, like whether God exists. But if atheism is true, why am I obligated to find out?"

Fitting the intrinsic goodness of truth into an atheistic worldview turns out to be exceptionally difficult, whereas it is a natural fit with Christianity. If a truth-loving God exists and commands us to seek the truth, then we can explain why truth-seeking is good and obligatory. We can even resolve the tension between truth-seeking and human flourishing because—if Christianity is true—the truth will always ultimately lead to our flourishing. No matter what hardships or difficulties attend truth-seeking here in this life, there will be no ultimate conflict between the truth and our joy, because God is the truth and will give everlasting flourishing to those who seek him.

In summary, we have good reasons to accept both premises. If a truth-loving God does not exist, then truth is not intrinsically good, and truth-seeking is not morally obligatory. But if we accept that truth is intrinsically good and that truth-seeking is morally obligatory, then a truth-loving God, such as the one described in the Bible, must exist.

Revelation and Scripture

Finally, to understand the evidence for God's existence from a Christian perspective, I'd like to elaborate on the concept of revelation. By "revelation," I'm referring not to the book at the end of the Bible filled with apocalyptic imagery but to the idea that God reveals himself to us. This concept is not another piece of the puzzle per se; it's better regarded as the frame in which the entire puzzle resides.

The God of the Bible is a revealing God, a God who makes his existence, his character, and his purposes known to humanity. There are two distinct categories of God's revelation: general revelation and special revelation.[23] General revelation is God's revelation to humanity through nature and reason. It is equally available to all people and is studied primarily through the disciplines of science and philosophy. Special revelation is God's revelation to humanity through Scripture. It was given to particular people or to particular groups in history, and is primarily studied through hermeneutics, the discipline of interpreting written texts.[24]

Recognizing these categories helps us understand why general revelation does not give us a complete picture of God. For instance, it's questionable whether the evidence discussed in the last two chapters can distinguish between the God of Christianity, the God of Islam, and the God of the Baha'i faith. While a study of general revelation can tell us broadly about God's existence and attributes, it cannot give us all that we need to know: Does God love us? What specifically does he require of us? Does he interact with history? Does he answer prayer? To answer these questions, we need more than just God's general revelation in nature; we need his special revelation in Scripture.

Imagine you are walking through the halls of some beautiful building. From your observations alone, you might be able to infer a great deal about the architect: he is a man of great intelligence, ingenuity, and love of beauty. But imagine that the architect taps you on the shoulder and begins speaking to you. You now have definitive and detailed access

---

23 See, for example, article 2 of the Belgic Confession:

> We know God by two means: First, by the creation, preservation, and government of the universe, since that universe is before our eyes like a beautiful book in which all creatures, great and small, are as letters to make us ponder the invisible things of God: God's eternal power and divinity, as the apostle Paul says in Romans 1:20. All these things are enough to convict humans and to leave them without excuse. Second, God makes himself known to us more clearly by his holy and divine Word, as much as we need in this life, for God's glory and for our salvation.

24 Special revelation could potentially include revelation not recorded in Scripture. For example, all of Jesus's teaching was inspired, yet we certainly do not have a record of everything he taught. However, Christians generally agree that *public* special revelation is limited to Scripture.

to this man's character. You can have a personal relationship with him in a way that would be impossible from staring at his work alone. The same is true of God. While there's much to be learned from general revelation in nature, we must not stop there and refuse to listen to God's voice in Scripture.

"But how," a skeptic might ask, "can we know what counts as 'Scripture'? Where do we find the supposed inspired words of God? In the Bible or the Qur'an or the Book of Mormon or the Vedas or some other book?" There are three ways to answer this question: one subjective and two objective.

First, subjectively, Christians experience God speaking to them through the Bible in a way they do not experience God speaking through other books. For example, while she was an atheist and a tenured professor of English at Syracuse University, Rosaria Butterfield began reading the Bible at the suggestion of Christian friends. She explains:

> I read the way a glutton devours. I read it many times that first year in multiple translations. At a dinner gathering my partner and I were hosting, my transgendered friend J cornered me in the kitchen. She put her large hand over mine. "This Bible reading is changing you, Rosaria," she warned. . . . I continued reading the Bible, all the while fighting the idea that it was inspired. But the Bible got to be bigger inside me than I.[25]

This is the way countless Christians have experienced and should experience the Bible.[26] We believe that it is Scripture because we sense

25 Rosaria Butterfield, "My Train-Wreck Conversion," *Christianity Today*, February 7, 2013, http://www.christianitytoday.com/.

26 It's an interesting historical corollary that the Bible is one of the most strictly regulated books in the world. Many nations have controlled or even prohibited the import, ownership, or distribution of Bibles, including Algeria, Brunei, China, Cuba, Iran, Laos, Mauritania, Morocco, North Korea, Saudi Arabia, and Turkmenistan. See the US State Department's annual "International

God speaking through it. Atheists presumably would not consider subjective, third-party testimony about the inspiration of the Bible to be particularly weighty, especially since the subjective experiences of Christians, Muslims, and Hindus regarding their respective Scriptures are contradictory. However, the atheist could always obtain firsthand confirmation of this claim by opening up the Bible for herself and asking God to speak through it if it is indeed his inspired revelation.

Second, we can recognize the Bible's inspiration through its world-view. Although some of the arguments proposed in the last two chapters would work for the Scriptures of some religions, they would not all work for the Scriptures of all religions. For example, religions based on books that do not cast humans as created in the image of God or that define God as a force rather than a person will have difficulty explaining why the universe follows rational laws we can discern. Likewise, religious writings which deny that the universe had a beginning will be difficult to square with the finite age of the universe. While arguments from natural theology can't necessarily tell us exactly which religious documents are inspired, they can help us determine which are the most consistent with God's general revelation. Moreover, if we include arguments like the trilemma (chap. 2), the resurrection (chap. 3), or the gospel (which I'll discuss in chaps. 7–9), it becomes exceptionally unlikely that any other book has a compelling claim to being inspired.

Third, and most importantly, the Bible can be recognized as Scripture through the teaching of Jesus. Jesus's teaching was utterly saturated with the Old Testament. Given that he was a first-century Jew, this is in no way surprising. Jesus viewed the Old Testament as fully inspired, fully authoritative, and fully reflective of a God of goodness, mercy, and love. Once we objectively conclude that Jesus viewed the Bible as God's

---

Religious Freedom Report for 2015," available at U.S. Department of State, https://www.state.gov/. While it's extremely doubtful that these nations recognize that the Bible is inspired and ban it as a result, they do seem to realize that the Bible is powerfully compelling and therefore dangerous, even if they think it is false.

special revelation, then the question of the Bible's inspiration rests on what we think of Jesus.[27] It is what we think of him that determines what we think of the Bible.

Before leaving this point, I'd also like to make an observation about the type of evidence I've presented so far. In many disciplines, knowledge of important truths requires a great deal of education and study. For example, it took the entire scientific enterprise hundreds of years to establish the existence of atoms, and it can take a student a decade

27 Of course, this argument technically applies only to the Old Testament, since the New Testament hadn't been written during the time of Jesus's ministry. Practically speaking, I find it very uncommon for people to accept the Old Testament as inspired on the basis of Jesus's authority and then to reject the New Testament. However, to complete the argument for the inspiration of the New Testament, there are a number of routes available.

First, Jesus commissioned his apostles to teach and preach authoritatively in his name. It's then reasonable to conclude that books written by the apostles or under the guidance of the apostles were divinely inspired.

Second, we could appeal to God's providential guidance of his people in recognizing his voice in Scripture. Just as God guided the Jewish people to accept the canonical books of the Old Testament as Scripture, we would expect God to guide the early Christian church to accept a set of canonical books as New Testament Scripture. Historically, that is precisely what we do see. Although there were some disagreements over exactly which books should be included in the New Testament canon, the core of the canon was well established within a couple of centuries after Jesus's death as Christians recognized the divine inspiration of certain books. See Michael J. Kruger, *Canon Revisited: Establishing the Origins and Authority of the New Testament Books* (Wheaton, IL: Crossway, 2012).

Finally, a fascinating argument that C. S. Lewis applied to the resurrection works even better, I believe, for the inspiration of the New Testament. He writes:

Supposing you had before you a manuscript of some great work, either a symphony or a novel. There then comes to you a person, saying, "Here is a new bit of the manuscript that I found; it is the central passage of that symphony, or the central chapter of that novel. The text is incomplete without it. I have got the missing passage which is really the centre of the whole work." The only thing you could do would be to put this new piece of the manuscript in that central position, and then see how it reacted on the whole of the rest of the work. If it constantly brought out new meanings from the whole of the rest of the work, if it made you notice things in the rest of the work which you had not noticed before, then I think you would decide that it was authentic. On the other hand, if it failed to do that, then, however attractive it was in itself, you would reject it.

See Lewis, "The Grand Miracle," in *God in the Dock: Essays on Theology and Ethics*, ed. Walter Hooper (Grand Rapids, MI: Eerdmans, 1970), 81–82. In my opinion, one of the most compelling arguments for the inspiration of the New Testament is how it fits into the narrative of the Old Testament in such a seamless and breathtakingly beautiful way.

or more to understand basic electronic structure theory. In contrast, arguments for God's existence can be understood by an eight-year-old. Moreover, without any prompting, an eight-year-old will ask questions that lead naturally to arguments for God's existence. While some arguments require quite a bit of philosophical or scientific sophistication, a child who wonders where the universe came from, or who listens in awe when she hears that math can predict the motion of planets, or who asks why some things are good and other things are bad is knocking on the door of theology.

Many skeptics will protest that our natural tendency to accept God as an explanation is a liability for theism rather than an asset.[28] Among them, atheist philosopher Daniel Dennett sees "hyperactive agent detection" in the origin of religion; he believes that evolution has primed us to see patterns and intelligence even in random and natural phenomena.[29] But, as we saw earlier, a supposedly evolved inclination to accept some conclusion does not make that conclusion false or absolve us of the need to weigh rational arguments for and against that conclusion. After all, evolution, by the same line of reasoning, may have primed us to believe certain basic mathematical propositions, like "Parallel lines never intersect," but it wouldn't follow that those propositions are false.

Regardless, this natural-tendency criticism misses the main point of my observation. The fact that the evidence for God's existence is so readily available shows that whatever objections atheists may have, they cannot argue that the evidence for God is inaccessible. The evidence for God's existence is all around us, in every aspect of our daily life, in our most basic moral experiences, and behind all of the *why* questions that children begin asking almost as soon as they can speak. In a sense,

---

28 Conversely, Christians could offer the rejoinder that our natural inclination toward theism is one of the many ways God has designed us to recognize and respond to his presence. See Justin L. Barrett, *Born Believers: The Science of Children's Religious Belief* (New York: Free Press, 2012).

29 Daniel C. Dennett, *Breaking the Spell: Religion as a Natural Phenomenon* (New York: Viking, 2006), 108–15.

theism comes naturally. It is atheism that must be learned.[30] By itself, that doesn't make theism true and atheism false, but it does support the biblical claim that "the heavens declare the glory of God" (Ps. 19:1) and that "[God's] invisible attributes, namely, his eternal power and divine nature, have been clearly perceived . . . in the things that have been made. So [people] are without excuse" (Rom. 1:20).

Evidence and Commitment

In summary, I've chosen six pieces of evidence that point to God's existence: the applicability of mathematics to nature, the origin of the universe, the explanation of the universe, the fine-tuning of the fundamental constants of physics, the existence of objective moral facts, and the intrinsic goodness of truth. The question before us is whether atheism or theism provides a better explanation for the evidence. Although atheistic responses to each of these pieces of evidence exist, in no case do I think that atheism provides as plausible an answer as theism. Indeed, many atheists acknowledge that some of these phenomena are currently inexplicable, even if they hold out hope that science or philosophy will one day be able to provide a better explanation.

However, the question of God's existence is unlike the majority of scientific and philosophical issues. In some situations, it's possible to adjust our behavior in proportion to our certainty. If we're uncertain whether it will be sunny or rainy on our hike tomorrow, we can pack both sunscreen and an umbrella. If we're not sure how long we'll need to use the lecture hall, we can reserve it for two hours rather than for only one. We can hedge our bets and leave our options open. But in other situations, this kind of partial commitment to exclusive alternatives is impossible. Greg Ganssle asks us to consider the decision to

---

30 "Children's minds are naturally tuned up to believe in gods generally, and perhaps God in particular." Barrett, *Born Believers*, 4. In addition to experimental evidence in support of his thesis, Barrett offers some fascinating anecdotes illustrating how difficult it is for parents to "dissuade [children] of belief in God" (5).

get into a car and drive on the freeway: "All of the available evidence convinces me that there is a less than 100 percent chance of reaching my destination safely. [But either] I get in the car and drive on I-95, or I do not. I cannot get in the car 99 percent."[31]

Choosing whether or not to trust in God involves the same kind of binary decision. Even if we are intellectually uncertain whether God exists, we will still make choices every day that reflect our posture toward God: Will we go to church? Will we pray? Will we lie? Will we steal? Will we forgive those who have wronged us? Will we ask God for forgiveness when we wrong others? Will we remain faithful to our spouses within marriage? Will we curse others in our hearts? Will we give generously to the poor? In every choice we make, we will live as if the biblical God does exist or does not. Given the way a person's relationship to God affects every area of his life, neutrality is impossible.

This observation is not evidence that God exists. The immediacy and profound relevance of a particular claim doesn't entail that the claim is true or that it is false. But it does mean that the question of God's existence is urgent. While we may genuinely desire more time to explore questions we've never before considered, any deferred decision is still an implicit no to God's authority over us and his offer of salvation to us.

If nothing else, we should come to realize that the existence of the biblical God is, quite literally, a question of life and death. Or, to put it more correctly, a question of death and life. We are, according to the Bible, dying men and women who are being offered our only hope for healing. If this claim is even possibly true, we ought to take it very seriously.

31 Ganssle, *A Reasonable God*, 41–42.

6

Arguments against God

The one who states his case first seems right,
until the other comes and examines him.

PROVERBS 18:17

IN THE TWO PRECEDING CHAPTERS, I provided evidence for God's existence. However, it would be unfair to present a case for God's existence without considering the case for God's nonexistence. In what follows, I'd like to review what I consider to be the three best and most common arguments against God's existence: the problem of evil, evolution, and divine hiddenness.

The Problem of Evil

The problem of evil was most famously formulated by Epicurus, who asked how evil could exist in a world ruled by a perfectly good, all-powerful God. Atheist philosophers since Epicurus have argued that the existence of evil is logically incompatible with God's existence.[1] To say that a perfectly good, all-powerful Being exists in a world containing

---

1   See, for instance, part 2 of Michael Martin and Ricki Monnier, eds., *The Impossibility of God* (Amherst, NY: Prometheus, 2003), 59–124.

evil is—they claim—like saying that a square circle exists: it is a logical contradiction. A slightly weaker but still powerful objection is that the amount of evil in the world makes it incredibly unlikely that God exists, even if it is not logically impossible.

Without question, the problem of evil is the most intellectually and emotionally formidable argument against God's existence. Few people can see and experience the horrendous evil in the world and not wonder how a good, loving God could allow it.

Given how frequently the existence of evil is used as evidence against theism, it may be surprising to learn that it is arguably an even bigger problem for atheism. Recall from the previous chapter that the moral argument proposed that the existence of objective moral facts is evidence for God's existence. In response, many atheists deny that moral facts exist at all. But to assert that the world is full of evil is to admit that there are, after all, objective moral facts about the pervasiveness of evil in the world. Far from being evidence against God, the existence of evil is therefore a powerful pointer to God.

C. S. Lewis writes of his own experience as an atheist:

> My argument against God was that the universe seemed so cruel and unjust. But how had I got this idea of *just* and *unjust*? A man does not call a line crooked unless he has some idea of a straight line. What was I comparing this universe with when I called it unjust? . . . Of course I could have given up my idea of justice by saying it was nothing but a private idea of my own. But if I did that, then my argument against God collapsed too—for the argument depended on saying that the world was really unjust, not simply that it did not happen to please my private fancies.[2]

To see how serious this point is, imagine a naturalist asking, "How can an all-loving, all-powerful God exist if evil spirits exist?" Our imme-

2   C. S. Lewis, *Mere Christianity* (New York: Macmillan, 1952), 45–46.

diate response would be to ask the naturalist whether he really believes that evil spirits exist. On the one hand, he might be posing an internal critique of Christianity. In that case, he would mean something like "Of course evil spirits don't exist. But Christianity *claims* they do, and that claim is incompatible with the existence of God. Therefore, Christianity is internally inconsistent." On the other hand, he might be posing an external critique of Christianity. In that case, he'd be saying something like "Yes, evil spirits really do exist. Therefore God cannot exist." If he is posing this kind of external critique, then before he continues his argument, he needs to explain exactly how the existence of supernatural evil beings is compatible with his belief—as a naturalist—that there is no supernatural realm at all.

A Christian can respond to an atheist who presses the problem of evil in precisely the same way. If the atheist is claiming that objective moral evil *actually* exists, then he has to answer the questions I raised in the last chapter's discussion of the moral argument: Where does this moral reality come from? What is the objective standard by which some action or event can be judged to be evil? If the universe and human beings are reducible to molecules in motion, why does anything have moral value?

For example, in 2015 atheist comedian Stephen Fry gave an interview in which he was asked what he would do if he died and discovered that God does exist. What would he say? Fry responded: "Bone cancer in children? What's that about? How dare you! How dare you create a world in which there is such misery that is not our fault. It's not right. It's utterly, utterly evil."[3] This ringing condemnation is powerful, but it depends crucially on the assumption that objective good and evil exist. Notice the moral language Fry employs. He is assuming that failing to prevent the suffering of the innocent is "utterly, utterly evil." But on what does he base his assumption that certain actions are objectively evil and morally blameworthy?

---

3   Stephen Fry, "Stephen Fry on God," interview by Gay Byrne, RTÉ One, February 1, 2015, https:// www.youtube.com/.

To insist that the world is not now as it ought to be is to assume that there is some way the world ought to be. To say that the world is broken is to assume that it has some purpose that has been thwarted. To say that humans are wicked is to assume that they have transgressed some objective moral standard that humans are obligated to obey. If there is no God, then what would these claims mean? Before deploying the problem of evil as an external critique of Christianity, the atheist needs to explain exactly how the existence of evil is compatible with atheism. If he comes to conclude, like many atheists, that there is no such thing as objective good or evil, then he cannot argue that the existence of evil is evidence against God's existence.

But let's grant that the atheist is not attempting to argue that evil actually exists. Instead, he could be arguing that Christianity is internally inconsistent. Since Christianity affirms both that God exists and that evil exists, can it reconcile these two ideas? I believe it can. However, I want to begin my discussion with a caveat.

Responses to the problem of evil need to be handled with care. The problem of evil is a philosophical question that should be addressed logically and rationally. But it is also a deeply personal subject for many people. No one can pass through life without suffering some kind of tragedy, whether it's the death of a friend or parent, betrayal, loneliness, disease, or depression. Any Christian who provides an answer to the problem of evil needs to recognize both the philosophical and personal sides of the question, as Jesus himself did. In the Gospel of John, Jesus's disciples see a man born blind and—following theological reasoning common at the time—ask him, "Rabbi, who sinned, this man or his parents, that he was born blind?" (John 9:2). Jesus rejects both alternatives and provides his disciples with a different answer. But he also stops and heals the man. Jesus views this interaction not merely as an opportunity for philosophical discussion but as an opportunity to display compassion and kindness to a human being made in God's image. I'll try to follow the same pattern, first addressing the philosophical issue and then approaching the problem from a more personal angle.

Philosophically, the problem of evil is answered by various "theodicies," or attempts to vindicate God's justice in the light of evil. Each theodicy hinges on the recognition that God can be opposed to evil but can still have morally sufficient reasons for permitting it. Rather than viewing each theodicy as a blanket explanation for all the evil we observe, we do better to view them as complementary and possibly overlapping explanations. Rutgers philosophy professor Dean Zimmerman has a helpful analogy in which he envisions all the instances of evil in the universe as a black circle on a whiteboard.[4] We can think of each particular theodicy as an eraser that explains a portion of the evil in the world and erases the corresponding sections of the circle. Even if no single eraser can erase the entire circle, the circle may be erased completely when all the theodicies are taken together. In what follows, I'll outline various major theodicies and explain how they account for evil in a logically consistent fashion.

One of the most important responses to the problem of evil is known as the "free-will theodicy," which holds that God could permit evil because he values human freedom: if God desires to create creatures with the capacity to freely choose to love him and do good, then they must have the capacity to freely choose to reject him and do evil. And, undoubtedly, many of the most grievous evils we see in the world today are the result of human beings misusing their freedom in order to sin.

However, an appeal to "free will" seems incomplete, because it does not easily account for another class of evils, which are known as natural evils. For example, how can free will explain why God allows natural disasters, like earthquakes or hurricanes? Or why he allows terminal illnesses in children? An appeal to free will also doesn't seem to account

4   A fellow philosopher attributed this illustration to Professor Zimmerman, but when I contacted him, he could not remember using it! Nonetheless, I think it is excellent and would like to give credit where it is presumably due.

for the degree to which our free choices harm bystanders. If God exists, why doesn't he prevent the free actions of evil people from causing such suffering in the world?

The theodicy of "soul building" answers some of these questions. Almost everyone recognizes that physical pain is not inherently evil. People willingly subject themselves to short-term physical pain at the gym or at the dentist's office for the sake of long-term benefits. The same is even true of emotional pain. We will willingly endure emotionally painful ridicule or rejection for the sake of standing up for causes we believe to be right. An analogy can then be made to God's allowance of evil. Some virtues like kindness or prudence seem to be achievable in a world with no evil. But it's difficult to imagine how people could display other virtues, like fortitude, patience, courage, and forgiveness, in a world devoid of evil. A bit of reflection both on our own lives and on the lives of others shows that the actions we most highly value, like self-sacrifice and love for enemies, are possible only because evil exists. In fact, the greater the evil faced, the greater and more valuable the virtue exhibited. Consequently, some of the evils we experience in this world could be logically necessary preconditions for the development of great moral good

To understand this theodicy, we need to dispel the wildly popular idea that God's primary role in the universe is to maximize our temporal comfort and enjoyment. For modern Americans, most of whom experience a historically unimaginable level of luxury, this assumption is natural but incorrect. Christian philosopher William Lane Craig explains:

> One reason that the problem of suffering seems so puzzling is that people naturally tend to assume that if God exists, then His purpose for human life is happiness in this life. God's role is to provide a comfortable environment for His human pets. But on the Christian view, this is false. We are not God's pets, and the goal of human life

is not happiness per se, but the knowledge of God—which in the end will bring true and everlasting human fulfillment.[5]

To put it another way, the universe is not a resort run by a kindly, slightly doddering, maître d' in the sky. If this conception of God were true, it would indeed be a mystery why God does not merely teleport us all onto a sunny beach with an endless supply of snacks and free WiFi. But if God is less interested in our physical comfort and more interested in producing in us a certain kind of character, then it makes much more sense that we face trials, hardships, and suffering that can produce in us forbearance, bravery, mercy, and compassion—virtues that wouldn't exist in a glorified day spa.

While "soul building" surely explains some of the evil we see in the world, it is likewise incomplete. Although it is not difficult to see how God can use some evil events to shape our character in positive ways, there are other events so horrific that it is hard to imagine how they could be justified by an appeal to the development of certain moral qualities. A skeptic could plausibly insist that while some evil may be absolutely necessary for the development of virtue, achieving that goal should take far less evil than we currently observe.

However, the theist could respond with a third observation: the interconnectedness of events means that evil is often inextricably linked with good. For example, if a man's wife dies and he marries another woman, or if a couple's infant daughter dies, causing them to have another child, it seems impossible to eradicate the evil without simultaneously eradicating the good that follows it. When one thinks of the extraordinary ways in which the choices we make have a ripple effect through history, it's plausible to think that some of the present evils we can see will result in future goods. In other words, it is not enough to look at an isolated event in the present. The evils that befall us may

---

5   William Lane Craig, *On Guard: Defending Your Faith with Reason and Precision*, 3rd ed. (Colorado Springs: Cook, 2010), 163.

indeed not be offset by immediate goods. But how will they shape our character in ten years? How will they shape the characters of our friends and family? How will they alter the path of our lives and the lives of those around us? How will they influence our future choices or values? Thus, God could be justified in permitting at least some evil for the sake of the morally compensating goods that will eventually result.[6]

Finally, the philosophical position known as "skeptical theism" holds that our inability to discover morally justifying reasons for God allowing any instance of evil is not a good reason to insist that he possesses no such reasons. Philosopher Stephen Wykstra asks, "Is it at all reasonable to think that if there were a justifying good for a particular evil, then we would likely discern it?"[7] Given the gap between God's knowledge and ours, Wykstra believes that the answer is a resounding *no*. He argues that to move from the claim "I see no good reasons for this evil" to the claim "There are no good reasons for this evil" places unwarranted confidence in our own very limited ability to recognize the significance of events and their effects.

For those of us who are parents, we see an immediate analogy to our relationship with our children. We bring all kinds of inexplicable pain into their lives when they are small: we vaccinate them, we put them to bed when they aren't sleepy, and we confiscate especially exciting pieces of electrical wiring and broken glass. Their inability to see or to understand our reasons for such actions does not mean that those

---

6   William Lane Craig comments:

> One has only to think of the innumerable, incalculable contingencies involved in arriving at a single historical event, say, the Allied victory at D-day. We have no idea of the natural and moral evils that might be involved in order for God to arrange the circumstances and free agents in them requisite to some intended purpose, nor can we discern what reasons such a provident God might have in mind for permitting some evil to enter our lives. Certainly many evils seem pointless and unnecessary to us—but we are simply not in a position to judge.

> Craig, "A Molinist View," in *God and the Problem of Evil: Five Views*, ed. Chad Meister and James K. Dew Jr. (Downers Grove, IL: IVP Academic, 2017), 46.

7   Stephen Wykstra, "A Skeptical Theist View," in Meister and Dew, *God and the Problem of Evil*, 116.

reasons do not exist. It would generally be an unwise and dangerous mistake for them to conclude that our actions are arbitrary and unloving. If this reasoning is true of the relationship between children and parents, how much more would it be true of the relationship between humans and a God whose wisdom infinitely exceeds our own? If we have a difficult time solving nonlinear differential equations, why think that we should be able to fathom all the workings of God's providence?

The solutions presented above are available to all theists and do provide explanations for the existence of evil. But frankly, I would find them deeply unsatisfying if they were our only answers to the problem of evil. While they are logically valid, they don't seem existentially sufficient in a world as fallen as ours. However, there are far greater resources available to Christians that are unavailable to theists in general. These responses not only speak to the philosophical problem of evil but address the personal dimension as well.

Here, it's helpful to recognize that the problem of evil is one that the biblical authors struggled with intensely. The question of how a just and good God can allow evil and suffering is one of the central issues in several books of the Bible, including Job, Ezekiel, Habakkuk, and Revelation. While certain segments of American evangelicalism tend to sugarcoat the Christian faith and suggest that following God will exempt us from suffering, the Bible paints a far more textured picture of serving God in the midst of pain, death, and sorrow. God did not inspire a quaint collection of inspirational jingles for us to sing on Sundays; he inspired the laments of men who were persecuted and oppressed and the cries of a people who saw their cities destroyed by war and famine. If the Bible is divinely inspired, then theodicy is not a hastily compiled response of nineteenth-century Christian apologists to the assaults of eighteenth-century skeptics, but is grounded in God's revelation to humanity. So how does the Bible reconcile the goodness of God and the reality of evil?

Evil and Eternity

One of the first considerations the Bible adds to a general theistic view of the problem of evil is its doctrine of eternity. According to the Bible, death is not the end of our lives. All of us will spend eternity in fellowship with God and with each other or separated from God forever. This claim affects the problem of evil in two ways.

First, it means that God can allow evil and suffering for the purposes of waking us up to our spiritual state and our need of forgiveness. When pressed, most people would theoretically admit that life is fragile and that the world is a dangerous place. If surveys are correct, the majority of Americans also believe that heaven and hell are real, and that our life on this earth has eternal consequences.[8] Yet, in the wake of the terrorist attacks of September 11, 2001, churches across the country were flooded with people who normally never attended. Why? Because people suddenly experienced the immediate, incalculable importance of what they claimed to have already believed. The events of 9/11 woke them up to a reality they intellectually affirmed but had not known existentially.

We tend to see temporal suffering and death as the worst things that can possibly happen to us. But if Christianity is true, we're wrong in that assumption. The worst suffering imaginable is an eternity in hell. This fact explains a great deal about the world we live in. When life is going well, when we have plenty of money, entertainment, romance, friendship, or whatever we value, the question of God's existence seems largely irrelevant. Everyone, whether a theist or an atheist, feels the tug of materialism, comfort, and complacency. But when a tragedy occurs, when we're forced to stare death and pain in the face, all our excuses and prevarications fall away. We have to confront the brokenness of our world and of our own lives and ask the questions that really mat-

---

8 The Pew Research Center's 2014 Religious Landscape Study reported that 89 percent of Americans believe in God, 72 percent believe in heaven, and 58 percent believe in hell. "U.S. Public Becoming Less Religious," Pew Research Center, November 3, 2015, http://assets.pewresearch .org/wp-content/uploads/sites/11/2015/11/201.11.03_RLS_II_full_report.pdf, pp. 3, 53, 55.

ter: Does God exist? Am I rightly related to him? Is there judgment to come, and am I prepared to meet it? If not, how can I find forgiveness? Reflecting on the existence of suffering, C. S. Lewis wrote, "God whispers to us in our pleasures, speaks in our conscience, but shouts in our pains: it is His megaphone to rouse a deaf world."[9]

But, second, putting evil in the perspective of eternity dramatically changes the way Christians should view it. While the existence of evil is very real, it is also temporary. The apostle Paul, who was repeatedly beaten, jailed, stoned, and whipped, wrote to the Christians in Corinth, "This light momentary affliction is preparing for us an eternal weight of glory beyond all comparison" (2 Cor. 4:17). The Bible claims that the worst suffering we experience on this earth will feel like nothing at all in the light of our eternal joy. Particularly relevant to the problem of evil is the idea that our present experience of suffering will actually be a part of the greater joy we experience in eternity.

Let me give a personal example. Just one week after my wife and I moved to North Carolina in 2010, I had a seizure and was diagnosed with a racquetball-sized brain tumor. A day later, on the eve of emergency surgery, I found myself saying goodbye to my parents, my pregnant wife, and my one-year-old son, who would never have remembered me. By God's grace, the operation was a success; the tumor turned out to be an incredibly rare variety that was benign. I'll never forget how the hospital room felt as I recovered; every inch of it was charged with God's glory, and every moment with my wife and son was pure joy. I appreciated all the gifts God had given me more than I ever would have without my illness. In retrospect, my stay in the hospital before and after the surgery was one of the sweetest times of fellowship with God in my life.

That, the Bible says, is how all our pain and suffering will appear through the lens of eternity. Not only will the pain be fleeting, but our joy will be even greater for having seen God deliver us out of it.

---

9   C. S. Lewis, *The Problem of Pain* (New York: Macmillan, 1962), 93.

Evil and Mercy

Second, when we ask, "Why is there evil in the world?" we have to also ask why God created the world in the first place. God created the universe for his glory; that is, for the display of his supreme, breathtaking love and perfect holiness.[10] But, according to the Bible, what is the greatest demonstration of God's love? The apostle Paul tells us: "God shows his love for us in that while we were still sinners, Christ died for us" (Rom. 5:8). God's goodness is most clearly seen in his mercy toward sinners, his love for his enemies, and his forgiveness of those who deserve his condemnation. Similarly, the holiness of God's moral perfection is most clearly displayed in his anger against sin and the exercise of his justice in punishing it.

These two considerations show us how evil not only can coexist with God's purposes for the world but also can actually further them. Evil can remain evil and yet can permit two great goods that would otherwise be impossible: the display of God's mercy to sinners and the display of God's judgment on sin.

Not only do God's mercy and justice reveal his glory; they are also sources of joy and comfort. If you've ever deeply regretted an offense you committed and have—against all hope—been forgiven by the one you've wronged, you know the happiness and freedom that forgiveness produces and the love it engenders toward the one who forgave you. The same will be eternally true of forgiven sinners in God's presence. While recognizing the love and care of God in meeting our daily needs, the biblical authors continually return with awe and amazement to God's forgiveness. The great nineteenth-century Baptist preacher Charles Spurgeon affirms: "The sweetest and the loudest note in our songs of praise should be of *redeeming love*. God's

---

10 A classic treatise on this thesis is that of eighteenth-century American theologian Jonathan Edwards, "A Dissertation concerning the End for Which God Created the World," Monergism, https://www.monergism.com/dissertation-concerning-end-which-god-created-world-jonathan -edwards.

redeeming acts towards his chosen are forever the favourite themes of their praise."[11]

Similarly, God's justice assures us that evil will not go unpunished. We can forgive those who wrong us and can pray for those who mistreat us because we know that God is the ultimate Judge, and justice is safe in his hands.

Evil and Incarnation

While these considerations offer what I believe is a good response to the problem of evil, they are sometimes still personally inadequate. When it is your son or daughter lying in a hospital bed, when it is your spouse who dies in a car accident, are these responses really sufficient? Alternatively, an atheist could still ask whether he has any reason to trust God. How can we be sure we are not pawns in some kind of cosmic game? How can we be expected not only to acknowledge that God exists but to actually worship this God who allows us to suffer in agony and despair? It is here that Christianity offers an answer other religions do not. Here Christianity points to the cross of Jesus Christ as the ultimate vindication of God's goodness in the face of evil and suffering.

God is an incarnational God, a God who enters into our pain. Even in the Old Testament, God suffered with his people. "In all their affliction he was afflicted," writes Isaiah (63:9). That solidarity was made inescapably clear when God entered human history in the person of Jesus Christ. In the miracle of the incarnation, God did not come to earth as a king or a philosopher but to live as a poor manual laborer, "a man of sorrows and acquainted with grief" (Isa. 53:3). Jesus's family thought he was insane (Mark 3:21). His closest friends often misunderstood him and, when he was arrested, abandoned him. In his final hours, he was stripped naked, publicly humiliated, mocked, beaten,

---

11 Charles H. Spurgeon, *Morning and Evening*, ed. Larry Piece and Marion Pierce (Green Forest, AR: New Leaf, 2010), entry for "December 1—Evening."

forced to carry the instrument of his execution through the streets, and nailed to a cross.

Yet the physical suffering that Jesus endured, although terrible and excruciating, was not the main component of his agony. The Bible tells us that Jesus was made a substitute for us, that he bore our sin. On the cross, Jesus experienced not just nails and thorns but God's furious wrath against evil. God caused the punishment that we deserve to fall on his own beloved son.

What does all this tell us? That we have a God who not only can sympathize with our suffering but has experienced it himself. Author Dorothy Sayers comments:

> For whatever reason God chose to make man as he is—limited and suffering and subject to sorrows and death—He had the honesty and the courage to take His own medicine. Whatever game He is playing with His creation, He has kept His own rules and played fair. He can exact nothing from man that He has not exacted from Himself.[12]

Theologian John Stott closes his reflection on the cross and evil in the following way:

> I could never myself believe in God, if it were not for the cross. . . . The only God I believe in is the one Nietzsche (the nineteenth-century German philosopher) ridiculed as "God on the cross." In the real world of pain, how could one worship a God who was immune to it? . . . He laid aside his immunity to pain. He entered our world of flesh and blood, tears and death. He suffered for us, dying in our place in order that we might be forgiven. Our sufferings become more manageable in the light of his. There is still a question mark

---

12 Dorothy L. Sayers, *The Greatest Drama Ever Staged* (London: Wyman, 1938), Project Gutenberg Canada, https://gutenberg.ca/ebooks/sayers-greatest/sayers-greatest-00-h.html.

against human suffering, but over it we boldly stamp another mark, the cross, which symbolizes divine suffering.[13]

When we see what Jesus suffered on the cross, it gives us a very concrete reason to trust God in the midst of a world filled with suffering.

For all these reasons, I do not believe that the problem of evil is an irrefutable objection to theism, much less to the Christian faith. While we can never look at a particular instance of suffering and know exactly why God has allowed it to occur, Christians can be confident that in all things God is good, and that in the end the Judge of all the earth will do right.

Evolution

A second major objection often raised to theism is the theory of evolution. The late neo-atheist Christopher Hitchens called Charles Darwin a greater emancipator than Abraham Lincoln for freeing humanity from the illusion of a Creator.[14] Richard Dawkins writes that "Darwin made it possible to be an intellectually fulfilled atheist,"[15] and the bulk of Dawkins's argument against God's existence in *The God Delusion* is based on evolution.[16] So is it true that evolution is incompatible with the existence of God? To answer that question, we need to define evolution carefully.[17]

Evolution can be summarized as "descent with modification." The narrative of modern evolution runs roughly as follows: At some point in

---

13 John Stott, *Why I Am a Christian* (Downers Grove, IL: InterVarsity Press, 2003), 62–63.

14 Christopher Hitchens, *God Is Not Great: How Religion Poisons Everything* (New York: Twelve, 2007), 66.

15 Richard Dawkins, *The Blind Watchmaker: Why the Evidence of Evolution Reveals a Universe without Design* (New York: Norton, 1996), 6.

16 Richard Dawkins, *The God Delusion* (Boston: Mariner, 2008), 188–89.

17 Two popular works that provide a broad overview of the evidence in support of evolution are Jerry A. Coyne, *Why Evolution Is True* (New York: Viking, 2009); and Richard Dawkins, *The Greatest Show on Earth: The Evidence for Evolution* (New York: Free Press, 2009). A higher-level and more mathematical treatment can be found in Martin A. Nowak, *Evolutionary Dynamics: Exploring the Equations of Life* (Cambridge, MA: Harvard University Press, 2006).

the earth's early history, a single self-replicating life-form emerged, if not from Darwin's "warm little pond" then from a sea of prebiotic chemicals.[18] Like organisms today, this original organism could reproduce to create new organisms with a nearly identical genetic code, except for small errors called "mutations," which occurred during replication. The vast majority of such mutations were either neutral or harmful. But, very infrequently, a mutation was beneficial and the new organism was able to produce more offspring than its neighbors. Eventually, the descendants of this new mutant organism came to dominate the population of its local environment. Occasionally, populations of organisms became reproductively isolated, often due to physical barriers like mountain ranges or oceans, but also due to genetic factors. These isolated populations then evolved independently, diverging until they became sufficiently distinct to be considered different species. Through these mechanisms, new species were generated, leading to the diversity we observe in the world today.

Described in this way, modern evolutionary theory rests on three foundational premises:[19] first, that species of life on earth have changed over the course of earth's history; second, that all species are descended from a single ancestral organism, an idea known as universal common descent; and third, that random mutation and natural selection are the primary drivers of modern biodiversity. Because a variety of views on evolution are accepted by conservative evangelical Christians, let alone by the Christian

18 Not all scientists agree on whether the term "evolution" should include the origin of the first life-form from nonliving matter, a process known as "abiogenesis." Writers like Richard Dawkins and Jerry Coyne favor a definition of "evolution" that deals only with the development of life *after* its origin. On the other hand, other scientists, like biologist and popular atheist blogger P. Z. Myers, argue that abiogenesis should be included in the concept of evolution. In what follows, I opt for the more conservative definition provided by Dawkins and Coyne, in which abiogenesis is not included under the umbrella of "evolution."

19 Coyne, *Why Evolution Is True*, 3–14. Coyne lists six components of "Darwinism": "evolution ["change over time"], gradualism, speciation, common ancestry, natural selection, and non-selective mechanisms of evolutionary change." However, Coyne later affirms that some of these components are "intimately connected" and that others—like gradualism—have been questioned while the theory is still left intact. Consequently, I've reduced the discussion to the three ideas that seem the most distinct and foundational.

church as a whole, I will do my best to represent all of them as fairly as I can without suggesting which I think is correct. Table 2 compares these views and highlights their major differences. So which of these various views conflicts with evolution? And does evolution conflict with God's existence?

Table 2. Major views of creation, design, and evolution

	Age of Earth	Change in Species?	Common Descent?	All Biodiversity by Natural Processes?
Young-earth creationism	6,000–50,000 years	Yes	Limited	No
Old-earth creationism	4.5 billion years	Yes	Limited	No
Intelligent design	N/A	Yes	N/A	No
Theistic evolution	4.5 billion years	Yes	Universal	Yes
Atheistic evolution	4.5 billion years	Yes	Universal	Yes

Surprisingly, the first premise, that species of life on earth have changed over earth's history, is accepted even by young-earth creationists. No one denies that the fossil record shows that species on earth have changed over earth's history. After all, there are no longer dinosaurs roaming the plains of the Dakotas. Moreover, many young-earth creationist organizations affirm not only that species have gone extinct but also that others have diverged from their original forms as they have adapted to environmental pressures.[20] While young-earth creationists depart drastically from

20 For example, in the 1961 book *The Genesis Flood*, which arguably launched modern "scientific creationism," authors John Whitcomb and Henry Morris argue that the "kinds" of animals enumerated in Genesis are different from the modern taxonomic category of "species" and that there are "amazing potentialities for diversification which the Creator has placed within the Genesis

other creationists and from evolutionists regarding the extent, timing, and timescale of the change of earth's species, they do not deny that it happened. So everyone accepts this first premise of evolutionary theory to some degree.[21]

The second premise is more controversial, but there is still more agreement than we might expect. Creationists, both those who hold to a young-earth view and those who hold to an old-earth view, accept *limited* common descent, just not *universal* common descent. In other words, they would affirm that many distinct modern species shared the same common ancestor but would place limits on the amount of change that can occur within a given population of organisms.[22] Additionally, at least some of those in the intelligent design community are willing to accept universal common descent wholesale, so that they would be in full agreement here with what modern evolutionary theory proposes.

The real source of conflict is the third premise, the idea that random mutation and natural selection are the primary drivers of all modern biodiversity.[23] Has science demonstrated that this third pillar of evo-

---

kinds" (66). Therefore, while the "total number of so-called species of mammals, birds, reptiles, and amphibians listed by [renowned biologist Ernst] Mayr is 17,600 . . . undoubtedly the number of original 'kinds' was less than this" (69). See John C. Whitcomb, and Henry M. Morris, *The Genesis Flood: The Biblical Record and Its Scientific Implications* (Phillipsburg, NJ: P&R, 1961).

21 It's possible to object that limiting earth's history to a few thousand years is tantamount to denying evolution. However, this objection seems incorrect. Scientists in the nineteenth century had no clear idea of the age of the earth, but many still accepted evolution. While a greatly compressed timescale for earth's history would render naturalistic evolution astronomically unlikely, it would not transmute the theory into some form of creationism. To put it another way, if you believed that all modern species evolved from a common ancestor through a process of unguided random mutation and natural selection *over the course of ten thousand years*, creationists would still not recognize your belief as a species of creationism.

22 For instance, in *The Genesis Flood*, the authors reproduce a diagram (fig. 4) that shows several distinct modern species of the genus Equus (onager, kiang, horse, zebra) sharing common ancestors of the horse kind. See Whitcomb and Morris, *The Genesis Flood*, 67. Of course, this kind of common descent is extremely different from the molecule-to-man evolution accepted by evolutionary biologists. Yet it explains why you'll occasionally find diagrams in young-earth creationist literature that look similar to phylogenic trees constructed by evolutionary biologists.

23 The importance of natural selection is such that it is sometimes discussed as if it were the only mechanism of evolution. However, that is incorrect. Genetic drift and other effects play important, nonadaptive roles in evolution. See Coyne, *Why Evolution Is True*, 122–24.

lutionary theory is true? I think the answer is no, for two reasons: one philosophical and the other scientific.

First, philosophically, the crux of the debate is what we mean by the word "random" when we talk about "random mutations." Scientifically, this word has a particular meaning. A random mutation is one that is not an adaptive response to the environment. In contrast, a nonrandom mutation is an adaptive response to the environment. In *Why Evolution Is True*, atheist evolutionary biologist Jerry Coyne explains: "The term 'random' here has a specific meaning that is often misunderstood, even by biologists. What this means is that *mutations occur regardless of whether they would be useful to the individual*."[24]

This kind of "randomness" says nothing at all about God's existence or his interaction with the world. It merely says that mutations appear to occur at a rate and in locations that are not necessarily beneficial, given the organism's environment. Unfortunately, people sometimes confuse this limited sense of randomness, meaning "nonadaptive," with a very different sense of randomness, meaning "absolutely uncaused, undirected, and unguided." It is this second kind of randomness that is problematic for theism, but only because it excludes God by definition. Even God cannot cause, direct, and guide an absolutely uncaused, undirected, unguided process. However, this second kind of randomness is not a scientific description of an event; it is a philosophical interpretation of the event. Summarizing this misunderstanding, Christian philosopher Alvin Plantinga writes:

> [It is claimed] that current scientific evolutionary theory is incompatible with Christian belief. This claim . . . is false. The scientific theory of evolution as such is not incompatible with Christian belief; what is incompatible with it is the idea that evolution, natural selection,

24 Coyne, *Why Evolution Is True*, 118.

is *unguided*. But that idea isn't part of evolutionary theory as such; it's instead a metaphysical or theological addition.[25]

This distinction between event and interpretation is well illustrated by how Christians view God's control over our own physical characteristics. Christians affirm with the Bible that God "knit [us] together in [our] mother's womb" (Ps. 139:13) and that everything, from our gender to our eye color, is sovereignly ordered by God. Yet our very existence depends on innumerable "random" events, from our parents' meeting to the fertilization of one particular egg by one particular sperm. Nonetheless, no Christian would conclude that the seeming randomness of these events rules out God's guidance, nor would a believer see a conflict between God's existence and embryology. Similarly, when it comes to our interpretation of "randomness" in random mutations, what we have is not a conflict between science and God but a conflict between naturalism and theism, two philosophical positions.

Second, even apart from philosophical considerations, this third pillar of evolutionary theory is the most difficult to prove experimentally. Creationists are willing to concede quite a large degree of biological change within populations, including all the types of changes we can observe today in phenomena like the emergence of antibiotic resistance in bacteria. Hence, proponents of evolution would have to show evidence that large-scale evolutionary changes can be driven by random mutation and natural selection. Unfortunately, because macroevolution occurs on geologic timescales of millions of years, this type of evidence is extremely sparse.

Here, we're not asking for evidence of common descent between different families of organisms; we're asking for evidence that random mutation and natural selection are sufficient to produce these different families. Both sides of the debate seem to agree that evidentiary support

25 Alvin Plantinga, *Where the Conflict Really Lies: Science, Religion, and Naturalism* (Oxford: Oxford University Press, 2011), 62–63.

for this third pillar is based upon a substantial extrapolation from the current observable evidence. Coyne writes that "given the gradual pace of evolution, it's unreasonable to expect to see selection transforming one 'type' of plant or animal into another—so-called *macroevolution*— within a human lifetime. Though macroevolution is occurring today, we simply won't be around long enough to see it."[26] While we can make a case that it's *reasonable* to extrapolate from microevolution ("small" changes) to macroevolution ("large" changes), it's difficult to argue that we have actually observed it.

To show how hard it is to distinguish "guided" evolution from "unguided" evolution on the basis of the evidence we have, I've found the following thought experiment to be helpful. Because the origin of life from nonlife is still such a mystery, some famous atheist biologists such as Nobel laureate Francis Crick[27] and even Richard Dawkins[28] have suggested that the first life-form might have been brought to earth by extraterrestrials. Let's assume for the sake of argument that this suggestion is correct and, what's more, that the aliens who brought life to our planet wanted to conduct an extended experiment on evolutionary dynamics. To do so, they returned to our planet every few millennia, sequestered certain species in pens, and selectively bred them over a few thousand generations until they diverged sufficiently from their ancestors to constitute a new species. Perhaps they even inserted new genes here and there through hyper-futuristic alien genetic engineering to further their experiments.

Obviously, this scenario is completely fanciful; I do not think that alien genetic engineers created life on earth. But I'd like us to consider

---

26 Coyne, *Why Evolution Is True*, 133.

27 Francis H. C. Crick and Leslie E. Orgel, "Directed Panspermia," *Icarus* 19, no. 3 (1973): 341–46.

28 From his interview with Ben Stein in the 2008 documentary *Expelled: No Intelligence Allowed*. To be clear, Dawkins is not saying that life was created by extraterrestrials. He explicitly denies that anyone knows how life began on earth, so his suggestion that life may have originated with extraterrestrials ought to be understood as a hypothetical speculation. However, he does refer to it as an "intriguing possibility." The interview is available at https://www.youtube.com/.

this question: How could we distinguish the intentional, directed creation of biodiversity through alien breeding from the unintentional, undirected generation of biodiversity though natural selection? Would there be any way to tell these two scenarios apart based on evidence from the fossil record or genetics? The answer seems to be no. All the genetic and molecular evidence would look exactly like it does now. But if that's the case, then it's very difficult to distinguish "guided" from "unguided" evolution on evidential grounds.

I believe that these two objections alone are sufficient to counter the claim that the current scientific evidence used to argue in favor of biological evolution is incompatible with belief in God. Philosophically, "random mutations" do not imply that God could not have guided evolutionary mechanisms, any more than embryology implies that God is not sovereign over our physical characteristics. Scientifically, it is very difficult to distinguish "guided" evolution from "unguided" evolution based on the evidence we have. For both philosophical and scientific reasons, it is possible to reject the claim that evolution demonstrates that God does not exist or that he is not the Creator of life on earth, whether through an evolutionary mechanism or not.[29]

The Hiddenness of God

Finally, the hiddenness of God is often proposed as evidence that God does not exist.[30] Atheists who advance this argument can affirm that there may be some evidence that God exists, such as the Big Bang, the fine-tuning of the universe, and the existence of objective moral facts. However, this limited evidence is far less than what we ought to expect. If the Christian God exists and loves us, and if our eternal destiny

---

29 For a critique of theistic evolution, see *Theistic Evolution: A Scientific, Theological, and Philosophical Critique*, ed. J. P. Moreland et al. (Wheaton, IL: Crossway, 2017). For a response, see Deborah Haarsma's review "A Flawed Mirror: A Response to the Book 'Theistic Evolution'" at https://biologos.org/.

30 See, for example, John L. Schellenberg, "Divine Hiddenness Justifies Atheism," in *Evil and the Hiddenness of God*, ed. Michael Rea (Stamford, CT: Cengage Learning, 2015), 61–70.

hangs in the balance, why isn't the evidence for his existence absolutely undeniable? Surely, a God who could create the entire universe could routinely perform unmistakable miracles, like regularly sending angels to materialize in the center of Times Square in the presence of thousands of witnesses. The absence of such extraordinary evidence is, then, an indication that this kind of God does not exist.

To answer this objection, we need to take a deeper look at the biblical doctrine of sin. According to the Bible, sin is not merely the breaking of God's rules; it stems from our inherent posture of rebellion toward God. To put it another way, if faith is essentially trust in God, then unbelief is essentially mistrust of God. We don't merely doubt his existence; we doubt his goodness. We distrust his claim that he knows what is best for us and that surrendering to his rule over our lives will bring us joy and freedom. The claim here is not that intellectual objections don't exist or that they are unimportant, but that they are not the primary obstacle between us and God. As surprising as it might seem, lack of evidence is not the ultimate reason for our unbelief.

If that claim sounds difficult to accept, a thought experiment might help. Imagine you have put this book down and are about to head to bed when Jesus suddenly appears in the middle of your living room. He shows you the nail prints in his hands and performs miracles, multiplying your avocado toast and fish sticks and turning your tap water into wine. In other words, imagine, for the sake of argument, that he gives you whatever evidence you need to completely convince you intellectually that he is God, that he died on the cross for your sins, and that he rose from the dead. The question I'd like you to consider is not whether you would believe that God exists or that Christianity is true, because we're granting for the sake of argument that these issues have been settled for you. The question is this: How do you feel about him?

At that moment, what if Jesus said to you: "Now that you know that I am God, I am calling you to become my disciple. That means you must take up your cross daily, dying to your own desires and demands, and seeking my will in all your decisions. I must be more important to you than any human relationship and even more important to you than your own life. You must put to death all the sins that you love and that seem so natural to you, even if it feels as difficult as plucking out your right eye or cutting off your right hand. Your money, your friendships, your sex life, your career goals, your entertainment, your entire ethical framework, your view of the Bible—everything must be reevaluated in light of who I am. I want you to devote your whole life to my mission, serving others, loving them, sacrificing for them, warning them about God's coming judgment, and pointing them to the forgiveness of sins and salvation that only I offer. Tell all your friends and family the bad news that they are sinners and the unimaginably good news that I died to rescue them from hell. Devote yourself to prayer, to worship, to friendship with other Christians, to membership in the local church. And do all of these things not grudgingly, but joyfully."

Be honest: how would you feel about Jesus now? I'll be honest. Part of me would feel claustrophobic. Even as a Christian, part of me wants to call the shots in my own life and wants to be my own ultimate authority. God's demand for our complete allegiance makes us feel uncomfortable. Why? Because deep down inside, we want to be our own gods. If that's the case, isn't it clear that evidence is not the ultimate issue? Even if we had all the evidence we needed to convince us intellectually that God exists and that Christianity is true, there would still be a volitional, emotional barrier between us and God.

That is why, at least from a Christian perspective, the objection from divine hiddenness is weak. I agree that God could have provided even more evidence than he did, so much evidence that atheism or skepticism of any kind would cease to exist. But why think that a world of theists who loathed God would be significantly more desirable to God than our current world?

God's purpose is to change hearts, not merely to change minds. Once we grant that a person can be completely intellectually convinced that

God exists and still fail to love God, we have to reevaluate whether God would necessarily provide more evidence than he has. If none of us can honestly say that there is nothing in the Bible that disturbs us, nothing about God's total claim over our lives that threatens us, and nothing about God's moral commands that offends us, then why think that lack of evidence is our main problem or that God ought to provide more?

However, even if the problem of divine hiddenness can be solved, perhaps an even more pressing question remains: If God's purpose in the world is creating people with new hearts who love him supremely and love their neighbors as themselves, has he made a way for our hearts to be changed? If our greatest problem is not a lack of evidence but a heart that is opposed to God, what can we do? What is God's solution to our deepest need? Those questions will be answered in the next three chapters.

7

The Gospel (Part 1)

The Uniqueness of Christianity

In Christ God was reconciling the world to himself,
not counting their trespasses against them.

2 CORINTHIANS 5:19

IN THE PREVIOUS FIVE CHAPTERS, I've run through several arguments for the truth of Christianity, starting with the identity of Jesus,
moving on to his resurrection, and closing with arguments for the
existence of God. I've also responded to some of the most common
objections to theism. Two conclusions are warranted.

First, I think it's difficult to claim that belief in Christianity is inherently irrational. Even if you are not persuaded that Christianity is true,
the arguments I've presented demonstrate that it's possible to believe in
Christianity on the basis of reason and evidence. The fact that someone
is a Christian does not prove that he or she has jettisoned reason and
is clinging to wishful thinking, prejudice, and dogmatism.

Second, it seems obvious that most Christians do not become Christians solely on the basis of the kinds of arguments I've provided. For

example, when I became a Christian in graduate school, I had only a vague understanding of arguments for God's existence or for the truth of Christianity. As a non-Christian, I had taken a course at Princeton on the historical origins of Christianity (popularly known as "The Faith Buster"), which presented the New Testament from an entirely secular, critical perspective, drawing heavily on the work of scholars like Bart Ehrman, Elaine Pagels, and the Jesus Seminar. Jesus was never portrayed as anything more than a wandering rabbi whose teachings had been edited and altered over decades before they were codified in the New Testament. I absorbed just enough history to know that Jesus was a real person and just enough theology to know that Christians believed that his death was fairly important. Yet, soon after taking that class, I became a Christian. I did not come to faith in Jesus as the consequence of a careful intellectual argument, nor do the majority of Christians. So what are we to conclude? Even if Christianity is not inherently irrational, can't it still be legitimately argued that most Christians' beliefs are unjustified?

Not necessarily. For one thing, claims that Christian conversion is inherently irrational must, to get off the ground, often assume that Christianity is false. After all, if Christianity is actually true, then the Bible's claims about the Holy Spirit's power to open our hearts and show us the truth of Christianity are presumably also correct.[1] If the Christian God really does exist, then he can make himself known to people directly through dreams, answered prayer, healings, miracles, and other forms of "religious experience." Only if we assume that Christianity is false can we safely assume that peoples' reports of having a religious experience that led them to Christ are also false.

C. S. Lewis's popular children's story *The Lion, the Witch and the Wardrobe* provides a helpful illustration of this point. At the beginning of the book, Lucy accidentally discovers a passage to the enchanted land

---

1   See an extended discussion in Alvin Plantinga, *Warranted Christian Belief* (New York: Oxford University Press, 2000). Part 3 is particularly relevant.

of Narnia through a wardrobe door. She returns with tales of a faun and a witch and a hundred-year winter, which her sister and brothers dismiss as false despite her insistence. While we can disagree over whether they were justified in dismissing her story, it seems clear that Lucy herself is justified in believing the evidence of her own senses, gathered on two different occasions that spanned several hours. Likewise, Lucy's siblings can't be certain that she is being irrational unless they are also certain that Narnia is only a figment of her imagination.

In the same way, arguing that we have no reason to accept the truth of Christianity on the basis of another person's religious experience is very different from arguing that they themselves have no reason to accept the truth of Christianity on the basis of their own religious experience.[2] If Christianity turns out to be true, and if the Holy Spirit really does enable us to experience it as true, then it is rational to believe that experience.

However, I would like to take a different route entirely. In the following chapters, I will argue that the gospel—that is, the central message of Christianity—is itself the best argument for the truth of Christianity. The Greek word for "gospel" is *euangelion*, which literally means "good news." This good news is summarized by the apostle Paul in his first letter to the Corinthians: "I delivered to you as of first importance what I also received: that Christ died for our sins in accordance with the Scriptures, that he was buried, that he was raised on the third day in accordance with the Scriptures" (15:3–4). I am claiming that this gospel, the good news that Jesus died for our sins and was raised to life for our justification, is evidence that Christianity is true.

---

2   We could argue that religious experiences are an unreliable method for determining truth, since Christians, Jews, Muslims, Hindus, and Buddhists all report mutually contradictory religious experiences. However, this approach is more difficult than it seems, because no one has access to anyone else's religious experience. Without experiencing another person's religious experience, we can't know whether it was similar enough to ours to give us reason to question its evidentiary value. What we can do in these cases is turn to objective evidence of the kind I'm presenting in this book to determine which religious experiences are likely to be veridical.

I suspect that Christians may be even more surprised by this claim than non-Christians. Most Christians see evidence for the truth of Christianity as a precursor to the gospel; we must first remove intellectual obstacles to the Christian faith and only afterward present the gospel. So how could the gospel itself give us a reason to believe that Christianity is true apart from any other evidence? How could the assertion that Jesus died for our sins be a reason to think that Christianity is true?

My claim is that the gospel presents us with two truths all of us must face as human beings: that we are all moral failures and that we all need a Savior. Of all the major world religions, only Christianity insists that we are radically morally corrupt people who are consequently alienated from a perfectly good God. And only Christianity insists that what we primarily need is not moral improvement but rescue. If these claims about the human condition turn out to be true, then they are compelling evidence for the truth of Christianity, which is unique in its assessment of the human condition.

Consider an analogy: imagine I'm playing pickup basketball at a park when I suddenly collapse. A crowd gathers, but they don't agree on what happened. Some people say I just tripped and should get up and "walk it off." Others suggest I twisted an ankle and may need a brace to finish the game. One person runs to get ice, another to get an ACE bandage, a third to get a bottle of Advil from the pharmacy across the street. All of them offer to help me up to my feet. While I'm lying on the ground a woman rushes up to me with a look of extreme concern. She says: "I'm a doctor. I saw this man fall and I know exactly what happened. We need to get him to a hospital immediately." She crouches down beside me and says urgently: "You can't feel your legs and you can't move. I'm going to call an ambulance; your life is in danger." I immediately tell the crowd, "Do exactly what she says."

The people around me are incredulous. They think she is wildly overreacting. They begin to question her credentials. They start to speculate loudly about her real, ulterior motives. Yet, in spite of their skepticism, I have reason to believe her. Why? Because I can't feel my legs and I can't move. Somehow she knew these two truths, even though no one else did. No matter how implausible her claims might seem to bystanders, I have crucial information they don't have. I have firsthand, immediate, and undeniable awareness of my own condition. Based on that knowledge, my trust in her is justified.

Note that my reaction here should not be attributed to wishful thinking. It would probably be far more comforting for me to believe that my injury is not serious than to admit that I need immediate hospitalization. My trust in the woman's competence has nothing to do with whether I hope she is correct or incorrect; instead, it is warranted by her unique insight.

This story explains how most people come to know that Christianity is true. People put their faith in Christ when they become personally aware of their own moral condition and their need for a Savior. The implicit reasoning behind their decision is easy to follow: Christianity is either true or false. If it is true, then its truth explains its unique ability to diagnose their spiritual condition. But if it is false, then it is an incredible coincidence that Christianity uniquely explains two deep, existential realities entirely by accident.

If we do have an immediate, internal awareness that we are radical moral failures and that we are in need of a rescuer, and if Christianity is the only religion that affirms these truths, then we have an excellent reason to believe in Christianity. But are these two claims true? And is Christianity really the only religion that teaches these truths?

Before answering those questions, let me address the discomfort that any discussion of a particular religion's uniqueness often engenders. Many people like to believe that all religions teach essentially the same thing: love, kindness, generosity, and compassion. Certainly, we can affirm that all major religions teach that such qualities are good and desirable. Moreover, there are many other doctrines that religions hold in common. Monotheistic religions like Judaism, Islam, and Christianity share a belief in a single Creator God. Buddhism and Hinduism share a belief in karma and reincarnation. Hinduism, Norse religions, and Greco-Roman religions share a belief in a multiplicity of gods.

However, some doctrines are distinctives of particular religions. This uniqueness does not necessarily imply superiority or inferiority. For example, there is nothing pejorative in asserting that Islam is unique in claiming that the Qur'an is God's final revelation to humanity or that Muhammad was God's ultimate prophet. Likewise, there is nothing deprecatory in saying that Buddhism is unique in seeing the Eightfold Path as the way to achieve enlightenment. To make these claims is not to pass judgment on the relative merits of Islam or Buddhism, but to register an objective fact about the content of Islamic and Buddhist teaching.

In the same way, my assertion that Christianity is unique in declaring that human beings are inherently sinful and need a Savior is an empirical claim. We can ask whether Christianity does indeed espouse these doctrines and whether it is unique in doing so before evaluating whether these doctrines are true or false.

A second issue to address is how we define Christianity and compare it with other religions. In both cases, I will refer to what has been taught historically by the major traditions within each faith. I'll also look only at the major world religions—namely, Christianity, Islam, Judaism, Hinduism, and Buddhism—since these five religions account for approximately 92 percent of all religiously affiliated individuals in the world.[3] It is certainly true that this kind of survey cannot account for smaller religions, for every possible variation within a religion, or for the beliefs of individuals. However, it will provide a broad overview of how the major world religions treat the topics of sin and salvation. It is within this context that I am claiming that Christianity is unique.[4]

---

3   "The Global Religious Landscape," Pew Research Center, December 18, 2012, https://assets.pew research.org/wp-content/uploads/sites/11/2014/01/global-religion-full.pdf, p. 9.

4   It's possible to object that Christianity is not completely unique since there could be local religions or smaller traditions within the world religions that—to some extent—affirm claims about our need for a savior. For example, Pure Land Buddhists within Mahayana Buddhism or the Tengalais

Christianity on Sin and Salvation

There are three main branches of Christianity: Catholicism, Orthodoxy, and Protestantism. Within each of these branches there is diversity of thought and practice so that it can sometimes be difficult to say what Christianity teaches about a particular issue. Fortunately, with regard to our two areas of interest, there is substantial agreement across all branches of the Christian church and throughout history. All Christians, whether Catholic, Orthodox, or Protestant, affirm that human beings are radically sinful. For example, the Catechism of the Catholic Church affirms that sin is "humanity's rejection of God and opposition to him,"[5] that we all have an "inclination toward evil and death," and that we are "in a fallen state."[6] Athanasius, known as the "Father of Orthodoxy," states:

> God has made man, and willed that he should abide in incorruption; but men, having despised and rejected the contemplation of God, and devised and contrived evil for themselves . . . received the condemnation of death . . . and from thenceforth . . . were being corrupted according to their devices; and death had the mastery over them as king.[7]

Or, as the Heidelberg Catechism succinctly puts it, "I am inclined by nature to hate God and my neighbor."[8]

---

within Vaishnava Hinduism are sometimes named as groups with a doctrine of salvation. It's not clear to me that these similarities are strong enough to undermine Christianity's uniqueness, but even if they were, we could modify our argument slightly to make it more robust to this kind of objection. Instead of concluding that the doctrines of sin and salvation are evidence that *Christianity* is true, we could alter our conclusion to say that *either* Christianity is true *or* one of these smaller religious traditions is true. We would then turn to the other arguments presented in this book to determine which of these alternatives is the correct one.

5 *Catechism of the Catholic Church*, 2nd ed. (Vatican: Libreria Editrice Vaticana, 2009), 97.

6 *Catechism of the Catholic Church*, 102.

7 Athanasius of Alexandria, *On the Incarnation of the Word*, trans. Archibald Robertson, chap. 4, New Advent, https://www.newadvent.org/.

8 Heidelberg Catechism, Q. 5, available at https://students.wts.edu/.

Likewise, all three major branches of Christianity affirm that we need not mere moral improvement but a rescuer who can do for us what we are unable to do for ourselves. In the Catholic Catechism, we read that "it is God who, in Jesus his eternal Son made man, 'will save his people from their sins'"[9] and that Jesus became a man *"in order to save us by reconciling us with God."*[10] Athanasius declares, "Seeing the race of rational creatures in the way to perish, and death reigning over them by corruption [Jesus] gave [his body] over to death in the stead of all";[11] and Jesus sacrificed himself because "no otherwise could the corruption of men be undone save by death as a necessary condition."[12] The London Baptist Confession states that Jesus perfectly obeyed God's law and then "underwent the punishment due to us, which we should have borne and suffered, being made sin and a curse for us," so that "by his perfect obedience and sacrifice of himself . . . [he] hath fully satisfied the justice of God, procured reconciliation, and purchased an everlasting inheritance in the kingdom of heaven."[13]

In his book *God Is Not One*, Stephen Prothero, the chair of the Department of Religion at Boston University, summarizes Christianity in this way:

> The [Christian] narrative arc typically runs from sin to salvation. . . . Sin refers [not just to particular transgressions but] more generally to the human propensity toward wrongdoing and evil. . . . Sinners cannot be admitted to heaven or granted eternal life, and there is nothing they can do on their own to merit salvation from sin. But happily Christianity is a "rescue religion," and this rescue was made possible as Jesus was dying on the cross. On that day, which Christians

9   *Catechism of the Catholic Church*, 108.
10 *Catechism of the Catholic Church*, 115.
11 Athanasius, *On the Incarnation* 8.
12 Athanasius, *On the Incarnation* 9.
13 The 1689 Baptist Confession of Faith, chap. 8, ARBCA, https://www.arbca.com/1689-chapter8.

celebrate as Good Friday, a sinless Jesus took our sins onto Himself.
. . . The "good news," therefore, is that anyone who hears this story,
confesses her sins, and turns to Jesus for forgiveness can be saved. Or,
as the Bible puts it, "the wages of sin is death; but the gift of God is
eternal life in Christ Jesus our Lord" (Romans 6:23).[14]

Christianity affirms both that human beings are radically sinful and
that we need a rescuer. But what about other religions?

Buddhism on Sin and Salvation

According to Buddhism, the central problem of human existence is
not sin but suffering. We see that emphasis in the core teachings of the
Buddha, which are known as the Four Noble Truths: "1) To live is to
suffer. 2) Suffering is caused by attachment. 3) To eliminate suffering
one must eliminate attachment. 4) One can eliminate attachment by
following the noble Eight-fold Path."[15] While Buddhists recognize a
moral dimension to life and even share many moral injunctions with
other religions, they do not see human beings as radically sinful and
alienated from God; indeed, some strands of Buddhism, such as Zen
Buddhism, are nontheistic.

The issue of our need for rescue is a bit more complicated. According to religious studies professor Huston Smith at the University of
California, Berkeley, the original teachings of the Buddha were entirely
focused on self-help. He explains:

[Buddha taught that] the way to the overcoming of self-seeking is
through the Eightfold Path [which is] a course of treatment. But it
is not an external treatment . . . from without. It is not treatment

---

14 Stephen Prothero, *God Is Not One: The Eight Rival Religions That Run the World* (New York: HarperOne, 2011), 71–72.
15 Winfried Corduan, *Neighboring Faiths: A Christian Introduction to World Religions*, 2nd ed. (Downers Grove, IL: IVP Academic, 2012), 320.

by pills, or rituals, or grace. Instead, it is treatment by training . . . [so that we can become] a different human being, one who has been cured of crippling disabilities.[16]

This same focus on achieving enlightenment through self-effort is preserved in the Theravada school of Buddhism.

In contrast, some traditions within the Mahayana school of Buddhism place great emphasis on supernatural grace obtained from the Buddha himself and other Buddhas who have already attained enlightenment. While there is a concept of a "savior" within these schools of Buddhist thought, the key question is, A savior from what? Because the fundamental problem within Buddhism is not sin but suffering, the Buddhist approaches a Buddha not for forgiveness and reconciliation with God but for help in achieving *nirvana*, a state of eternal bliss and liberation from desire. Moreover, the aid of a Buddha is helpful but not required to achieve nirvana. With sufficient commitment, a Buddhist could achieve nirvana on his own, without the need of a savior.

Hinduism on Sin and Salvation

In Hinduism, the fundamental problem that must be overcome is the cycle of reincarnation, or *samsara*. Bad actions in our present lives will result in bad *karma*, leading to suffering in one's next reincarnation, while good actions will lead to a better reincarnation. Bad actions include not only moral violations but any violation of our duty, or *dharma*.[17] The final goal of Hinduism is *moksha*, freedom from the cycle

16 Huston Smith, *The World's Religions: Our Great Wisdom Traditions*, 2nd ed. (New York: HarperSanFrancisco, 1991), 104.

17 Apparently, it is difficult to translate the word *dharma* into English, because it is a complex concept. Dayanand Bharati writes: "For an average person *dharma* is a comprehensive word which includes spiritual, moral, social and even secular values. . . . The difference between sin and *adharma*, though they look like one and the same, is basic and foundational. Sin is transgression of some spiritual and moral law and can be universal, whereas *adharma* (though it includes sin in some contexts), also relates to social regulations which are not universal." See Bharati, *Understanding Hinduism* (New Delhi: Munshiram Manoharlal, 2005), 22–23.

of reincarnation, although different schools of Hinduism disagree on what happens to us after we achieve moksha.

Moksha can be achieved through three main paths: the way of knowledge, the way of works, and the way of devotion. The way of knowledge is grounded in the Vedantic philosophical idea that while our bodies, thoughts, and all physical objects are illusions (*maya*), each individual soul (*atman*) is real because it is identical to the "world soul" (*Brahman*). A follower on the way of knowledge seeks to experience the reality of his own divinity through withdrawal from the world and meditation. The way of works is characterized by fulfilling one's duty to others and to society without regard to the fruit of one's labors. Huston Smith compares this commitment to service to a "radical reducing diet" that is "designed to starve the finite ego" so that the practitioner can achieve transcendence.[18] Finally, the way of devotion enlists the help of one of Hinduism's many gods to attain moksha. Rather than pursuing moksha through meditation or works, the devotee seeks it as a gift from the god to whom he is committed.

As with Buddhism, Hinduism diverges from Christianity in its conception of the human condition. While Hinduism acknowledges the existence of moral failings, it does not see human nature as universally and radically corrupted. Indeed, the doctrines of reincarnation and *karma* guarantee that human beings are not all equal in their spiritual maturity, because of their behavior in past lives. For example, Hindu monk Swami Bhaskarananda writes: "Reincarnation . . . gives a person the opportunity to gradually evolve spiritually through the various valuable experiences he acquires in his different incarnations. Eventually he reaches the acme of his spiritual progress through God-realization."[19]

With respect to rescue, there are apparent similarities between the devotional path (*bhakti yoga*) and Christian reliance on Jesus Christ as

18 Smith, *The World's Religions*, 41.
19 Swami Bhaskarananda, *The Essentials of Hinduism: A Comprehensive Overview of the World's Oldest Religion*, 2nd ed. (Seattle: Viveka, 2002), 94–95.

Savior. The *bhakta* seeks grace from his god as a gift, just as a Christian seeks salvation from God as a gift. However, the nature of the gift being sought is of central importance. The Hindu is not necessarily seeking forgiveness for his rebellion, mercy in the face of God's judgment, or reconciliation with God. Even more importantly, the path of devotion is only one of the paths to moksha. Because liberation from samsara can be achieved through the way of knowledge or the way of works, it would be incorrect to claim that Hinduism teaches that we require rescue.

Islam on Sin and Salvation

As an Abrahamic religion, Islam is much closer to Christianity than either Hinduism or Buddhism in its conception of God and the universe. Islam affirms that there is only one God, who is the Creator and Sustainer of the universe, and who is good, just, and holy. Islam also recognizes that sin is a moral offense that provokes God's wrath and makes us liable to his judgment.

However, there are also major differences between the Christian and the Islamic understandings of sin. To begin with, Muslims deny that our natures are corrupted by sin. Instead, we are born in a state of natural purity (*fitra*) and learn to sin through the influences of our environment, family, and society. John Esposito, professor of religion at Georgetown University, writes that according to Islam, "sin is not a state of being; it is the result of an act of disobedience, failure to do or not to do what God commands or prohibits. Human beings are not sinful by nature."[20] Muslim author Suzanne Haneef, a convert from Christianity, concurs, writing that "every human being comes into the world innocent and sinless" and that we inscribe our actions "upon the unblemished *tabula rasa* [blank slate] of [our] nature."[21] Prothero writes,

---

20 John L. Esposito, *Islam: The Straight Path*, 3rd ed. (New York: Oxford University Press, 1998), 27.

21 Suzanne Haneef, *What Everyone Should Know about Islam and Muslims*, 11th ed. (Chicago: Kazi, 1993), 182.

"[Muslims believe that every] human being is born with an inclination toward both God and the good."[22]

From this different view of sin follows a very different view of the nature of salvation. Because sin is a matter of disobedience to God's will, the solution is simple: obedience. Esposito observes: "Repentance is simply remembering or returning to God's path, the straight path of Islam. There is little or no emphasis on feelings of shame and disgrace or guilt."[23] At the last judgment, all human beings will be "responsible for their own actions and will be judged according to the record found in the Book of Deeds. . . . There is no redemption, atonement, or intercession through an intermediary."[24] Haneef again agrees, writing that because human beings can approach God directly, "there is no need for a Savior, and in any case God Most High alone can save."[25] Prothero adds: "Sin is not the problem Islam addresses. Neither is there any need for salvation from sin."[26] While Islam has an understanding of God's mercy and forgiveness, there is very little sense that God rescues.

Judaism on Sin and Salvation

Comparing the beliefs of Judaism with Christianity is complicated by several factors. Most significant is the fact that Judaism is both a religion and an ethnicity, so that a person who identifies as ethnically Jewish may nonetheless hold few Jewish religious beliefs. For example, in 2013, a Pew research survey found that 68 percent of Jews affirmed that being Jewish is compatible with not believing in God.[27] A second complicating factor is the existence of Messianic Jews, who identify as Jews but believe that Jesus is the Messiah. From a Christian perspective,

---

22 Prothero, *God Is Not One*, 31.

23 Esposito, *Islam*, 28.

24 Esposito, *Islam*, 30.

25 Haneef, *What Everyone Should Know*, 183.

26 Prothero, *God Is Not One*, 31–32.

27 "A Portrait of Jewish Americans," Pew Research Center, October 1, 2013, http://www.pew forum.org/.

this stance is not problematic since all of Jesus's earliest followers (and Jesus himself!) were Jews who worshiped in the temple and saw Christianity not as a new religion but as the fulfillment of God's promises in the Old Testament. Yet most Jews would strenuously object to the idea that a person can be Jewish and still accept Christian doctrine.[28] For these reasons, I'll focus on rabbinic Judaism, which emerged after the destruction of the Jewish temple by the Romans in AD 70. Rabbinic Judaism stands in clear and often self-conscious distinction from Christianity and is the origin of the three major Jewish denominations of Orthodox, Conservative, and Reform Judaism.

Because Judaism and Christianity view the Hebrew Scriptures, or the Old Testament, as divinely inspired, they share many beliefs about the nature of God and our ethical duties. Like Muslims and Christians, Jews believe that sin is an offense against God. However, Jews—like Muslims—disagree with Christians on the radical nature of sin. For example, in his book *Entering the High Holy Days*, Rabbi Reuven Hammer states plainly: "Judaism teaches that human beings are not basically sinful. We come into the world neither carrying the burden of sin committed by our ancestors nor tainted by it."[29] The Jewish Virtual Library states: "Jews believe that man enters the world free of sin, with a soul that is pure and innocent and untainted. . . . Man sins because he is not a perfect being, and not, as Christianity teaches, because he is inherently sinful."[30]

Regarding our need for rescue, Jewish and Christian beliefs also differ. Professor Prothero writes that in Judaism: "The solution [to our distance from God] is return—to go back to God and to our true home. The techniques for making this journey are two: to tell the story

28 The 2013 Pew survey cited above found that only 34 percent of Jews believed you can be Jewish while affirming that Jesus is the Messiah.

29 Reuven Hammer, *Entering the High Holy Days: A Complete Guide to the History, Prayers, and Themes* (Philadelphia: Jewish Publication Society, 2005), 30.

30 "Issues in Jewish Ethics: Judaism's Rejection of Original Sin," The Jewish Virtual Library, https://www.jewishvirtuallibrary.org/.

[of God's actions in history] and follow the law—to remember and to obey."[31] Similarly, Professor Michael Fishbane writes, "Through devoted obedience to the prescriptions of the Torah [God's law] and its rabbinic elaborations, Judaism has taught that one might lead a life of divinely guided sanctity and ascend along just this path to religious perfection and communion with God."[32] In other words, reconciliation with God is accomplished not by God's rescue of radically sinful human beings but by remembering God and obeying his good and life-giving law.

Problems and Solutions

In this chapter, I've compared the views of the largest world religions with the Christian views of sin and rescue. Let me repeat that my analysis here is in no way an indictment of other world religions. It is entirely possible for someone to read my description of Hinduism or Judaism and to find them more attractive than the Christian view, which might seem unnecessarily pessimistic. In this section, I am only demonstrating that the Christian approach to these questions is unique.

In *God Is Not One*, Professor Prothero reaches the same conclusion. According to Prothero, the idea that religions differ only on nonessentials is "a lovely sentiment but [is] dangerous, disrespectful, and untrue. . . . The world's religious rivals do converge when it comes to ethics, but they diverge sharply on doctrine, ritual, mythology, experience, and law."[33] His thesis is that each religion articulates both a fundamental problem to be overcome and a solution to that problem. Religions are distinct not only in what cures they prescribe but also in what disease they are trying to cure.

Prothero is not a Christian trying to proselytize his readers (he describes himself as "religiously confused"). At no point does he suggest

---

31 Prothero, *God Is Not One*, 253.

32 Michael A. Fishbane, *Judaism: Revelation and Traditions* (San Francisco: Harper & Row, 1987), 15–16.

33 Prothero, *God Is Not One*, 2–3.

that one religion is better than another because of the differences between them. He is simply trying to assess each religion objectively and to make empirical statements about their beliefs. Table 3 summarizes his views of the five major world religions I've discussed. It dovetails well with the descriptions I've already provided.

Table 3. Prothero's assessment of the fundamental human problem and its solution as described by various world religions

	The problem to be solved is . . .	The solution is . . .
Buddhism	Suffering	Awakening
Hinduism	Samsara ("wandering")	Moksha ("release")
Islam	Pride	Submission
Judaism	Exile	Return to God
Christianity	Sin	Salvation

Prothero explains his thesis as it pertains to Christianity in the following way:

> While it may seem to be an act of generosity to state that Confucians and Buddhists and Muslims and Jews can also be saved, this statement is actually an act of obfuscation. Only Christians seek salvation.
>
> A sports analogy may be in order here. Which of the following—baseball, basketball, tennis, or golf—is best at scoring runs? The answer of course is baseball, because *runs* is a term foreign to basketball, tennis, and golf alike. Different sports have different goals. . . . To criticize a basketball team for failing to score runs is not to besmirch them. It is simply to misunderstand the game of basketball. . . . Just as hitting home runs is the monopoly of one sport, salvation is the monopoly of one religion. If you see sin as the human predicament and salvation as the solution, then it makes sense to come to Christ.[34]

34 Prothero, *God Is Not One*, 22–23.

But should we see sin as the fundamental human predicament and salvation as the solution? Why think that we are, in the words of the Book of Common Prayer, "miserable offenders," who need to throw ourselves on the mercy of God and trust in the free gift of salvation he offers in Jesus? I'll answer those questions in the next chapter.

8

The Gospel (Part 2)

Christianity and Sin

None is righteous, no, not one.

ROMANS 3:10

IN THE PREVIOUS CHAPTER, I argued that Christianity is unique among major world religions in teaching that we are radically corrupt sinners who need divine rescue. By itself, the uniqueness of Christian teaching on these two subjects is not evidence that Christianity is true. For example, many humanists believe that human beings are basically good and would consequently see the Christian view of sin as evidence that Christianity is false. To argue that these doctrines have evidentiary value, we have to show that they are not just unique but true. Are they? Let's begin by taking a closer look at the biblical view of sin.

Are We Radically Morally Corrupt?

The Bible teaches that we are all radically corrupted by sin. The word "radically" here is not merely being used as an intensifier; in other words, I am not primarily saying that we are "really, really, ridiculously morally corrupt." Instead, "radically" should be understood to mean "at a fundamental level." At our root, we are morally corrupt. Sin is like an infection or a poison that has tainted all humanity and expresses itself in our thoughts, words, and actions.

Sin is not just "breaking the rules." Sin is our rebellion against God. We were created to love and value God supremely, but instead we love and value other things supremely. As a result, there is a deep relational separation between us and God, who is the source of all goodness. One consequence of this separation from God is that our thoughts and actions are evil. Another consequence of this separation is that our hearts are darkened and our consciences are deadened. Not only do we willfully perform wrong actions, which our consciences condemn, but we can also do evil without the reproach of our consciences.

Consider a few of the depressing, but candid, assessments of the biblical authors:

The LORD saw that the wickedness of man was great in the earth, and that every intention of the thoughts of his heart was only evil continually. (Gen. 6:5)

Against you, you only, have I sinned
    and done what is evil in your sight,
so that you may be justified in your words
    and blameless in your judgment.
Behold, I was brought forth in iniquity,
    and in sin did my mother conceive me. (Ps. 51:4–5)

Since they did not see fit to acknowledge God, God gave them up to a debased mind to do what ought not to be done. They were filled with all manner of unrighteousness, evil, covetousness, malice. They are full of envy, murder, strife, deceit, maliciousness. They are gos-

sips, slanderers, haters of God, insolent, haughty, boastful, inventors
of evil, disobedient to parents, foolish, faithless, heartless, ruthless.
Though they know God's righteous decree that those who practice
such things deserve to die, they not only do them but give approval
to those who practice them. (Rom. 1:28–32)

None is righteous, no, not one;
  no one understands;
  no one seeks for God.
All have turned aside; together they have become worthless;
  no one does good,
  not even one.
Their throat is an open grave;
  they use their tongues to deceive.
The venom of asps is under their lips.
  Their mouth is full of curses and bitterness.
Their feet are swift to shed blood;
  in their paths are ruin and misery,
and the way of peace they have not known.
  There is no fear of God before their eyes. (Rom. 3:10–18)

According to the Bible, our primary problem is not a lack of self-
affirmation, a bad environment, or even material poverty; our primary
problem is our sin.

If human nature has been fundamentally corrupted by sin, then
we'd expect to see its traces all over human history. Similarly, we'd
expect to see sin infecting every part of life, every stratum of society,
and every culture. Finally, we'd expect that honest self-reflection
would show us a bent in each of our lives toward self-absorption,
wickedness, and willful blindness. So, what do we see when we mull
over the pages of human history or current events or our own lives?
The answer is not pretty.

Sin in the World

In his award-winning book *The Blank Slate: The Modern Denial of Human Nature*, Stephen Pinker, an atheist and professor of evolutionary psychology at Harvard, challenges the popular myth that "the human mind has no inherent structure and can be inscribed at will by society or ourselves."[1] Marshalling evidence from cognitive science and anthropology, Pinker rejects the claim that we are born with an undefined and infinitely malleable disposition, and argues instead that all human beings are born with a "complex human nature" that includes preferences, emotions, and patterns of thought. Some of these aspects of human nature are morally neutral, like our ability to use language. Some are even morally positive, like our capacity for compassion. But others are profoundly negative.

For example, Pinker devotes an entire chapter to the human propensity for violence, beginning with Winston Churchill's statement "The story of the human race is war. Except for brief and precarious interludes there has never been peace in the world; and long before history began murderous strife was universal and unending."[2]

Contrary to the myth of the Noble Savage, violence and warfare are not the products of modern nation-states vying for political power. They have existed as long as human beings have existed. Pinker cites the work of anthropologist Lawrence Keeley, who found that among indigenous peoples from eight geographically dispersed tribes, war accounted for between 8 percent to almost 60 percent of all male deaths.[3] In contrast, during the twentieth century, which included two world wars and innumerable bloody conflicts, war accounted for less than 2 percent of male deaths in Europe and the United States. Other anthropologists have found that

1　Steven Pinker, *The Blank Slate: The Modern Denial of Human Nature* (New York: Penguin, 2002), 2.
2　Pinker, *The Blank Slate*, 306.
3　Pinker, *The Blank Slate*, 57.

90 percent of hunter-gatherer societies are known to engage in warfare, and 64 percent wage war at least once every two years. . . . [Of] 99 groups of hunter gatherers from 37 cultures . . . 68 were at war at the time, 20 had been at war five to twenty-five years before, and all the others reported warfare in the more distant past.[4]

Pinker concludes: "Modern foragers, who offer a glimpse of life in prehistoric societies, were once thought to engage only in ceremonial battles. . . . Now they are known to kill one another at rates that dwarf the casualties from our world wars."[5]

Genocide offers another example of the depths of human depravity. In *Genocide: A World History*, Stanford professor Norman Naimark catalogs some of the unspeakable cruelty visited by men on their fellow human beings, from the Crusades, to the invasion of the Mongols, to settler genocides in the Americas, Africa, and Australia, to the Armenian genocide, to the Holodomor in Ukraine, to the Holocaust, to the Khmer Rouge in Cambodia, to ethnic cleansing in the Balkans. A few representative quotes from chroniclers of these atrocities will suffice to capture the brutality of which human beings are capable:

On one occasion, when the locals had come some ten leagues out from a large settlement in order to receive us and regale us with victuals and other gifts . . . the Christians were suddenly inspired by the Devil and, without the slightest provocation, butchered, before my eyes, some three thousand souls—men, women and children—as they sat there in front of us. I saw that day atrocities more terrible than any living man has ever seen nor ever thought to see. [Dominican friar Bartolomé de Las Casas on the behavior of the conquistadores][6]

4 Pinker, *The Blank Slate*, 57.
5 Pinker, *The Blank Slate*, 306.
6 Norman M. Naimark, *Genocide: A World History* (New York: Oxford University Press, 2017), 40.

It is impossible for me to convey what happened to those 6,400 defenseless women, virgins, and brides, as well as children and suckling
infants. Their heartrending cries and doleful pleas brought down the
deaf canopies of heaven. The police soldiers . . . would even boast to
some of us about how they had committed tortures and decapita-
tions, cut off and chopped up body parts with axes and how they
had dismembered suckling infants and children by pulling apart their
legs, or dashing them on rocks. [Armenian cleric Grigoris Balakian,
describing scenes from the Armenian genocide][7]

[Prisoners] were hit on the neck or on the head with iron bars that
were nearly one meter long. After that, Pol Pot men cut the victims'
throats or ripped their bellies open to pluck out the liver. Then the
bodies were thrown into the pits and covered over. At first, 5 or 6 were
killed each day, but the number shot up day by day, and by 1977 the
Pol-Pot-Ieng Sary gang had killed from 130 to 150 prisoners a day.
[a former prison official describing the actions of the Khmer Rouge][8]

In the majority of massacres there is evidence of multiple acts of
savagery, which preceded, accompanied or occurred after the deaths
of victims. Acts such as killing of defenseless children, often by beating them against walls or throwing them alive into pits where the
corpses of adults were later thrown; the amputation of limbs; the
impaling of victims; the killing of persons by covering them in petrol
and burning them alive; the extraction, in the presence of others,
of the viscera of the victims who were still alive . . . the opening of
wombs of pregnant women, and other similarly atrocious acts. [The
Commission on Historical Clarification, describing Guatemalan
atrocities against the Mayans][9]

7   Naimark, *Genocide*, 73.
8   Naimark, *Genocide*, 99.
9   Naimark, *Genocide*, 109.

It is tempting to think that only criminals and sociopaths are responsible for such horrors and to exempt ourselves from the population of individuals capable of such evil. But the truth is that we are not exempt. Reflecting on the human propensity for violence, Pinker writes: "History and ethnography suggest that people can treat strangers the way we now treat lobsters. . . . [Certain] tactics can flip a mental switch and reclassify an individual from 'person' to 'nonperson,' making it as easy for someone to torture or kill him as it is for us to boil a lobster alive."[10] It is this capacity to "flip a switch" and turn our fellow human beings into "viruses" and "vermin" fit for extermination that should terrify us.

We see the sinfulness of humanity displayed not only in war and genocide but also in diverse sets of psychological studies and surveys on general populations. In 1993, psychologists Douglas Kenrick and Virgil Sheets asked 312 undergraduates if they had ever had thoughts about killing someone. Seventy-three percent of males and 66 percent of females admitted to having had such fantasies. Fifty-two percent of males and 37 percent of females "reported that their most recent fantasy had lasted more than just 'a few minutes' (i.e., 'hours', 'days', or longer)." About 30 percent of males and more than 15 percent of females admitted to having such fantasies "frequently."[11]

Because definitions of sexual abuse and study methodologies vary, the precise number of children who experience childhood sexual abuse is difficult to specify. However, a recent meta-analysis of worldwide abuse rates concluded that 13 percent of females and 6 percent of males under the age of eighteen had experienced "contact sexual abuse," defined as "touching/fondling, kissing," while 9 percent of girls and 3 percent of boys had experienced forced intercourse.[12]

10 Pinker, *The Blank Slate*, 320–21.
11 D. T. Kenrick and V. Sheets, "Homicidal Fantasies," *Ethology and Sociobiology* 14, no. 4 (1993): 231–46.
12 J. Barth et al., "The Current Prevalence of Child Sexual Abuse Worldwide: A Systematic Review and Meta-Analysis," *International Journal of Public Health* 58, no. 3 (2013): 469–83.

A WHO multicountry study published in 2006 found high incidences of violence against women across numerous countries and
cultures. Of fifteen geographically and demographically diverse sites,
all the countries surveyed except Japan showed rates of physical abuse
greater than 20 percent, with many sites climbing into 30-some or 40-
some percent. Across most of the sites, approximately 15 percent of the
women surveyed reported having experienced "severe" abuse, which
was defined as "[being] hit with fist or something else that could hurt,
. . . kicked, dragged, or beaten up, . . . choked or burnt on purpose, . . .
threatened [or attacked with] a gun, knife, or other weapon." At sites
in Ethiopia and Peru, the percentage of women who had experienced
"severe" violence reached 35 and 50 percent, respectively. In thirteen
of the sites chosen, more than 10 percent of the women had also experienced "sexual violence," with incidences as high as 50 percent in
Bangladesh and 59 percent in Ethiopia.[13]

The potential for normal individuals to participate in potentially
lethal violence is highlighted by a series of famous psychology experiments. Beginning in the 1960s, Yale psychologist Stanley Milgram re-
cruited subjects to participate as "teachers" in what he claimed was an
experiment on learning. In the presence of a supervising "experimenter,"
a "teacher" was told to read a list of word pairs to a "learner," who had
been strapped to an electric chair. If the learner answered questions
incorrectly, the teacher was instructed to administer an electric shock,
increasing the voltage each time a mistake was made. Unbeknownst
to the teacher, the shocks were fake and both the learner and the experimenter were actors. The real experiment probed what percentage
of teachers would be willing to apply potentially lethal voltages to the
learners. As the experiment progressed, the teacher could hear the
learner uttering cries of pain, complaining of a heart condition, and

13   Claudia Garcia-Moreno et al., "Prevalence of Intimate Partner Violence: Findings from the WHO
     Multi-Country Study on Women's Health and Domestic Violence," *The Lancet* 368, no. 9543
     (2006): 1260–69.

begging to be released. Eventually, the learner fell completely silent and stopped answering questions. In spite of these deterrents, 65 percent of the participants were willing to administer the highest voltage. A 2006 experiment replicated Milgram's results, finding very little change in the compliance rates.[14]

Based on these data, it's difficult to argue that humanity's problems are not widespread or that they are superficial. As a race, we seem capable of astonishing levels of cruelty and evil. Note that I haven't invoked a Christian or even a religious code of ethics. I'm focusing solely on egregious behaviors like genocide, torture, murder, child sexual abuse, and violence against women, which most of us recognize as grossly immoral.

Could we argue that such actions are learned? Perhaps children are naturally innocent, kind, and peaceful and are driven to sin only by their environment or bad parenting. This explanation was, and still is, emotionally appealing to me. Who can witness the toothless grin of a baby, hear the giggles of a toddler, or see the wonder with which a preschooler greets each snowfall and not assume that young children are free from the evil inclinations that plague us as adults?

For most people, myself included, the romantic idea that children are innately good and pure collides with the realities of parenting. As a father of four wonderful children whom I love more than I could have imagined, I nonetheless find myself marveling at the patterns of selfishness that spring naturally from their hearts. Where did my two-year-old learn to hit and bite and scratch? Why would my four-year-old rather break a toy than share it with her sister? Where does my six-year-old learn to scream at me or sneer at her siblings? They are not imitating Mommy and Daddy; it's not as if my wife and I shriek at and bite each other every night. They are not imitating television or movies, which we dutifully monitor to ensure that their entertainment is filled to

14 Jerry M. Burger, "Replicating Milgram: Would People Still Obey Today?," *American Psychologist* 64, no. 1 (2009): 1–11.

the brim with messages about sharing and compassion. Their friends don't goad them into hoarding their toys and kicking their siblings. The problem is not that the outside world is corrupting them but that there is some principle of self-centeredness buried deep inside them.

And isn't that the obvious conclusion? If children really are born with pure and blameless desires, where are all the pure and blameless adults? Why is it that children born into loving homes with loving parents and every possible advantage can still turn into murderers? If children are naturally good, why is parenting so crucial to a child's moral development? Left to themselves, children will not chart a course toward greater and greater love, but will rapidly spiral into complete self-absorption. Without ceaseless instruction and tenderness, no children will learn to share, to obey their parents, or to treat others as they want to be treated. Good and generous behaviors take careful, methodical, intentional, and enduringly patient parenting. Bad and selfish behaviors flourish like weeds in the fertile soil of the human heart.

It is not just our intuition as parents that illuminates our children's sinful tendencies but the empirical data on childhood development as well. While we certainly have instincts toward pro-social behavior, a dark bent in our nature appears as soon as we can interact with the world. Consider some of the experimental findings: Children are known to exhibit aggressive behavior from the earliest stages of life. A 2006 study of 2,253 young children asked parents if their children had exhibited aggressive behavior, defined as "behavior that may cause physical harm to people, animals, or objects [which includes] hitting, kicking, and fighting." "Of the 12-month-olds, 52% according to their mothers and 46% according to their fathers showed at least some form of physically aggressive behavior, sometimes or often." Those percentages climbed to 80 percent and 74 percent for twenty-four-month-olds, and were 78 percent and 68 percent for thirty-six-month-olds.[15]

---

15 Lenneke R. A. Alink et al., "The Early Childhood Aggression Curve: Development of Physical Aggression in 10- to 50-Month-Old Children," *Child Development* 77, no. 4 (2006): 954–66.

A study of approximately ten thousand Canadian schoolchildren specified three types of aggressive behavior: "kicks, bites, hits other children," "gets into many fights," and "reacts with anger and fighting." The researchers found that 68.8 percent of two-year-olds could be categorized as, on average, displaying one or more of these behaviors "sometimes" or "often."[16]

While children generally learn to control their physically aggressive behavior as they grow older, bullying increases as they age. A study from the Netherlands probed the incidence of bullying in a sample of eleven thousand children ages five and six. They identified four forms of victimization: physical victimization ("being hit, kicked, pinched, or bitten"), verbal victimization ("being teased, laughed at, or called names"), relational victimization ("[being] excluded by other children"), and material victimization ("belongings of a child were hidden or broken"). Sixteen percent of the students engaged in physical victimization of others either weekly or monthly, while 22 percent of the students engaged in verbal victimization of others either weekly or monthly. Altogether, 30 percent of these kindergarten-age students engaged in bullying of one form or another.[17]

A study in the *Journal of the American Medical Association* reported the results of a survey of over fifteen thousand schoolchildren from grades six through ten. Students filled out a questionnaire that defined bullying as doing or saying "nasty and unpleasant things" to a fellow student or teasing a schoolmate "repeatedly in a way he or she doesn't like." According to self-reports, 27 percent of boys and 23 percent of girls admitted to bullying others "once or twice" in the current term. Twenty-six percent of boys and 14 percent of girls admitted to bullying

16 Sylvana M. Côté et al., "The Development of Physical Aggression from Toddlerhood to Pre-Adolescence: A Nation Wide Longitudinal Study of Canadian Children," *Journal of Abnormal Child Psychology* 34, no. 1 (2006): 71–85.

17 Pauline W. Jansen et al., "Prevalence of Bullying and Victimization among Children in Early Elementary School: Do Family and School Neighborhood Socioeconomic Status Matter?," *BMC Public Health* 12, no. 494 (2012).

others "sometimes" or "weekly" in the same period of time. In all, 53 percent of boys and 37 percent of girls self-reported engaging in bullying. These reports considered only harassment of a weaker child by a stronger child; they didn't even take into account quarreling or fighting between students of "about the same strength," which was explicitly excluded by the questionnaire.[18]

It's possible to dismiss such studies by insisting that this behavior is a natural part of child development; obviously, small children haven't yet learned to control their urges or to regulate their external behavior in socially acceptable ways. But that is *precisely* my point. The behavior that we see is natural. We are born with the natural tendency to supremely value our own desires and to satisfy them regardless of whether we hurt others in the process. There is an unmistakable trajectory from the self-centeredness of our childhood to the self-centeredness of our adolescence and to the self-centeredness of our adulthood. In war and genocide and rape, we are witnessing adults act on the same sinful urges that lead a toddler to snatch a toy or bite his playmate. Extreme circumstances and a bad environment may reveal or exacerbate our inherent sinfulness, but they do not create it.

To be clear, I am certainly not arguing that behind their adorable facade, children are coldhearted monsters. Jesus himself blessed children and called his followers to imitate their trust and humility. In children, we see transparency, self-forgetfulness, lack of guile, unrestrained affection, awestruck appreciation of beauty, playfulness, and many other wonderful qualities that fade as we grow older. But alongside and underneath these qualities is the same inordinate love of self that is the root of all sin.

The metaphor of a disease is helpful here. Every human being is born with the moral equivalent of cancer, which infiltrates every aspect of our development. In children, the cancer hasn't spread as far as it has in

---

18 Tonja R. Nansel et al., "Bullying Behaviors among US Youth: Prevalence and Association with Psychological Adjustment," *Journal of the American Medical Association* 285, no. 16 (2001): 2094–2100.

adults, so in children we see glimpses of the kind of innocence we were all meant to have. Nevertheless, they are infected just as we are, and, apart from God's intervention, the disease will corrupt us all entirely.

In light of such evidence, the conclusion that human beings as a whole are sinful seems inescapable. But we can't stop there. Admitting that human beings are sinful can be a mechanism for avoiding or suppressing a more difficult truth: *we* are sinful. The sinfulness of humanity is not simply a problem "out there"; it is a problem "in here." Each of us needs to come to terms with his or her own corruption and moral failure.

Sin in Our Hearts

How do we really begin to recognize our sin? We can start with the standards we expect other people to follow. We all want others to treat us with love, gentleness, respect, and charity. Each of us can immediately call to mind certain unkind words and actions that hurt us deeply. How many times have we been shocked by the pettiness, indifference, or disdain of others?

Yet, while we expect other people to adhere to certain standards of kindness and compassion, do we? Can we look back at our lives and truly claim that we have lived as we ought to have lived and as we wished other people lived? Can we look at our past, which may be strewn with broken friendships, betrayals, jealousy, gossip, and bitterness, and say that we've never been to blame? Is there an ex-girlfriend or ex-boyfriend or ex-spouse whose life we've damaged irreparably? Has there never been a schoolmate or colleague who, in the loneliness of his room, has cursed our cruelty or our bullying? These actions may not rise to the level of war, genocide, crime, or the more egregious behavior highlighted in the last sections. But they are part of everyday human life, emphatically reminding us that sin is the air we breathe, what we inhale and exhale, as we go about our daily business.

Moreover, our self-perception is usually based on our conduct at our very best moments and on the most charitable possible interpretation of our actions. Most of us are continually repeating a narrative in which we're the good guys. When there's conflict, it's because our good intentions have been misunderstood. We've done our best, but other people have been selfish or jealous or vindictive. We're the reasonable, sensitive, compassionate ones. But is that really an accurate reflection of our character? Knowing our capacity for rationalization and self-justification, we ought to doubt the stories we tell ourselves. If we take a hard look at our lives as dispassionately as possible, we'll find a great deal that we would like to forget.

Here's an interesting test: Imagine that scientists invented a smartphone app that could read your mind and broadcast your thoughts over a portable speaker.[19] If all your most private thoughts—your sexual urges, your jealousy, your anger, your self-righteousness—were made audible for everyone to hear for just one day, where would you go? To the beach? To the mall? To an outdoor concert in your hometown? To your neighbor's Christmas party? To your daughter's dance recital? To church? To your workplace? Would you even leave your house?

This thought experiment doesn't probe some objective standard of morality but involves only our own sense of shame. The fact that we are hesitant to expose our inner lives to others shows not only that our thoughts are often filled with darkness but also that we know they are and don't want them exposed. It is unbearable for us to imagine people seeing and hearing what actually goes on inside us each day. In some ways, it's even unbearable for us to admit these truths to ourselves, which is why we lie to ourselves and others.

Thus far, we've only discussed our own standards. But most of us recognize that an individual's standards do not determine what is or is not ethical. Peter Singer, the Ira W. DeCamp Professor of Bioethics at Princeton University and one of the most influential ethicists of our

---

19 This illustration is modified from an illustration Tim Keller used, citing Francis A. Schaeffer. It appears to have come from Schaeffer, *The Church at the End of the Twentieth Century*, 2nd ed. (Westchester, IL: Crossway, 1985), 49–50.

time, argues that morality requires us to do as much good as possible to as many people as possible every moment of our lives. In *Practical Ethics*, he writes, "An action [is] right if it produces more happiness for all affected by it than any alternative action and wrong if it does not."[20] According to Singer, this standard of morality requires—among other things—veganism, strict limitation of carbon emissions, and radical financial giving to the global poor. As an atheist, Singer does not base his ethics on the existence of God but insists that they are consistent with a purely naturalistic view of the universe. Let us assume, for a moment, that he is correct. Have any of us lived up to this standard of universal good will? Have we even come close? No.

If you work a full-time minimum-wage job in the United States, you are in the 85th percentile of annual income worldwide.[21] Billions of men, women, and children survive on a few dollars a day. How much do we do to alleviate their suffering? What percentage of our income do we spend on luxuries and frivolities, and what percentage do we spend on saving the lives of the desperately poor? Our own inner cities and poor rural areas are often filled with broken families, impoverished children, and single mothers struggling on welfare. Do we joyfully donate our time and talents to share their burdens?

When we examine ourselves honestly, we find that we do not want to alleviate the suffering of others if it comes at too high a cost to us. We find in ourselves an overpowering desire to remain ignorant of their condition in order to protect our own happiness. We would rather entertain ourselves with romantic comedies and action movies than comfort real people in need. We would rather buy luxuries like designer clothes and high-end electronics than make radical monetary sacrifices.[22] We would rather eat takeout and play video games than

---

20 Peter Singer, *Practical Ethics*, 3rd ed. (Cambridge: Cambridge University Press, 2011), 3.

21 Readers can calculate their own percentile at https://www.givingwhatwecan.org/.

22 This definition of "luxury" is extremely conservative. In his chapter on wealth and poverty, Singer notes that "even a bottle of water is a luxury if there is safe drinking water available free." Singer, *Practical Ethics*, 215.

visit lonely shut-ins in retirement homes. Reflecting on these realities, atheist Sam Harris says:

> Are we culpable for all the preventable injury and death that we did nothing to prevent? We may be, up to a point. The philosopher Peter Unger has made a persuasive case that a single dollar spent on anything but the absolute essentials of our survival is a dollar that has some starving child's blood on it. Perhaps we do have far more moral responsibility for the state of the world than most of us seem ready to contemplate.[23]

So far, I haven't made any appeal to God in this section. By these wholly secular standards, we can see that there is something seriously wrong with us. But what if we consider religious standards? In particular, let's consider the standard that Jesus set for human beings by looking at his famous parable of the good Samaritan:

> And behold, a lawyer stood up to put him [Jesus] to the test, saying, "Teacher, what shall I do to inherit eternal life?" He said to him, "What is written in the Law? How do you read it?" And he answered, "You shall love the Lord your God with all your heart and with all your soul and with all your strength and with all your mind, and your neighbor as yourself." And he said to him, "You have answered correctly; do this, and you will live."
>
> But he, desiring to justify himself, said to Jesus, "And who is my neighbor?" Jesus replied, "A man was going down from Jerusalem to Jericho, and he fell among robbers, who stripped him and beat him and departed, leaving him half dead. Now by chance a priest was going down that road, and when he saw him he passed by on the other side. So likewise a Levite, when he came to the place and saw

---

23 Sam Harris, "The Limits of Discourse: As Demonstrated by Sam Harris and Noam Chomsky," Sam Harris (blog), May 1, 2015, https://samharris.org/the-limits-of-discourse/.

him, passed by on the other side. But a Samaritan, as he journeyed, came to where he was, and when he saw him, he had compassion. He went to him and bound up his wounds, pouring on oil and wine. Then he set him on his own animal and brought him to an inn and took care of him. And the next day he took out two denarii and gave them to the innkeeper, saying, 'Take care of him, and whatever more you spend, I will repay you when I come back.' Which of these three, do you think, proved to be a neighbor to the man who fell among the robbers?" He said, "The one who showed him mercy." And Jesus said to him, "You go, and do likewise." (Luke 10:25–37)

The context in which Jesus delivers this parable is important. He is asked by a Jewish religious expert how a person can achieve eternal life. Most likely, the lawyer in this passage is attempting to elicit a dismissive response from Jesus regarding God's law. Jesus's compassion, love, and gentleness toward sinners, prostitutes, and other social outcasts is well known to his contemporaries, and many assume (as they do today) that it reveals a permissive attitude toward sin. But when Jesus affirms that the keeping of God's law is required to inherit eternal life, the man is uncomfortable. How do we know? Because he attempts to "justify himself." He wants to believe that he has indeed kept the law and deserves God's blessing. Jesus can't possibly mean that anyone we meet is our neighbor. If he does, then all of us, like the lawyer, stand condemned as lawbreakers. God's law can't possibly demand that we love all people—rich or poor, Jew or Gentile, male or female, friend or enemy—just as much as we love ourselves. Can it?

Jesus tells the parable of the good Samaritan to show that an active, eager, sacrificial, universal, counter-conditional love for others is *exactly* what God's law demands. At the time, Samaritans and Jews are bitter enemies. Yet, Jesus says, it is the Samaritan who obeyed God's law by loving his Jewish neighbor, while the priest and the Levite, fellow Jews, did not. Jesus's message is stunning: God's law demands love like the

Samaritan's. Not a love that is limited to people who look like us or think like us or love us in return, but a love that extends even to our enemies.

It is in the harsh light of the Golden Rule ("whatever you wish that others would do to you, do also to them," Matt. 7:12) that we are most terribly exposed. If I accepted Singer's ethical standards, I could imagine achieving a right moral standing through extreme effort. At least in principle, I could grit my teeth and radically alter my behavior to place the appropriate weight on the happiness of the poor and suffering. It is conceivable that through discipline, self-denial, and sheer will-power I might even achieve some significant measure of improvement. However, Jesus taught that God's commands apply not just to our actions but to our thoughts, our motivations, and our desires.

It is possible to act ethically with regard to the poor but to do so out of grinding obligation rather than out of love. In the parable of the good Samaritan, Jesus points out that real love motivates us to give joyfully and extravagantly, without counting the cost. When we truly love our neighbor, the question is not What is the minimum amount I am ethically required to give? but What is the maximum amount I am permitted to give? At first, this ethic of love strikes us rightly as beautiful. Yet, if we take it seriously, we will recognize that by its very goodness, it condemns us. We might improve our external behavior by a tremendous exertion of will, but how can we change our loves, our desires, and our affections?

Moreover, the fact that such a tremendous exertion of will would be required to change our behavior only shows us more clearly how selfish our hearts naturally are. We don't normally have to try to breathe or force ourselves to drink water when thirsty or make ourselves eat when hungry. Conversely, we don't expend great effort to avoid eating pencil shavings or slamming our hands repeatedly in car doors. Things that are natural come easily to us. If something takes immense effort, it must be unnatural to us. This principle demonstrates that we do not naturally love our neighbors as ourselves; the harder we try to be good, the more we show how unnatural it is.

There are depths to our pettiness, lust, anger, and self-obsession that we suppress because we cannot bear what they reveal about us. Where our affections should have been focused outward on God and other people, they have curved back inward onto us. This fact explains why no amount of social reform or education or even religious coercion can fix us. History is littered with the wreckage of attempts to cure our problems. Communist regimes meant to bring equality and dignity to the poor collapsed into totalitarianism, poverty, and corruption. The attainment of money and fame has led celebrity after celebrity into isolation, despair, and even suicide. The material prosperity of the American dream has done nothing to fill our inner emptiness, so we numb ourselves with alcohol, drugs, sex, and entertainment to hide from reality. When we take an honest look at our own hearts, the misery we have inflicted on ourselves and others, and the state of our world, the Christian explanation becomes not only plausible but unavoidable: something is deeply, radically wrong with us.

9

The Gospel (Part 3)

Christianity and Salvation

There is salvation in no one else, for there is no other name
under heaven given among men by which we must be saved.

ACTS 4:12

EVEN IF REFLECTION ON THE TRAGIC, destructive path of human history and careful introspection convince us that human beings are radically corrupt, is there a reason to admit that we need rescue? While they don't identify our fundamental problem in quite the same way as Christianity, other worldviews and religions offer alternative solutions that sound quite reasonable. Secular philosophies say that we can solve our problems through better education, a different form of government, income redistribution, a return to traditional values, social activism, or therapy. Other religions say that we can solve our problems through good deeds, morality, obedience to God's law, prayer, meditation, rituals, or ascetic practices. From a Christian perspective, many of these suggestions would certainly improve the world we live in. So why think that the Christian solution offers something distinct and necessary?

In spite of the vast differences, all the prescriptions listed above have one thing in common: they all assume that we can fix ourselves. Christianity alone claims that what we need most is a Savior, a rescuer, someone who will do for us what we cannot do for ourselves. Just as the biblical authors declare our desperate moral guilt, they also declare the gracious forgiveness that God has provided:

> For God so loved the world, that he gave his only Son, that whoever believes in him should not perish but have eternal life. (John 3:16)

> There is no distinction: for all have sinned and fall short of the glory of God, and are justified by his grace as a gift, through the redemption that is in Christ Jesus. (Rom. 3:23–24)

> By grace you have been saved through faith. And this is not your own doing; it is the gift of God, not a result of works, so that no one may boast. (Eph. 2:8–9)

> Let the one who is thirsty come; let the one who desires take the water of life without price. (Rev. 22:17)

So do we have reason to think that we need a rescue that comes to us freely and entirely unmerited?

I believe we do. Almost all other systems of thought, whether secular or religious, are based on the premise that we can atone for our moral failures. In other words, God's judgment works like a ledger or a checking account: if we accumulate enough moral credit, we can offset our moral liabilities. But any reflection on the actual nature of moral failure shows that such reasoning is extremely dubious. In contrast to the idea of a moral ledger, the Bible offers two metaphors for sin that demonstrate our need for salvation: sin as *transgression* and sin as *slavery*.

Sin as Transgression

The idea that sin is a transgression of God's moral law is perhaps the most common understanding of sin: God gave us the Ten Commandments and the Golden Rule, and breaking these commands is a sin. As I argued in the previous chapter, that understanding of sin is only partial, but—as far as it goes—it is correct. However, very few people connect the idea of sin as transgression to the implausibility of the "moral ledger" view of salvation.

How does the Bible treat the transgression of God's law? In the Old Testament, the Ten Commandments and the surrounding stipulations of the Mosaic law were not just a moral code but the legal code of the nation of Israel. As a result, breaking the Mosaic law carried not only spiritual consequences but civil punishments as well, many of which strike us as extremely harsh. While it's very important to understand the cultural and historical context of these laws,[1] one walks away from the Old Testament with the unmistakable impression that a transgression of God's law is a serious offense incurring serious penalties. To cite just one example, consider God's warnings of the consequences of Israel's failure to keep his law:

> But if you will not obey the voice of the LORD your God or be careful to do all his commandments and his statutes that I command you today, then all these curses shall come upon you and overtake you. Cursed shall you be in the city, and cursed shall you be in the field. Cursed shall be your basket and your kneading bowl. Cursed shall be the fruit of your womb and the fruit of your ground, the increase of your herds and the young of your flock. Cursed shall you be when you come in, and cursed shall you be when you go out.
>
> The LORD will send on you curses, confusion, and frustration in all that you undertake to do, until you are destroyed and perish quickly

[1] See, for example, Paul Copan, *Is God a Moral Monster? Making Sense of the Old Testament God* (Grand Rapids, MI: Baker, 2011).

on account of the evil of your deeds, because you have forsaken me. (Deut. 28:15–20)

This passage and many others like it are representative of what we find in the Old Testament: the keeping of God's law is rewarded, and the breaking of God's law is punished. But isn't the idea of keeping God's law to avoid God's punishment and merit God's blessing an Old Testament idea? Isn't the New Testament completely different?

Actually, no. Consider the judicial language used by Paul in his letter to the Romans:

[God] will render to each one according to his works: to those who by patience in well-doing seek for glory and honor and immortality, he will give eternal life; but for those who are self-seeking and do not obey the truth, but obey unrighteousness, there will be wrath and fury. There will be tribulation and distress for every human being who does evil, the Jew first and also the Greek, but glory and honor and peace for everyone who does good, the Jew first and also the Greek. For God shows no partiality.

For all who have sinned without the law will also perish without the law, and all who have sinned under the law will be judged by the law. For it is not the hearers of the law who are righteous before God, but the doers of the law who will be justified. (Rom. 2:6–13)

As we saw in the parable of the good Samaritan, Jesus also affirmed that the way to inherit the kingdom of heaven was to keep God's commandments. Conversely, Jesus taught that the breaking of God's commandments merited his wrath:

Not everyone who says to me, "Lord, Lord," will enter the kingdom of heaven, but the one who does the will of my Father who is in heaven. On that day many will say to me, "Lord, Lord, did we not prophesy in your name, and cast out demons in your name, and do many mighty works in your name?" And then will I declare to them, "I never knew you; depart from me, you workers of lawlessness." (Matt. 7:21–23)

As in the Old Testament, the consistent theme of the New Testament, including the statements of Jesus himself, is that sin is a transgression of God's law and that "the wages of sin is death" (Rom. 6:23).

What relevance does the biblical view of God's law have to the idea of a "moral ledger" that balances our moral debts and our moral credits? Upon reflection, it makes the idea of a moral ledger highly implausible.

Imagine you have committed a serious offense, like the first-degree murder of a six-year-old girl. Let's also assume that the state has conclusive evidence of your guilt and that you have confessed to the crime. When you're brought to trial, does the judge declare you guilty or innocent on the basis of your net moral behavior? Does she total up your good deeds and weigh them against the heinousness of your crime? Of course not. The question the court considers is whether or not you have broken the law. At best, your overall moral behavior might persuade the judge to soften the sentence; but it would never persuade her to declare you innocent. It would be sheer insanity to stand before the judge, confess to the crime, and then coolly insist that your good behavior should convince the judge to declare you not guilty.

From a moral perspective, the situation is even more dire. Think of the little girl whose life you ended, or the weeping parents remembering the child they loved and cherished. Imagine addressing the parents in the following way: "Yes, I killed your little daughter. But I do many good things. I pay my taxes. I volunteer at a homeless shelter. I'm a loving father. Overall, I think my many good deeds make up for this one offense. Besides, killing your daughter took just a few minutes. I spend 99.99 percent of my time not murdering children."

Would the insistence that your good deeds outweigh your bad deeds convince the judge of your innocence? Would it even move her to leniency? No, just the opposite. Your protests would make you a hundred times more morally repugnant than if you had said nothing. The fact that you can stand in front of your victim's family and offer excuses shows that you have no real grasp of the seriousness of your actions. The only acceptable response is to acknowledge your guilt and recognize that nothing you can do could make up for your crime.

If this reasoning applies to our imperfect human notions of justice, how much more would it apply to the justice of a morally perfect God? If a single crime is enough to make us guilty in the sight of human courts, how much more does a lifetime of moral compromise, evasion, sin, and the silencing of our conscience render us liable to God's judgment? Viewed from the standpoint of God's law, none of us can plead innocence.

Even more troubling is the realization that our very attempts to live a morally exemplary life are often tainted and sustained by pride. The more successful we are in living up to our own standards or society's standards—or even God's standards, outwardly—the more we tend to look down on others whom we regard as moral failures. Whether these others are "moral degenerates" who fail to live up to our standards of religious devotion and sexual purity or "hate-filled bigots" who fail to live up to our standards of tolerance and acceptance, in either case we are exalting ourselves and our own performance. Pride is the rock on which the hopes of the self-achieving moralist are perennially dashed. God's law is not meant to be a template by which we can save ourselves; rather it is meant to humble us by showing us how far short we fall so that we can throw ourselves on God's mercy in Christ.

The only cure for pride is not a more resolute attempt at humility—which is often just another expression of our pride—but grace. Grace alone can save us from our arrogance because grace alone leaves no room for boasting. Only if salvation is an entirely free gift and not something we achieve can we be set free from the insufficiency of our own efforts and the deadly burden of our own pride.

Sin as Slavery

A second biblical metaphor for sin is that of *slavery*. In one sense, we sin freely because we are acting out of our own desires. But in another sense, we are slaves to sin.

In his letter to the Romans, Paul asks, "Do you not know that if you present yourselves to anyone as obedient slaves, you are slaves of the one whom you obey, either of sin, which leads to death, or of obedience, which leads to righteousness?" (Rom. 6:16). Jesus expressed the same thought in response to religious leaders who took offense at his suggestion that he could free them from their slavery. He told them: "Truly, truly, I say to you, everyone who practices sin is a slave to sin. The slave does not remain in the house forever; the son remains forever. So if the Son sets you free, you will be free indeed" (John 8:34–36). According to the Bible, we choose to sin, but we are also shackled to sin and trapped in it, like a prisoner chained to his bed and locked in a cell.

To use modern terminology, we might substitute the word *addiction* for *slavery*. An addiction is any destructive habit that we are powerless to stop and that controls our lives. The addict may be in denial and may insist that he can stop at any time. Or he may know that the addiction is destroying his life and is literally killing him. Either way, the addiction is his master and he is its slave. We see these signs so clearly when the addiction is to drugs or alcohol. But what if the addiction is to sin?

Suppose someone offered you a million dollars to perfectly obey the interpersonal ethical standards of the Bible for just one month. Naturally, certain behaviors would have to be avoided: no looking at pornography, lying, gossiping, extramarital sex, or dishonesty. But even your patterns of thought would have to change: no more greed, lust, self-righteousness, boasting, envy, and pride. How long would it be before your first lustful thought? How long before you'd snap at one of your children or your spouse or your coworker? How long before you'd begin feeling superior to all the people who aren't even trying to obey God's commands? After your inevitable failure, if your benefactor graciously allowed you to start over and try for another month, could you (or I) do it this time? Or the next time? Or the next?

We don't even need to consider perfect adherence to biblical standards to see that we have a problem. How many times have we identified areas where we fail to live up to our own moral standards and yet have found ourselves unable to change? For example, in reading the previous chapter, your conscience may have been bothered about your level of financial giving, your involvement with the poor, or your sexual purity. You may have resolved to give more or to try harder. Yet it is more than likely that within a few weeks all your resolutions will have faded beneath the far weightier desire for your own pleasure and comfort.

What these thought experiments show us is that we can't not sin. Abstaining from sin even for the shortest period of time is exhausting. Our attempts at reformation are usually short-lived and superficial. Eventually, we throw up our hands and say: "This is so pointless. It's not worth it. I'm not hurting anyone. If it ever becomes a real problem, then I'll deal with it."

That's the language of addiction. We are all sin addicts.[2]

Like the judicial metaphor, the metaphor of sin as slavery undermines the idea of a "moral ledger." What use is it to the alcoholic to total up all the hours he has been sober and compare them to the hours he has been drunk? Is the heroin addict any less an addict because he helps his mother do the laundry? Moral debits and credits are irrelevant to our condition because all the credit in the world can't cleanse our hearts.

Seeing sin as slavery is also a useful complement to a judicial understanding of sin. Imagine a heroin addict who has lost his job, has

2   Of course, this metaphor, like all metaphors, breaks down if pushed too far. Addiction to drugs or alcohol can be treated through various forms of rehabilitation, and some people do succeed in throwing off addictions without external help. Additionally, while some might deny that we are morally culpable for our addictions, we are definitely morally culpable for our sin. As a metaphor, though, the idea of sin as an addiction helps us to realize that our problem is far deeper than mere "bad behavior."

lost all his friends, has been estranged from his wife and children, and has become a drug dealer to support his own habit. He's arrested and is brought before a judge on charges that could send him to prison for decades. The bailiff calls his case, and he stands up, trembling with fear. But to his amazement the judge says: "I'm waiving all the charges against you. In fact, I'm granting you permanent immunity. You will never again be brought to court on drug charges. You're free to go."

In joy, the man turns to leave. But then he stops. He haltingly approaches the bench and whispers: "Your honor, I'm so grateful. But please, sir, I've lost everything. I've destroyed my family. My daughter won't even speak to me. If you send me out there, I know I'll end up back on drugs. Please, sir, could you help me? Could you find a place for me in rehab. I don't just want to be free. I want to be well." The prisoner has realized that as important as forgiveness is, he needs more. He needs transformation. He needs to be healed.

In the same way, we certainly need forgiveness, but we need more than just forgiveness. We also need transformation. We need someone to rescue us out of bondage, to break our chains, and to lead us into freedom.

The Gospel of Grace

In opposition to any salvation that originates with us, Christianity insists that salvation is by grace. We are saved not by our good works or by our good intentions but by God's unmerited favor and unconditional love. The cross of Jesus offers us what no other religion does: a perfect atonement for our sins that is not achieved by us but given to us as a free gift. God's gracious rescue and restoration provide an answer to both problems I raised in this chapter.

Let's first consider the issue of sin as slavery. Because sin has enslaved us, it cannot be cured by forgiveness alone. A forgiven addict is still an addict. Even worse, to an addict who has been awakened to the fact that his addiction is killing him, forgiveness without healing is tragically incomplete. When we realize that our sin is poisoning us, poisoning our relationship to others, and poisoning our relationship to God, we don't merely want it forgiven; we want it healed.

God's answer to the sin dwelling in our hearts is regeneration. When we turn to Jesus in repentance and trust, God not only forgives us but also transforms us. Jesus offers us a redemption that not only saves us from wrath but also restores us.[3] When God rescues us, he fills us with his presence to give us new affections and new desires.

Now, clearly, Christians do not become morally perfect the moment they trust in Christ to rescue them. Far from it. The Bible is filled with commands to Christians to fight against their evil inclinations, to struggle against sin, and to resist temptation. Ask Christians throughout history and they will tell you that the Christian life is a battle. The presence of a battle in the heart of every Christian is not an indictment of Christian doctrine but a confirmation of it. There is now a new principle of love at war with the natural self-absorption of our hearts. God will not cease waging that war against our sin until it is conquered. To someone who is sick with sin and longs for rescue, this is the greatest news in the world. The struggle between the goodness of God and the evil in our hearts is like the pain of the surgeon's knife. God is removing the cancer of sin and will not stop until we are finally free of it. It is through God's power and God's sustaining grace that we fight sin, knowing that he will deliver us from it because of his love for us.

---

3   The idea that Jesus's atonement frees us from both the punishment and the power of sin is the inspiration for the first stanza in Toplady's famous hymn:

> Rock of Ages, cleft for me,
> Let me hide myself in Thee;
> Let the water and the blood,
> From Thy wounded side which flowed,
> Be of sin the double cure,
> Save from wrath and make me pure.

Augustus Toplady, "Rock of Ages," 1776, https://hymnary.org/.

Next, let's address the issue of sin as transgression. As I documented in chapter 7, the message that Jesus saves us from our sins is affirmed by every historic branch of Christianity. However, they differ on how that salvation is accomplished and, in particular, how Jesus atoned for our sins. The answer is multifaceted, but in what follows, I will present the historic Protestant answer to this question, primarily because I believe it is the most consistent with the Bible but also because it clearly addresses the judicial problem I noted in the first section of this chapter.

In the book of Isaiah, which scholars unanimously agree was written centuries before Jesus's birth, we find the following enigmatic passage:

Who has believed what he has heard from us?
    And to whom has the arm of the LORD been revealed?
For he grew up before him like a young plant,
    and like a root out of dry ground;
he had no form or majesty that we should look at him,
    and no beauty that we should desire him.
He was despised and rejected by men,
    a man of sorrows and acquainted with grief;
and as one from whom men hide their faces
    he was despised, and we esteemed him not.

Surely he has borne our griefs
    and carried our sorrows;
yet we esteemed him stricken,
    smitten by God, and afflicted.
But he was pierced for our transgressions;
    he was crushed for our iniquities;
upon him was the chastisement that brought us peace,
    and with his wounds we are healed.
All we like sheep have gone astray;
    we have turned—every one—to his own way;

and the LORD has laid on him
  the iniquity of us all. . . .

Yet it was the will of the LORD to crush him;
  he has put him to grief;
when his soul makes an offering for guilt,
  he shall see his offspring; he shall prolong his days;
the will of the LORD shall prosper in his hand.
Out of the anguish of his soul he shall see and be satisfied;
by his knowledge shall the righteous one, my servant,
  make many to be accounted righteous,
  and he shall bear their iniquities.
Therefore I will divide him a portion with the many,
  and he shall divide the spoil with the strong,
because he poured out his soul to death
  and was numbered with the transgressors;
yet he bore the sin of many,
  and makes intercession for the transgressors.
    (Isa. 53:1–6; 10–12)

Non-Christian scholars are divided on the identity of the "servant" of the Lord in this passage, but it's hardly surprising that Christians see it as referring to Jesus. If Christians are correct, then we see in this passage that Jesus's atonement can be summarized in a single word: substitution.

Throughout the Old Testament, God revealed both his law to the Israelites and the penalties for breaking it. To obey God's law was to choose life, but to disobey it was to choose death. In the New Testament, we learn that every human is faced with the same choice: life through obedience or death through disobedience. Yet every one of us has chosen death. Through millions of sins both large and small, through acts of overt and covert rebellion, through sins of commission and omission, through our failure to love justice and do mercy, through our greed and hedonism, through our open immorality and hidden self-righteousness, we have violated God's requirements over and over. The sentence of death hangs over the head of every person on earth.

Except for one.

Jesus of Nazareth kept God's law. He loved God with all his heart, mind, soul, and strength. He loved his neighbor as himself. He traveled from village to village with no place to lay his head, but he never coveted anyone else's food or shelter or possessions. He was despised and rejected, but he turned the other cheek. He comforted widows and orphans in their distress. He had compassion on the sick and suffering. He poured out his life doing good. This was God's chosen King, the eternal Son of God, with all the beauty, kindness, and holiness of divinity. Of all the people who have ever lived, here is the one man—the only man—who ever fully and completely deserved God's blessing.

Yet, at the end of his life, Jesus was greeted not with thunderous applause but with scorn and spitting. He was not dressed in a king's robe; he was stripped naked. He was not embraced as a hero but beaten as a criminal. The hands that blessed children and comforted widows were torn by nails. He wasn't given a crown of gold but bore a crown of thorns. In the moment of his deepest need, all his friends left him. And on a Roman cross, he gasped out his last hours in torture and abandonment. Why?

Because he was taking our place. All his life, Jesus had taken our place. He fulfilled the law that we should have kept, loving God and loving his neighbor. On the cross, he took the punishment that we deserve, bearing our sins and enduring the wrath of God. The story of salvation is the story of exchange. Jesus takes our sin so that we can have his righteousness. Jesus bears our curse so that we can have God's blessing. Jesus, the Son of God, is treated like a rebel so that rebels like us can be accepted as sons.[4]

Substitutionary atonement solves the problem of how God can be both just and the justifier of those who trust in Jesus. God's very

4   This description of the gospel can be found many places. See, for instance, J. D. Greear, *Gospel: Recovering the Power That Made Christianity Revolutionary* (Nashville: B&H, 2011), 45–58.

goodness demands that sin is treated justly. When we, as humans, look at a history strewn with murder, rape, adultery, theft, and every kind of evil, we know that real justice cannot simply wink at such horrors and wave them away. We feel intuitively that criminals must pay for all the misery, all the tragedy, and all the pain they have inflicted. How much more must a perfectly holy, omniscient God demand that every sin be met with perfect, impartial, and inexorable justice?

Yet the Bible also declares that God loves mercy, that God is not merely loving but is love itself, that mercy triumphs over judgment. So how can God be both fully just and fully merciful? How can he punish sin perfectly and yet forgive sin completely?

Only through the cross. Out of love for sinners, God sent his only Son to stand in our place. He so identified with us and united himself to us that he took on our burdens and our sins as if they were his own. The cross provides the final answer for how a holy God can forgive the unforgivable in us.

> On the mount of crucifixion
> fountains opened deep and wide;
> through the floodgates of God's mercy
> flowed a vast and gracious tide.
> Grace and love, like mighty rivers,
> poured incessant from above,
> and heav'n's peace and perfect justice
> kissed a guilty world in love.[5]

Not only does Christianity uniquely expose the depths of our sin; it also uniquely shows how God has gone to unimaginable lengths to rescue us from it.

---

5   From the hymn "Here Is Love," by William Rees, 1855, trans. William Edwards, 1915, https://hymnary.org/.

To return to the question I posed at the beginning of chapter 7: How do most Christians come to realize that Christianity is true? How is their belief justified, if not through knowledge of traditional apologetic arguments? My claim is that this "argument from the gospel" explains how the vast majority of Christians come to recognize the truth of Christianity.

Most Christians can't defend the reliability of the Gospels or the historicity of the resurrection. Very few Christians have studied natural theology. Not all Christians put their faith in Christ as the result of dreams and visions, or dramatically answered prayer. But all Christians have an awareness of their sin and a recognition that they need a Savior. When Christians hear the message of the gospel, they know it identifies two deep existential truths they have never heard articulated by any other religion or ideology. Thus, like the injured man on the basketball court, they are justified in placing their lives into the hands of the only one who has correctly identified their condition.

Objections to the Christian View of Salvation

Of all the arguments for God's existence, the "argument from the gospel" is usually met with the most resistance. Let me try to address the main objections in what follows.

"My Sin Isn't That Bad"

By far, the most common objection to the argument of these last three chapters is a rejection of the seriousness of sin. Almost everyone realizes that he or she is not morally perfect, that we all have character flaws, and that we make mistakes. However, we are often extremely hesitant to affirm that we are sinners. Moral perfection, we insist, is far too high a standard; and our transgressions are, after all, fairly minor. Therefore, Christianity's diagnosis and its proposed cure are excessive.

The difficulty in responding to this claim is that we seem to be hitting philosophical and existential bedrock. Speaking personally, my awareness of my own moral failure is so central to my experience that to deny it would be as difficult as denying the existence of the external universe. It would be easier for me to believe that I am living in a computer simulation than to believe that I am a moral success. The universality of feelings of guilt, shame, and regret; the reality of our consciences; and the evidence from human history seem to make it next to impossible to deny our sinfulness.

However, it may help to consider that the only alternative to a humble confession of our sin is confidence in our own righteousness. One of the reasons that prostitutes and tax collectors flocked to Jesus was that they knew they were failures. They knew they needed forgiveness and transformation. On the other hand, the moral, religious people rejected him, because they refused to admit that they were just as helpless and corrupt as those they despised.

In the same way, our view of our own sin will lead us into one of only two postures toward those we consider the "bad people." Either we can say, "Thank God that I am not like *those* people; I am one of the good people," or we can say: "The same sin that lives in their hearts lives in mine. I am no different than anyone else. God have mercy on me, a sinner." According to the gospel, the only thing separating us from those we might otherwise despise most is not our goodness but God's grace. That knowledge leads to a genuine humility and gentleness toward those we would be tempted to look down on. Embracing the gospel puts our pride to death. Nothing else will.

If we're still not convinced that we're sinners, let me offer a suggestion that might sound extremely odd coming at the end of a book arguing for the truth of Christianity: don't bother with the evidence for Christianity yet. Until our sin becomes an unavoidable existential reality in our lives, we will see Christianity as—at best—a harmless social pastime. Even if we come to believe intellectually that Christianity is true, we will never actually "repent and believe the good news," since we think we have nothing much to repent of and therefore no good news to believe.

C. S. Lewis puts it this way:

Christianity simply does not make sense until you have faced the sort of facts [about our sinfulness] I have been describing. Christianity tells people to repent and promises them forgiveness. It therefore has nothing (as far as I know) to say to people who do not know they have done anything to repent of and who do not feel that they need any forgiveness. It is after you have realised that there is a real Moral Law, and a Power behind the law, and that you have broken that law and put yourself wrong with that Power—it is after all this, and not a moment sooner, that Christianity begins to talk.[6]

If you don't believe you're a moral failure in need of rescue, it might be more profitable for you to put down this book and pick up Jesus's Sermon on the Mount from the Gospel of Matthew (chaps. 5–7), or the entire Gospel of Luke, or Lewis's *Mere Christianity*, or Charles Spurgeon's *All of Grace*. And if you're willing, I'd recommend doing so in a posture of prayer. Ask God, if he exists, to show you the truth about who you are, and be willing to listen if he answers. Jesus himself declared that he had come not to call the righteous but sinners (Mark 2:17). If you are a righteous person who does not need a Savior, then Jesus has not come for you.

"The Concept of 'Sin' Is Unhealthy and Morally Paralyzing"

Another objection is that obsessing over our own sinfulness is psychologically unhealthy and lazy. The first charge, I believe, is easily dealt with. Constantly thinking about our own sinfulness is indeed unhealthy if we are not actually sinful. In the same way, constantly thinking about pancreatic cancer is unhealthy if we do not actually have cancer. But these thoughts are unhealthy *only if they are untrue.*

6   C. S. Lewis, *Mere Christianity* (New York: Macmillan, 1952), 38–39.

On the other hand, if you actually have pancreatic cancer, then there is nothing healthier than thinking about treatment options, even drastic ones. Only if you are already very confident that you are not sinful do you need to worry that believing in your own sinfulness is morbid.

The charge of laziness is a bit more complicated. It usually emerges from a worry that Christianity's insistence that we are saved by God's grace gives us a license (and perhaps even a desire) to sin. After all, if God forgives us freely, why not go on sinning?[7] Wouldn't it be better to believe in a god who demanded that we earn salvation through our good deeds?

First, it needs to be emphasized that questions of truth can't be decided by pragmatic considerations. For example, we can't reject the idea that pancreatic cancer needs to be treated with chemotherapy on the grounds that this belief might not motivate the patient to exercise. Exercise is excellent, but it does not cure pancreatic cancer. If we are addicted to sin and if our moral transgressions are indelible, then we need God to rescue us, whether or not we think fear of hell or desire for heaven might be a better motivation to moral behavior.

Second, this objection is based on a serious misunderstanding of the nature of repentance. To repent of sin is not only to stop performing certain actions but to change our whole way of thinking about God and about sin. Real repentance necessarily results in a new way of living. Imagine a farmer who has, for years, drunk from a certain well in his fields. After a long hot day, taking a cool, refreshing drink gives him great pleasure. But one day, a local official shows up at his door and announces that the EPA has discovered that all the wells in the area are heavily contaminated with arsenic. The farmer might disbelieve this information, or he might believe it. But if he truly believes it, he will definitely not continue drinking from the well. Similarly, if we have truly "changed our mind" about God and sin, then we will act differ-

---

7   The Bible itself raises the same objection before rejecting it emphatically: "What shall we say then? Are we to continue in sin that grace may abound? By no means! How can we who died to sin still live in it?" (Rom. 6:1–2).

ently. If our behavior is unchanged, then there is good reason to think we have not truly repented.

Moreover, true repentance produces a joyful obedience to God motivated by love and gratitude that fear or a mere sense of duty could never produce. The threat of prison might coerce an abusive husband to change his behavior, but his heart will be just as selfish and violent as before. Only a true repentance that involves seeing himself as he really is and treasuring his wife for who she is will transform both his behavior and his heart. Far from inhibiting moral behavior, the gospel is a tremendous catalyst for moral behavior. When we are no longer motivated by the fear of punishment, we are finally free to serve God out of gratitude and joy.

"If God Transforms Christians, Why Are They So Awful?"

What about the objection that the Christian view of salvation is invalidated by the hatefulness of Christians? If Christians are truly "born again" when they put their trust in Jesus, why are there so many bitter, angry, judgmental Christians? The answer is complicated.

First, we should be careful that we're not caricaturing all Christians as hateful bigots the way others might (wrongly) caricature all Muslims as violent terrorists. As a Christian, I've had the privilege of attending a number of healthy churches and can say with complete truthfulness that the Christians I've known were always among the most generous, kind, and compassionate people I knew wherever I went. Anecdotal evidence is of limited use because we will always find professing Christians whose lives are unchanged by the gospel and professing Christians whose lives are transformed by the gospel. The Bible is quite clear that not all those who profess faith in Christ have actually trusted in and been transformed by Christ. So, unless we are able to sort out who is who, comparisons are difficult.

That said, there is statistical evidence that committed Christians do fare significantly better than both nominal Christians and the nonreligious over a wide range of behaviors, from use of pornography[8] to divorce, adultery, and criminality,[9] to charitable giving.[10] I am hesitant to even mention this data, because it could give the impression that I think "moral behavior" is synonymous with Christianity or that Christians are saved because of their good behavior, which, as I've argued in this chapter, is precisely the opposite of the Christian gospel. Suffice it to say that while Christians do still sin in grievous ways and fall far short of the standard to which God calls us, I do not think it's valid to argue that the gospel is false on the basis of the unchanged lives of Christians.

Lewis offers us one final word of warning:

If what you want is an argument against Christianity . . . you can easily find some stupid and unsatisfactory Christian and say, "So there's

---

8   While concluding that pornography is still a major problem for Christians, a 2016 Barna survey found that "practicing Christians are more than three times less likely to use porn than other teens and adults (13% compared to 42%)." See "Porn in the Digital Age: New Research Reveals 10 Trends," Barna Group, April 6, 2016, https://www.barna.com/.

9   See Bradley R. E. Wright, *Christians Are Hate-Filled Hypocrites . . . and Other Lies You've Been Told: A Sociologists Shatters Myths from the Secular and Christian Media* (Minneapolis: Bethany House, 2010). For example: "Contrary to popular belief, Christians and members of other religions have lower divorce rates, about 42%, than do the religiously unaffiliated, about 50% [and] 60% of [Evangelicals who never attend church] had been divorced or were separated compared to only 38% of the weekly attendees" (133). "Among Christian respondents almost 6% of the men who rarely attended church reported hitting, shoving, or throwing something at their partner in the previous year, compared to only 2% of the weekly attending men [and 6–8 percent of the religiously unaffiliated]" (136). "16% of Evangelicals reported that they had committed adultery at some time in their life. . . . Mainline Protestants, Catholics, and Jews all reported similarly low levels of 14 to 16%. Black Protestants and the religiously unaffiliated reported the highest rates of extramarital sex, at about 25%" (139). "Overall, Protestants were the least criminal of the respondents. For example, 9% of the Protestants had been arrested, which was less than the 11% of Catholics, 13% of other religions, and 15% of the religiously unaffiliated. . . . Weekly attendees [at churches] had crime levels that were about half as high as the other, less-frequently-attending Protestants" (145).

10   The average nonreligious person in the United States gives 0.7 percent of his or her income to charity, while the average Christian gives 2.9 percent, and the average Christian who regularly attends church gives 6.2 percent. Similarly, the fraction of people who give away 10 percent or more of their income each year is 0.6 percent for the nonreligious, 9.4 percent for all Christians, and 17.9 percent for Christians who regularly attend church. See table 2.1 in Christian Smith, Michael O. Emerson, and Patricia Snell, *Passing the Plate: Why American Christians Don't Give Away More Money* (Oxford: Oxford University Press, 2008), 30.

your boasted new man! Give me the old kind." But if once you have begun to see that Christianity is on other grounds probable, you will know in your heart that this is only evading the issue. What can you ever really know of other people's souls—of their temptations, their opportunities, their struggles? One soul in the whole creation you do know: and it is the only one whose fate is placed in your hands. If there is a God, you are, in a sense, alone with Him. You cannot put Him off with speculations about your next door neighbors or memories of what you have read in books.[11]

"No Historical Adam Means No Need for a Savior"

Traditionally, Christians have believed that humanity arose from an original human pair, Adam and Eve, whose disobedience to God led to the corruption of humanity. To my surprise, the claim that we have no need for a Savior because there was no historical Adam is fairly common on the Internet. This objection may arise partially from a misunderstanding of Christian doctrine. For instance, Christopher Hitchens protests that "the agony [of Jesus's crucifixion] was *necessary* in order to compensate for an earlier crime in which I also had no part, the sin of Adam."[12] Similarly, Jerry Coyne writes, "If there was no original sin transmitted to Adam's descendants, then Jesus's Crucifixion and Resurrection expiated nothing: it was a solution without a problem."[13] Both of these statements seem to imply that, according to Christianity, Jesus died only to save us from Adam and Eve's sin.

This notion is wildly incorrect. While Catholics, Protestants, and the Orthodox differ on precisely how the fall is connected to our sin,[14]

---

11 Lewis, *Mere Christianity*, 182–83.

12 Christopher Hitchens, *God Is Not Great: How Religion Poisons Everything* (New York: Twelve, 2007), 209.

13 Jerry A. Coyne, *Faith versus Fact: Why Science and Religion Are Incompatible* (New York: Viking, 2015), 128.

14 Briefly, the Orthodox generally believe that Adam's fall corrupted us but did not render us guilty, while Catholics and Protestants believe that the fall rendered human beings both corrupt and guilty.

they all emphatically agree that Jesus came not only to reverse the consequences of Adam's sin but also to save us from the myriad sins we each personally commit. Even if Adam and Eve had never sinned, our personal sin would still require redemption through Jesus. To put it another way, the doctrine of a historical fall is an explanation of *why* human beings are sinful, not the basis for the claim that we *are* sinful.

Think about the following illustration: In the 2007 Will Smith film *I Am Legend*, humanity is almost entirely wiped out by a pandemic that kills billions and turns most of the few survivors into vampire-like creatures. The pandemic was accidentally caused by a measles virus genetically modified by Dr. Alice Krippin to cure cancer. Will Smith's character is an Army virologist desperately trying to find an antidote. Imagine a person living in this terrifying alternate reality. Will all their vampire problems be solved if they deny that the Krippin virus ever existed? Will they have any less need of a cure for vampirism? Can they now blithely wander down dark alleys in the middle of the night with no need to fear for their lives? Of course not. In the same way, we can recognize the radical sinfulness of humanity and our need for a Savior without any reference to an explanation for why humanity is in this state.

While I affirm the importance of the doctrine of a historic Adam,[15] it is distinct from the two issues I've discussed in this chapter. Even if we reject the traditional Christian understanding of *why* we are so radically sinful, that in no way diminishes the fact that we *are* radically sinful and need a Savior.[16]

---

15 See, for example, Tim Keller's white paper "Creation, Evolution, and Christian Laypeople," Bio-Logos, February 23, 2012, https://biologos.org/.

16 As someone with no expertise in population genetics, I find it difficult to evaluate the evidence for or against a historical Adam. An up-to-date discussion of the genetic evidence against the existence of a single ancestral pair from a Christian perspective can be found in Dennis R. Venema and Scot McKnight, *Adam and the Genome: Reading Scripture after Genetic Science* (Grand Rapids, MI: Brazos, 2017). A valuable resource is a paper by Professor Kenneth Keathley that examines three different proposals from conservative Christians on how to reconcile a historical Adam with the findings of genetics: Kenneth D. Keathley, "Rescuing Adam: The Approaches to Affirming the

"Why Did Jesus Have to Die?"

Finally, many people are repelled by the idea of substitutionary atonement. Why couldn't God just forgive? Why did Jesus have to die? Couldn't God have found some other way?

Two responses are in order.

First, what would it mean for God to "just forgive" our sin? Is that even possible? Pastor Tim Keller offers the following illustration: Imagine that a stranger enters my home and breaks a lamp on my table. I have only two options. On the one hand, I could refuse to forgive him and force him to pay the cost of the lamp. On the other hand, I could choose to forgive him. In that case, I absorb the cost of the lamp myself, either by buying a new one or by going without light in my house. In either case, someone pays the debt.[17]

In the same way, when others hurt us deeply, we can retaliate, inflicting the same harm on them that they did to us. Or we can forgive them. But forgiveness itself is costly. Whenever we see them, we choose to put aside our hurt, we forgo retaliation, we swallow our anger. We pay the debt ourselves. In a moral universe, we can't ask the debt to evaporate. When it comes to our sin, the most we can hope is that God will absorb the moral debt we incurred. And he did. In the person of his Son, he paid our debt in nails and tears and a crown of thorns and a cry of "Eloi, eloi, lama sabacthani" ("My God, my God, why have you forsaken me?" Mark 15:34).

Second, as pressing as this question sounds, I don't think it's relevant. I remember wrestling with exactly this issue when I began graduate

---

Historical Adam," *Southeastern Theological Review* 8, no. 1 (2017): 55–76. On balance, I think that from a secular perspective genetics provides some evidence against a single ancestral human pair (which is actually a separate claim from the existence of a historical Adam) but that such evidence cannot definitively rule out a single ancestral pair, mainly because quantitative models that project tens to hundreds of thousands of years into the distant past are sensitive to assumptions that are difficult to test.

17 Timothy Keller, *King's Cross: The Story of the World in the Life of Jesus* (New York: Dutton, 2011), 100–101.

school. I had been attending church with my future wife, I had heard the gospel, and I was beginning to see my own sinfulness and my need for rescue. However, I was stuck on the question *why*: Why the need for a crucifixion? Why did it have to be this way? I'm not entirely sure when the answer came to me, but it seems so clear in retrospect: What if it simply *is* this way? If it cost the very life of God's Son to rescue me, who am I to turn down that sacrifice? If God's forgiveness really was so infinitely costly, how dare I refuse it?

In these last three chapters, I've argued that Christianity is unique in its presentation of two fundamental truths about each of us: that we are all moral failures and that we all need a Savior. On the one hand, Christianity has what is perhaps the most radically pessimistic view of humanity of any religion or worldview. We are fallen and hopelessly corrupt. The horrors we see around the world, throughout history, and in our own lives are not aberrations but symptoms of the evil that lives in all our hearts. On the other hand, Christianity has a radically optimistic view of God's grace. Although we are all equally fallen, we are all equally redeemable. If salvation were based on our goodness, our effort or our ability, then there would be a scale of redemption: some people would be more deserving of salvation than others. But if salvation is based not on our merit but only on God's mercy, then no one is outside its scope, and no one can boast in his or her own goodness.

These two doctrines, which lie at the very heart of Christianity, have incredible explanatory power. They explain why we see such misery in the world today. They explain why even the best of us are stained with evil. They explain why many of us have an insatiable longing for reconciliation and acceptance that we seek to fill with money, careers, or human relationships. They explain why our moral striving cannot cleanse us. The gospel is not just the central message of Christianity; it is the best evidence for its truth. Speaking personally, Christianity is the only religion or worldview or philosophy that correctly identifies the disease I know I have and the cure I know I need.

10

Conclusions

Why will you die, O house of Israel?

EZEKIEL 18:31

LET'S RETURN TO THE QUESTION with which this book began: "Why should we think that Christianity is true?" We are now better equipped to give an answer.

Chapter 2 outlined C. S. Lewis's trilemma: Jesus was a liar or a lunatic or the Lord. More succinctly, Jesus makes such outrageous claims of authority and demands such complete allegiance that he is either an evil megalomaniac or God. Because this argument depends on the general historical reliability of the biblical accounts of Jesus, I showed that the historicity of the Gospels is supported by numerous lines of evidence, ranging from the accuracy of textual transmission and corroboration by non-Christian writers to confirmation by archaeology and onomastic studies. If the biblical picture of Jesus is generally accurate, then each of us is confronted with the person of Jesus himself speaking to us through the Bible and calling us to repentance and faith. We can reject him or accept him, but we cannot evade him.

Next, we examined evidence for the resurrection of Jesus, the claim that Jesus rose physically from the dead after being crucified. Although this claim has obvious religious implications, it is also a historical claim that can be studied through historical investigation. As it turns out, a number of well-known non-Christians are willing to concede that there is historical evidence for the resurrection, including but not limited to the historicity of the empty tomb, the numerous appearances of Jesus after his death, and the conversion of skeptics like the apostle Paul. The debate turns not on whether there is any evidence at all but on the strength of the evidence: Is it sufficient to compel belief? My contention is that the implausibility of the alternative naturalistic explanations of the evidence, like the hypothetical existence of a "twin Jesus," ought to make skeptics uneasy. If skeptics must resort to what are—by their own admission—highly implausible theories to avoid the Christian explanation, then can they really claim that their skepticism is rooted in the evidence? Or is it driven by their assumptions about the existence of God?

In the fourth and fifth chapters, I outlined some of the evidence for God's existence. According to the Bible, the universe is the product of an infinitely powerful, infinitely wise, perfectly good, and perfectly holy Creator. Several features of the universe support this claim. That the universe possesses a deep and deeply beautiful mathematical structure, that it appears to have come into being in the finite past, and that the laws of physics are exquisitely finely tuned for life all fit naturally into a biblical framework but prove much more difficult to explain if God does not exist. The existence of God also provides a basis for objective moral values and duties that is not available to atheism. In particular, our moral obligation to seek true answers to ultimate questions about reality is predicated on the existence of a God who commands us to seek such knowledge. While it may be possible to construct alternate explanations for some of these phenomena, I argued that the evidence is much more consistent with theism than with atheism.

Chapter 6 explored the three most common objections to belief in God: the problem of evil, evolution, and divine hiddenness. I argued, first, that evil is a problem for all worldviews, not just for Christianity. The existence of objective evil arguably poses an even greater difficulty for atheists than for theists, because atheists lack the resources of theism to explain what grounds the concepts of good and evil. In contrast, Christianity has rich resources to draw upon in explaining why a good and loving God could permit the existence of evil. Second, I carefully defined evolution and showed that the main disagreement between a Darwinian view of naturalistic evolution, on the one hand, and intelligent design or theistic evolution, on the other, is in how we understand the "randomness" in "random mutation." If we define these words carefully, we do not run into problems affirming God's guidance of natural processes. Moreover, we find that it is very hard to imagine observations that would rule out intentional or supernatural intervention in large-scale evolutionary processes, which is the source of most of the discomfort surrounding evolution among conservative Christians. Finally, I addressed the alleged lack of evidence for God's existence, pointing out not only that evidence is readily available but also that volitional obstacles rather than a lack of evidence constitute the fundamental barrier between us and God. In the absence of compelling evidence for atheism, the arguments of natural theology then provide us with good reasons to believe that God exists.

Although we can know something of God from the universe he created and from our moral experience, we should not stop there. On the Christian view, God reveals himself through both his works in nature and his words in Scripture. If the God who created the entire universe and all of its beauty has spoken into human history, then it seems only natural that we should want to know him intimately. Yet we find that it is far more comfortable to settle for an impersonal, deistic force or a benevolent Santa Claus in the sky than to risk contact with a holy, righteous, and morally perfect God. A real God issuing real moral commands is threatening. Why? Because we are sinners. The subject of our alienation from God through sin and the solution that Christianity offers was the focus of chapters 7–9.

The final major section of the book was devoted to the idea that the Christian understanding of sin and salvation is itself evidence that Christianity is true. Of the five world religions that account for more than 90 percent of all religious adherents on the planet, Christianity is unique in identifying humanity's fundamental problem as sin and the fundamental solution as salvation, or rescue. While other religions share many beliefs with Christianity, they differ in their views of the seriousness of human moral failure and its remedy. By itself, this distinctiveness does not prove that Christianity is true, since many religions are distinctive in one way or another. But if we have evidence that we truly are moral failures and that we need comprehensive rescue instead of moral improvement or self-help, then we have good reasons to believe that Christianity is true.

The universality and depth of human sinfulness can be seen in many ways. An overview of human history shows that there has never been a time when human beings weren't killing, torturing, and abusing each other. Wars and genocide have swept across the planet leaving a bloody wake. Human violence is not a product of modern living conditions but is found in the most distant and isolated people groups. Babies begin to exhibit aggressive behavior as soon as they can communicate. The biting and scratching of infants give way to the tantrums of toddlers, the bullying of young children, the rebellion of adolescents, and the selfishness of adults.

Apart from empirical studies of human violence, each of us has immediate access to our own hearts and knows how far we fall short of our own standards, let alone God's standards. Anger, lust, bitterness, jealousy, and self-righteousness lurk just beneath the surface of our actions, which is why we are so hesitant to let other people see inside our lives. To admit the truth is to confess that we are in desperate need, that we are moral failures, and that we are enslaved to our self-absorption.

This admission is a blow that our pride desperately resists. Yet the evidence of history and our own honest introspection reveal that it is the plain truth, even if it is almost impossible for us to stare it in the face.

The good news of Christianity is that no matter how terrible our sin, there is salvation in Christ. In his old age John Newton, a former slave trader who authored the hymn "Amazing Grace," said, "My memory is nearly gone, but I remember two things: that I am a great sinner and that Christ is a great Savior."[1] *Christianity never seeks to minimize our sin. It does not downplay our wickedness or gloss over our rebellion. But it magnifies God's love. It offers restoration and reconciliation to us not because we are good but because God is good.* In his life, death, and resurrection, Jesus acted as our substitute. He lived the life that we should have lived, loving God and loving his neighbor perfectly. And on the cross, he died the death we deserved to die as rebels against our good and gracious Creator.[2] In his resurrection, Jesus announced that the penalty for our sin is fully paid and offered us healing and forgiveness, not on the basis of our good deeds but despite our bad ones.

This last argument is the way most people come to know the truth of Christianity.[3] While people can be convinced (and I hope are convinced!) by other arguments, a profound awareness of our sin and need for rescue is not only necessary but sufficient to lead us to trust in Christ.

What's Missing from This Book

Given the extensive discussions in this book on topics as diverse as textual criticism, evolutionary theory, and world religions, some

---

1   Jonathan Aitken, *John Newton: From Disgrace to Amazing Grace* (Wheaton, IL: Crossway, 2007), 347.

2   Tim Keller has used this summary of the gospel in many places. For instance, it can be found in Timothy Keller and Kathy Keller, *The Meaning of Marriage: Facing the Complexities of Commitment with the Wisdom of God* (New York: Dutton, 2011), 69.

3   Although I do not know if this argument has been developed elsewhere, it contains echoes of Pascal's anthropological argument. See Douglas Groothuis, *Christian Apologetics: A Comprehensive Case for Biblical Faith* (Downers Grove, IL: InterVarsity, 2011), 418–37.

readers may wonder why there was so little discussion of Christian doctrine, particularly issues that are especially troubling to modern people. For example, how could a loving God send anyone to hell? Doesn't Christianity squelch creativity and individuality? Why is God so vengeful and angry in the Old Testament? Why is the Christian sexual ethic so backward and repressive? In books of this sort, which argue for the truth of Christianity, such questions are usually given a prominent place.

I do not think these issues should be lightly dismissed, and I highly recommend Tim Keller's *The Reason for God* for those who would like to explore the answers Christianity provides.[4] However, I deliberately set those issues aside to make an extremely important point: the truth of Christianity (or of anything else, for that matter) does not depend on whether we like it. We may at first find Christianity disgusting, repressive, repugnant, and deserving of an entire thesaurus entry's worth of pejoratives. But, for all that, Christianity might still be true.

This reminder is vital for us today, in a culture driven by consumerism and personal autonomy. We naturally assume that any product that does not meet every one of our precise specifications can and should be discarded for a better model. The problem with this approach is that Christianity is not a product, and God is not trying to market it to us.

Perhaps it will help to turn the tables. Imagine an atheist trying to convince a Christian that God does not exist. The Christian responds to the atheist's reasoned arguments by saying: "I just can't believe in a universe without a loving God. It sounds so sad and miserable. What about suffering people who die in despair without any hope of redemption? What about the purposelessness of life? What about all the moral practices that you say are acceptable but that I've been taught are wrong? No, I refuse to believe in a reality like that!" The atheist would presumably make the same point I am making: reality does not require

---

4   Timothy Keller, *The Reason for God: Belief in an Age of Skepticism* (New York: Penguin, 2008).

our approval, and our feelings don't alter the truth. Reality is reality, and if we accept it at all, we must accept it on its own terms, not ours.

In this way, theology done properly is a great deal like science done properly. As scientists, we don't refuse to move beyond our assumptions about the way reality "ought to be." We may indeed have preconceptions and intuitions and favored theories. Everyone does. But at the end of the day, we need to be willing to submit ourselves to the way things actually are, not the way we want things to be. In a wonderful, though apocryphal, exchange between Albert Einstein and Niels Bohr, Einstein objects to the disturbing randomness of quantum mechanics by saying, "God does not play dice with the universe." Bohr replies, "Albert, stop telling God what to do with His dice."[5] While Einstein and Bohr were discussing physics rather than theology, we should ideally have the same attitude toward God. God is who he is, and our preferences don't change that. Our emotions and affections need to be brought into line with God's character, not vice versa.

The need for some semblance of objectivity in theology is part of what makes the Bible so important. If the Bible is inspired by God, then our attitude toward it reflects our attitude toward him. Yes, many things in the Bible are hard to understand. Yes, there are things in the Bible that I misinterpret. I am not denying that there will always be an element of subjectivity—at best—and insincerity—at worst—in our reading of the Bible. But at the end of the day, are we willing to say to God: "You are God and I am not. I trust that your ways are right, even when I don't understand them"? Or will we insist that God conform to our standards and our preferences before we yield our lives to him?

---

5 Quantum mechanics has always engendered resistance due to its staggeringly counterintuitive implications. While explaining quantum mechanics, Richard Feynman cautioned his students: "Do not keep saying to yourself, if you can possibly avoid it, 'But how can it be like that?' because you will get 'down the drain,' into a blind alley from which nobody has escaped. Nobody knows how it can be like that." Feynman, "The Character of Physical Law" (lecture series at Cornell University, 1964), quoted in John Gribbin, *Q Is for Quantum: An Encyclopedia of Particle Physics* (1998; repr., New York: Simon & Schuster, 2000), 9.

That's more than a question about the Bible; it's a question about our hearts. In a culture like ours, in which feelings are exalted, we need to be reminded that our feelings must be restrained by and conformed to the truth of who God is.

The View from Somewhere

Hopefully, I've been able to convince you that there is at least some evidence for the truth of Christianity. However, you may still have many questions. You may see what look like inconsistencies within the Christian faith that make you hesitant to consider it. You may also feel that the complicated responses of Christian philosophers, theologians, and apologists wouldn't be necessary if Christianity were true.

If so, it's worth keeping in mind that every worldview has points of tension that require philosophical defenses; the existence of vigorous philosophical disagreement over a claim does not show that the claim is false.[6] Moreover, we can't evaluate religions or philosophies except on the basis of another religion or philosophy. There is no "view from no-where" that gives us an accurate picture of the strengths and weaknesses of every worldview apart from any underlying assumptions whatsoever.

For example, Christianity has traditionally taught that there is no salvation outside of Christ. But does this teaching make Christianity less likely to be true or more likely to be true? It depends on your underlying assumptions about the nature of reality. If you assume, like conservative Muslims, that there is one true path to God, then this teaching makes Christianity seem more likely to be true because it, like Islam, rejects the idea that all paths to God are equally valid. On the other hand, if you're a religious inclusivist, this teaching makes Christianity seem less

---

6   If philosophical disagreement over a claim entailed its falsity, then nearly all philosophical claims would be false, since there are hardly any views on which philosophers are in complete agreement. In 2009, Philpapers did an interesting survey of 3,226 professional philosophers. On only one question out of thirty was the consensus greater than 80 percent (81.6 percent of philosophers agree that we can be non-skeptical that external reality exists). Of the other twenty-nine questions, the most popular answers rarely achieved the consent of more than 60 percent of those surveyed.

likely to be true since it conflicts with your belief that all religions are equally valid. Either way, your evaluation of Christianity won't be a completely objective assessment. It will be colored by your prior beliefs about the nature of reality.

Even seemingly uncontroversial objections like purported scientific errors or logical contradictions are based on philosophical precommitments. For instance, the application of the laws of logic to religion assumes that the laws of logic are universally valid and as applicable to spirituality as to everyday reasoning, an idea that not every religion affirms. Appeals to the findings of science are honeycombed with all kinds of philosophical assumptions about the regularity of nature, the reliability of our senses, and the validity of induction. Lest there be any doubt, I am not arguing that the laws of logic or the scientific enterprise should be abandoned. Christianity affirms both. I'm merely observing that there are few, if any, self-interpreting observations that stand entirely outside of any philosophical or religious framework.

For this reason, we should be willing to recognize and critically examine our own worldviews alongside our critical examination of Christianity. Three questions are particularly relevant: What does my worldview explain? Is it coherent? And is it livable? First, *what does it explain?* That is, what features of my own experience and of reality in general does my worldview acknowledge and address? Conversely, what features of my own experience and of reality does my worldview reject as illusory or meaningless? Second, *is it coherent?* Do its beliefs "fit together," or are they logically contradictory? Third, *is it livable?* Can I operate consistently within my worldview in practice, or is it a purely theoretical construct that I must abandon as soon as I enter the real world? In thinking critically about worldviews, we can't exempt our own, whether we're Christians, Buddhists, atheists, pantheists, or agnostics. Realizing that our own worldviews have apparent inconsistencies that require careful analysis means that apparent inconsistencies within Christianity are no reason to peremptorily reject it.

If you're not a Christian, ask yourself: What are the major obstacles between me and the Christian faith? Does Christianity entail certain moral or theological positions I strongly dislike? Has my experience with professing Christians so repulsed me that I want no part of their religion? Do doctrines like the deity of Christ or the sovereignty of God appear incomprehensible? It's worth making a list of your objections and being as honest as possible. What would it take for you to move from skepticism to faith in Christ?

But what if the arguments in this book have moved you to seriously consider Christianity? What comes next? How do you become a Christian? The answer is simple, if shockingly out of fashion: repent and believe. "Repent and believe in the gospel" is the message with which Jesus began his ministry (Mark 1:15), and it is the message that Christians proclaim today.

The Logic of Repentance

Before I explain these terms any further, let me take a brief detour to avoid a fatal misunderstanding. When people hear the word *repentance*, they immediately think of moral reformation. They conjure up lists of immoral behavior they need to stop and moral behavior they need to start. Now, I have no problem with people turning from their immoral behavior and seeking to live morally. The world would be a better place if people stopped lying, committing adultery, and oppressing the poor. But repentance goes far deeper than mere behavioral change.

The Greek word for "repentance" is *metanoia*, which literally means "change of mind." Repentance is a radical change of mind about sin and about God. If the essence of sin is loving and valuing anything more than God, then repentance is coming to the realization that God is more beautiful and more valuable than anything else. Repentance leads to changed behavior, but it is far more than changed behavior.

Imagine two teenage boys who have drifted apart from their parents. For years, they both sit sullenly through dinner, roll their eyes at every comment, and mock their parents in public. But one day, they both decide to repair their relationships. They begin carrying on conversations at meals. They start doing their neglected household chores. They speak respectfully. They even awkwardly submit to the occasional hug. All this behavior continues until the day of their high school graduation. Then the first son leaves home and never speaks to his parents again, while the second son's gradual transformation continues. Why?

The first son wanted his parents to buy him a car for graduation and realized he would be more likely to get one if he was a dutiful child. When his parents didn't deliver, he abandoned his polite behavior and turned his back on them for good. In contrast, the second son had accidentally stumbled across an old photo album he had crammed under his bed. He found dozens of pictures that brought back all kinds of happy memories from his childhood: making cushion forts, celebrating birthdays, taking vacations. He realized how much his parents loved him and how badly he was treating them. It suddenly broke his heart. He could no longer go on acting as he had; he no longer wanted to.

These two sons exemplify the difference between behavior modification and biblical repentance. When we see God as supremely valuable, our behavior inevitably changes. We begin to love what he loves and abhor what he abhors. We begin to speak to him in prayer and listen to his voice in Scripture. We begin to follow Jesus's commands and join with other Christians in the local church. But when God is calling us to repent, he is not primarily calling us to improve our behavior. He is calling us to give him the place in our lives that he has always deserved. Seen this way, repentance is not a state of impulsive, emotional fervor; instead, it's an entirely rational response to reality.

Think for a moment of the Christian view of God. He is the author of every truly beautiful thing you've ever seen or heard or experienced. His voice whispers to you in the rustling leaves and in the patter of rain. God is the ground and source of all good, whether you see it in the love between friends, in the devotion of a husband to his wife, or in a toddler clasping her mother's hand. You can see his grandeur in the night sky or from a cliff overlooking the ocean. Even the greatest beauty the world has to offer is only the barest glimpse of God's infinite and all-satisfying goodness.

Forget for a moment whether Christianity is true or false. Hypothetically, if Christianity is true, what is the only rational response to a God like this? Worship. Utter delight, awe, praise, and amazement. A repentant heart supremely values this infinitely good God not merely because he commands it but also because he is so consummately worthy of it. In contrast, an unrepentant heart is not merely wicked; it is irrational. Anyone who would trade the eternal, certain, and infinite pleasure of knowing and delighting in God for the fleeting, uncertain, finite pleasures of this life is a madman. As C. S. Lewis says, "We are half-hearted creatures, fooling about with drink and sex and ambition when infinite joy is offered us, like an ignorant child who wants to go on making mud pies in a slum because he cannot imagine what is meant by the offer of a holiday at the sea."[7]

But there is a problem. None of us fully and completely gives God the significance in our lives that he truly deserves. Speaking personally, I struggle to keep God in my thoughts for more than a few minutes at a time. I'm sluggish in prayer, dull in joy, and complacent in service. If we were honest with ourselves, many of us would have to admit that we find it easier to take pleasure in watching a YouTube cat video than in worshiping the Creator of the entire universe. While this might seem like a minor, unavoidable failing, it is the root of all the most spectacular evil we commit. We murder because we do not properly value the image of God in other human beings. We steal because we value created things more than their Creator. We covet because we don't truly believe that God is what we most need. Ultimately, whenever we

---

7   C. S. Lewis, *The Weight of Glory and Other Addresses* (1949; repr., New York: HarperSanFrancisco, 1980), 26.

violate God's law, whether in small ways or large, we do so because we value our own desires more highly than we value God.

If our repentance is always flawed, imperfect, and half-hearted, how can anyone be saved? And where does true repentance come from? Can we just grit our teeth and resolve to love God more?

The answer to those questions is found in the second half of Jesus's command: "Believe the gospel."

By Grace through Faith

The great nineteenth-century Baptist preacher Charles Spurgeon opens his book *All of Grace* this way:

> A minister called upon a poor woman, intending to give her help; for he knew that she was very poor. With his money in his hand, he knocked at the door; but she did not answer. He concluded she was not at home, and went his way. A little after he met her at the church, and told her that he had remembered her need: "I called at your house, and knocked several times, and I suppose you were not at home, for I had no answer." "At what hour did you call, sir?" "It was about noon." "Oh, dear," she said, "I heard you, sir, and I am so sorry I did not answer; but *I thought it was the man calling for the rent.*" . . . Now, it is my desire to be heard, and therefore I want to say that I am not calling for the rent; indeed, it is not the object of this book to ask anything of you, but to tell you that salvation is ALL OF GRACE, which means, *free, gratis, for nothing.*
>
> Oftentimes . . . our hearer thinks, "Ah! now I am going to be told my duty. It is the man calling for that which is due to God, and I am sure I have nothing wherewith to pay. I will not be at home." No, this book does not come to make a demand upon you, but to bring you something. We are not going to talk about law, and duty, and punishment, but about love, and goodness, and forgiveness, and mercy, and eternal life. Do not, therefore, act as if you were not at

home: do not turn a deaf ear, or a careless heart. I am asking nothing of you in the name of God or man. It is not my intent to make any requirement at your hands; but I come in God's name, to bring you a free gift, which it shall be to your present and eternal joy to receive.[8]

If a superficial understanding of repentance is one fatal mistake, then a merit-based understanding of repentance is another. If we see repentance as something that we give to God to earn forgiveness, then we will obscure the gospel.

The Christian message is good news, not good advice.[9] The gospel is an announcement of what God has done to rescue hopelessly sinful human beings, not advice on how we can improve ourselves and earn our salvation. Salvation is, as Spurgeon wrote, "all of grace," meaning that it is entirely and completely unmerited, undeserved, and free. There is nothing we can do to earn it. It is ours to receive as a gift.

The gospel provides the answer to the questions posed at the end of the previous section. First, the gospel is the news that Jesus came to live a perfect life, to suffer, to die for my sins, and to rise to life to secure salvation for me. Those sins include not just my immoral behavior but also my coldness toward God, my indifference, and my half-hearted repentance. After all, Jesus said that the greatest commandment is to "love the Lord your God with all your heart and with all your soul and with all your strength and with all your mind" (Luke 10:27). I have broken this commandment no less than the others. Yet Jesus covers over even my imperfect repentance with his perfect forgiveness.

Second, the gospel is the power that fuels love for God. Clenching your fist and setting your will to love God is not only insufficient but, on reflection, dishonoring. Imagine that your spouse came to you and

8   Charles Spurgeon, *All of Grace* (Fort Worth, TX: RDMc, 2001), 9–10.

9   This phrase has been repeated so frequently that it's difficult for me to find the original source. I've heard it in sermons from Tim Keller and J. D. Greear, and it appears in books by N. T. Wright and Michael Horton, but I don't know who first articulated it.

said: "I've resolved to love you. I know it's my moral obligation. As a conscientious spouse, I'll grit my teeth and do it, even if it kills me." Wouldn't you feel insulted? All of us want to be loved not out of a sense of obligation but spontaneously. In the same way, a heart overflowing with gratitude and gripped with God's beauty confers more honor on God than half-hearted service motivated only by duty or fear.

The gospel is what creates this spontaneous, overflowing love toward God. When we clearly see and embrace the amazing news that God so loved us that he sent Jesus to rescue us, it is then that we begin to truly treasure God. Only the sight of the Son of God suffering in the place of sinners will finally break our hardened hearts and set God in his rightful place. In one of his holy sonnets, the English poet John Donne captured this dynamic perfectly:

> I, like an usurp'd town to another due,
> Labor to admit you, but oh, to no end;
> Reason, your viceroy in me, me should defend,
> But is captiv'd, and proves weak or untrue.
> Yet dearly I love you, and would be lov'd fain,
> But am betroth'd unto your enemy;
> Divorce me, untie or break that knot again,
> Take me to you, imprison me, for I,
> Except you enthrall me, never shall be free,
> Nor ever chaste, except you ravish me.[10]

What we need is not ultimately more information or more resolve or more zeal. We need God to overthrow and crush our stubborn, irrational, defiant self-reliance so that he can bind us up. We need him to make us new people who value him supremely and trust in him to save us. We need him to heal our blind eyes so they can see his beauty.

10 John Donne, "Holy Sonnets: Batter My Heart, Three-Person'd God," Poetry Foundation, accessed September 3, 2021, https://www.poetryfoundation.org/.

A Christian is someone who has obeyed Jesus's command to repent and believe the good news. Christians have turned to God and turned their lives over to God, recognizing that he is their greatest good. They have trusted God's promise that he will forgive their sins and reconcile them to him not on the basis of their good works but on the basis of Jesus's work on the cross for them. Repentance and belief are not confined to the moment we become Christians; they characterize the believer's whole life. Every day of our lives, we turn again to God as our greatest good and trust again in his promise to bless us for Christ's sake.

The Good News of the Kingdom

One final aspect of the biblical message that is occasionally neglected by evangelical Christians is the centrality of God's kingdom. Jesus's command to "repent and believe" was prefaced by this announcement: "The time is fulfilled, and the kingdom of God is at hand" (Mark 1:15). The kingdom of God is his breaking into human history to bring healing and salvation. Although the kingdom of God will come fully and finally at the end of history, we can have a foretaste of it now. When we become Christians, we begin to experience the healing of God in our own lives, and we become agents for bringing God's healing into the world. One day, God will wipe away every tear from every eye; therefore, Christians strive to comfort the suffering and bind up the brokenhearted. One day, God will heal all disease and sickness; therefore, Christians serve in hospitals and clinics around the world bringing medicine and healing in Christ's name. One day, justice will roll down like waters, and righteousness like a mighty stream;[11] therefore, Christians work for justice today.

Just as Christians are called out of sin and into God's kingdom, we are also called out of our alienation and into God's family. God's kingdom

---

11   See Amos 5:24, which was cited by Martin Luther King Jr. in his famous "I Have a Dream" speech.

is made visible among his people, the church.[12] Christians were never meant to live in isolation from each other. It is in the church that we learn to love one another and tear down the barriers that our sin has erected between ethnic groups, genders, and socioeconomic classes. It is in deep friendship and transparency with other followers of Jesus that we learn to confess our sin, give and receive forgiveness, and celebrate the gospel in baptism and the Lord's Supper.

I realize that many people have been hurt by broken, lifeless churches, but we shouldn't assume that this experience is the norm. The churches to which I have belonged in Berkeley, New Haven, and Durham were filled with people from diverse ethnic, racial, educational, and political backgrounds. Through the church, I have become friends with former drug addicts and alcoholics, refugees, university professors, stay-at-home moms, and hedge-fund managers. We loved each other not because we had so much in common socially, ethnically, economically, and educationally but because we shared a common commitment to Jesus Christ. My current church has ministries to refugees, the homeless, orphans and widows, prisoners, unwed mothers, and at-risk youth. It invests tens (perhaps hundreds) of thousands of hours and millions of dollars into caring for the least-served members of our community. It actively supports dozens of foster families in our congregation and offers matching funds to the many families pursuing adoption. All of these activities enumerate only the official functions of the church. Informally, I've seen Christians all around me serving the common good through daily acts of mercy, kindness, and compassion. The sacrificial love of the Christians I've known flows out of a passionate desire to see God's kingdom come.

If you are still not ready to commit to Christ, spend time with his followers and among his people. Serve with them. Study the Bible with them. Get to know them. God is not limited to working within and

---

12 In the Bible, the word *church* refers not to a building or an institution but to people gathered together in the name of Christ.

through the church, but it is the primary means through which God extends his salvation into the world.

The Step of Faith

People occasionally refer to Christian belief as a "leap of faith," a decision to blindly accept a proposition in the absence of any evidence. This claim is incorrect, for two reasons. First, there is no absence of evidence when it comes to Christianity. The evidence for God is all around us, the evidence for the lordship of Jesus Christ ripples through history, and our need for the gospel grips every heart. But, second, and more subtly, this claim misunderstands the nature of faith. As I discussed in chapter 4, biblical faith is not mere intellectual assent to a proposition but personal trust.

In this sense, you and I exercise faith on a daily basis. When you get into an airplane trusting that it will carry you safely to your destination, when you place yourself under the knife of a surgeon trusting that she can restore your health, or when you say your marriage vows trusting that your spouse will honor them, you are exercising faith. Indeed, when it comes to the ultimate questions of life, the absence of faith is an impossibility. The Christian is resting all the weight of his life on the truth of the gospel; if it is false, then "we are of all people most to be pitied" (1 Cor. 15:19). The choices and sacrifices Christians make would be sheer foolishness if they were based on a lie. In the same way, the Muslim is resting all the weight of his life on the truthfulness of Muhammad's message and the Buddhist is resting all the weight of his life on the veracity of the Buddha's message. Even the atheist and the agnostic are resting the weight of their lives on God's nonexistence; if it turns out in the end that God does exist, they will look back on their lives and realize they have squandered them, investing in things that don't matter and ignoring things that do.

For this reason, it's better to think of commitment to Christ as a step of faith rather than a leap of faith. Coming to a personal trust in

God is not a matter of whipping yourself into an emotional frenzy to believe something for which you have no evidence. Instead, it is a decision to move from contemplating a truth to actively relying on it. Picture a man standing at the end of a pier as a boat is about to embark. He is intellectually confident that the boat is seaworthy, that it has an experienced and trustworthy captain, and that it will reach its destination. He "believes in" the boat. But does he have faith in the boat? Not until he steps onto the deck and entrusts himself to it. He must transfer his weight from the shore to the boat, trusting it to carry him safely home. The Puritans used to speak of faith as "recumbency," placing all the weight of one's life on the truth of the gospel. Saving faith means entrusting yourself and the weight of your whole life to Jesus, saying to him: "I am yours. I trust in you to rescue me."

I remember the night that the claims of Christianity first came home to me. I had been attending church for a few weeks with my future wife, Christina, and had realized that I could no longer dismiss the gospel as intellectually indefensible. But the fact that I had to take Christianity seriously was troubling to me. I began to ask Christina about all of the unacceptable consequences if Christianity were true: What about devout followers of other religions? What about hell? What about people who had never heard the gospel? What she said surprised me. She said she didn't have all the answers. In retrospect, I think this response was powerful in part because it demonstrated that Christianity is not based on a God we invent and whom we completely understand. Instead, it is based on a God who is real and who reveals himself as he is, whether we can understand him or not. Her response also meant that I couldn't go on demanding answers to keep Jesus at bay. If Jesus was who he claimed to be, then he didn't have to give me explanations to deserve my allegiance. He was not offering to solve all my most perplexing theological puzzles. He was commanding me to repent and believe.

For me, the biggest obstacle to faith in Christ was the realization that it would mean complete and abject intellectual humiliation. Becoming a Christian would mean admitting that the most uneducated, backward, Bible-thumping Christian with a gun rack over his mantelpiece and antlers on his pickup truck knew more about God than I did. It would mean that all my carefully constructed spiritual-but-not-religious beliefs would have to be abandoned and that I'd have to enter God's presence like a little child. It was terrifying. But I remember telling God: "I don't know who you are anymore. I don't even know if Jesus is your Son. But if he is, I'm willing to follow him." Although I had a long, long way to go theologically, I think that's the night I became a Christian.

Where are you, spiritually? Are you a Christian who is trying to better understand the evidence for the Christian faith? Are you an agnostic who is not really sure what you believe? Are you someone who has been deeply wounded by the church? Are you an atheist who thinks that Christianity is a fairy tale concocted by ignorant, flea-infested, leprosy-ridden Bronze Age sheep herders (thank you, Reddit)?

No matter who you are, you need the gospel. The bad news is that we are sinners. We stand justly condemned before God, not in spite of his goodness but because of it. His goodness is fundamentally opposed to all the hatred, the slander, the cowardice, the lies, the anger, the violence, the gossip, the lust, and the selfishness in our hearts. But the good news is that God is a God who rescues sinners. God so loved the world that he sent Jesus to rescue it, taking the filthy garments of our sin and offering us the robes of his righteousness.

Take him at his word. Trust him. He is worth it.

Acknowledgments

I'VE BEEN WORKING ON THIS BOOK for years, really ever since I became a Christian in graduate school. Along the way, many people have shaped my theology, my thinking, and my character.

At UC Berkeley, Barry Wong and Carrie Bare mentored me as graduate ministry workers with CRU and InterVarsity. Keith Casner, Derek Chiang, Eric Friedman, Justin Hastings, Andrew Hwang, Mike Jaasma, Jon Touryan, and the other members of my men's Bible study welcomed me and guided me as a brand-new Christian.

In New Haven, Pastor Ian Maddock, Pastor Josh Moody, Pastor Jay Ridenour, Gerard Considine, Rob Dunlop, Jonathan Gough, Jim Hebda, Jon Hinkson, Dave Schwaderer, Nic Tecu, and many other friends at Trinity Baptist Church taught me, supported me, and loved me. The elders there gave me my first experience preaching and teaching apologetics. Imran Babar and Jeremy Blum talked theology, science, and life with me over lunch and sharpened me as iron sharpens iron.

In Durham, Pastor Brad O'Brien, Pastor Peter Park, and Pastor J. D. Greear have given me innumerable opportunities both to learn and to teach. When John Pearson asked me over lunch, "When are you going to write your book?" I finally started taking this project seriously. The Chambers, McKibben, Moody, Privratsky, and St. John families, and many other families, have supported me and mine in Bible studies throughout the last decade.

Online, I've been encouraged and prodded by other Christian scholars and apologists, including Dr. Rob Bowman, Dr. Tim McGrew, Dr. Bob Stewart, and Tom Gilson.

My parents, Mary and Ashok, and my brother, Ryan, have shown me the unconditional support and love that I want to show to my own children.

I owe a great debt to my in-laws, Rick and Lenore Brown, for giving me one day a week to devote to my reading and writing. I'm also deeply grateful that they raised such a wonderful daughter.

To my wife, Christina, who first showed me what Christian character looks like: I am forever in love.

To my children, Adrian, Alia, Ellie, and Evan: thank you for putting up with my absentminded parenting as I worked out arguments and phraseology in my head during snack time.

And to Dr. Pat Sawyer, without whose efforts and energy this manuscript would be sitting on a hard drive to this day: thank you for your friendship and mentorship.

To God be the glory, forever and ever. Amen.

General Index

Scripture Index